Phonics and Spelling Through Phoneme-Grapheme Mapping

By Kathryn E. S. Grace, M.Ed., CAGS

REALLY GREAT READING

Printed in the United States of America

Published and Distributed by

REALLY
GREAT
READING

P.O. Box 46, Cabin John, MD 20818-0046 ▪ 866-401-READ (7323)
www.ReallyGreatReading.com

Dedication

Dedicated to my parents, Howard and Katherine Sherman, who made me realize from an early age that all children have special gifts and that education should never be taken for granted. And to my children and students, who will forever be my teachers.

Acknowledgments

I am extremely appreciative of my husband, Robert, and our three sons (James, Jeffrey, and Jonathan) for their willingness to continually share me with my students.

I am especially grateful to my mentor, Dr. Blanche Podhajski of the Stern Center for Language and Learning, who always believed we could make a difference; to my colleagues and friends, Marilyn Varricchio and Jackie Earle-Cruickshanks, for their tremendous intellectual and personal support; to Dr. Louisa Moats and Dr. Reid Lyon for my enlightened postgraduate training and their relentless pursuit of literacy for all children; to my dear public school colleague and friend, Tanya Carpenter, for her wisdom, encouragement, and courage; to my sister, Theresa Marshall, for helping me type when my hands could do no more; to my teacher siblings Rachel Straw and Ron Sherman, who gave me endless inspiration; and to my youngest son Jonathan who, from a very young age, never complained when I perfected this technique on him.

About the Author

Kathryn Grace has devoted her personal and professional life to promoting literacy across the United States. She holds a Master's Degree in Reading and Language Arts from the University of Vermont and a Certificate of Advanced Graduate Study in Language and Learning Disabilities from St. Michaels College in Colchester, Vt. While there, she studied under both Dr. Reid Lyon and Dr. Louisa Moats - leading experts in the field of learning disabilities and literacy. Kathryn was a mentor, contributing author and teacher trainer for the TIME for Teachers literacy project in Williston, Vt. and an adjunct professor at Trinity College. She has received numerous awards for teaching excellence and literacy advocacy.

Kathryn created the process of Phoneme-Grapheme Mapping (PGM) in 1983 while teaching in a Vermont classroom. It has been instrumental in helping students of all ages better understand the alphabetic principle - the idea that the sounds (phonemes) of spoken language are represented by letters and groups of letters (graphemes). PGM starts with speech sound awareness and highlights phoneme-grapheme relationships by depicting the internal details of both spoken and written words through a series of intricate mappings. Its multi-sensory process is highly effective and engaging for students of all ages.

Ms. Grace has delivered numerous presentations on the PGM process over the past several decades including numerous workshops at IDA's annual conference and for school districts and literacy organizations across the country. Since 1995, Phoneme-Grapheme Mapping has been highlighted in Dr. Louisa Moats' acclaimed LETRS program where it helps teach the logic of English orthography to teachers.

Contents

Foreword

I have been looking forward to this publication for a long time. In the LETRS professional development manuals, I presented the ideas around which *Phonics and Spelling Through Phoneme-Grapheme Mapping* was developed, hoping that every teacher would soon be able to obtain this outstanding instructional tool. This program, fully classroom tested and theoretically sound, exploits a fundamental fact about the relationship between speech and print: the 44 speech sounds (phonemes) in English are represented by graphemes, not letters. Graphemes are letters and letter combinations that correspond to individual speech sounds and that are used in largely predictable patterns and sequences. Kathryn Grace's innovative and effective approach highlights phoneme-grapheme relationships, depicting for students the internal details of both spoken words and written words and the patterns by which print represents speech. This program embodies the true meaning of "the alphabetic principle," which is much discussed and seldom taught in such an engaging, logical, organized, and complete fashion. With this program, in the regular classroom or the intervention group, students will learn the fundamentals of word structure for both reading and spelling. It's powerful; it's fun. Thank you, Kathryn, for giving us this work.

—*Louisa Moats*
Author, *Language Essentials for Teachers of Reading and Spelling* (LETRS)

Preface

The sequential, systematic, and explicit lessons in *Phonics and Spelling Through Phoneme-Grapheme Mapping* are a direct outcome of my experience teaching young students and incorporating of best practice based on empirical research.

- *Phoneme-Grapheme Mapping* strengthens phonemic awareness while simultaneously building an association of sounds to the spellings of words.

- Its multisensory elements help to bridge the brain's phonological and orthographic processors to strengthen learning and recall.

- *Phoneme-Grapheme Mapping* supports the development of automaticity and fluency with reading and spelling for all ages in one-on-one tutoring and in small-group and whole-group settings.

- *Phoneme-Grapheme Mapping* provides the one-to-one correspondence easily grasped and familiar to young students as a math concept but lacking in sound-to-spelling relationships.

Phoneme-Grapheme Mapping was created to help students understand the reality that the number of sounds (phonemes) they hear in a word may be different from the number of letters that represent those sounds. This procedure employs a variety of mapping methods to illustrate the complex, *yet predictable,* phoneme/grapheme relationships in our written language. By mapping sounds to print, students acquire a metacognitive approach to decoding, spelling, and reading skills.

Recently, one of my third grade students, Kyle, demonstrated his newfound confidence in word study. He discovered an exception to one of the new spelling patterns he had just learned in class. When a fellow student challenged his discovery, he eagerly announced, "Let's take it to spelling courtroom. Letters lie, but sounds speak the truth." Kyle beamed with pride over the new venue he had just given his classmates to share and question their word knowledge. Then he turned to me and coyly said, "You can put that in your book, Mrs. Grace, if you use my name."

To all the Kyles in our classrooms, thank you for teaching me and making teaching you such a rewarding experience.

Introduction

Educators, eager to implement current reading research outcomes when teaching young students to read, are finding themselves at a crossroads. Teachers have learned that phonemic awareness (the ability to isolate, manipulate, segment, and blend speech sounds) is a critical early skill and the foundation for developing decoding and spelling ability. A commonly employed phoneme awareness task is to ask students, using colored cubes or tiles, to isolate and touch one cube or tile for each sound in a word. However, teachers observe that even with this enhanced ability to segment the sounds in words, some students do not readily transfer this skill to their independent reading and writing. Educators ask, *"How* do we take students to the next level of connecting sounds with the letters that represent those sounds in written text, especially when there is not a one-to-one correspondence between the sounds and letters?" *Phonics and Spelling Through Phoneme-Grapheme Mapping* provides an accessible, trustworthy, and systematic process to help take students to successful levels of understanding and applying the sound/symbol relationships found in the English language.

Research on Combined Phoneme and Symbol Instruction

Phoneme-Grapheme Mapping is based on research that supports the combined — not isolated — instruction of the phonemes in words with the letters used to represent them. We have learned through research on phoneme awareness that early instruction linking speech sounds to alphabetic symbols strengthens phonemic awareness, decoding skills, spelling, and word reading. Here are a few of the many supportive findings in the literature:

- It is imperative that early learners acquire a practical knowledge of phoneme/grapheme and grapheme/phoneme correspondences. It is a bidirectional process that has become unitized and can be applied to decoding and spelling. (Ehri, 2022)

- Children need to know how to distinguish phonemes within pronunciations of words and how these map onto graphemes within the spellings of words. Both print and speech are involved. (Ehri, 2022)

- Instructional models with explicit teaching of phonologic and orthographic relationships produced results wherein students demonstrated advanced knowledge of the internal structures of words (Blachman, Schatschneider, Fletcher, & Clonan, 2003).

- When students with deficit word level skills received small group, explicit instruction in phonemic awareness and phonemic decoding, they achieved scores solidly within the average range (Torgesen, Rashotte, Alexander, & MacPhee, 2003).

- When phoneme awareness activities are paired with the alphabetic symbols that represent the sounds, phonemic awareness abilities and decoding abilities improve more rapidly (Adams, 1990).

- The skills involved in phoneme segmenting and blending bear a strong relationship to word recognition skills (Perfetti, Beck, Bell, & Hughes, 1987).

- The effectiveness of phonological training is significantly improved when students are assisted to directly apply their phonemic knowledge to reading and spelling tasks (Bradley & Bryant, 1985).

- Students in programs that emphasize phonemic awareness and the alphabetic code outperform students who do not receive this instruction on measures of invented and standard spelling (Tangel & Blachman, 1995).

English Isn't Crazy

A common misunderstanding among the general community of English spellers is that the English orthography is crazy, having unpredictable and unreliable sets of rules and exceptions that make it impossible to understand. This misconception has fueled a belief system among educators that our language has so many exceptions that rules shouldn't be taught at all. Yet the spelling patterns of English *are* predictable and logical, if one understands the layers of language represented in our English orthography. Spelling predictability, in fact, is based on these factors: sound/symbol correspondences, syllable patterns, orthographic rules, word meaning, word derivation, and word origin (Moats, 2000).

Table 1 was created by Kathryn Grace and is based on a 1966 study by Hanna, Hanna, Hodges, & Rudorf of the 17,000 most commonly used words. As you can see, approximately 96 percent of the words in our language can be accessed through explicit instruction in phonology, word patterns, structural analysis, and categories of syllable types. The lessons in *Phoneme-Grapheme Mapping* teach students to read and spell through a highly motivational, concrete, and carefully monitored format that helps students to become metacognitive about the rules and patterns of written English. Although the lessons are often used to teach spelling, teachers see an immediate transfer to independent decoding, including decoding of multisyllabic words.

Table 1 Spelling Pattern Predictability			
Characteristic	**Description**	**Example**	**Portion of English Words**
Predictable and consistent	• By sound-symbol correspondences alone	• pan, must, that	Approximately 50% of words in our language.
Predictable and frequent—one error per word if only phoneme/ grapheme mapping is used	Determined by: • Position of a phoneme in a word (initial, medial, or final) • Syllable stress • Phonemic environment (e.g., soft c and g)	• rain vs. ray baby vs. bake • con TENT vs. CON tent • cent vs. cost gym vs. cage back vs. bank wrench vs. watch	An additional 36% of the words in English are then "regular."
Predictable but infrequent	• Word relatives/word families	• kind, mind, blind • old, fold, mold	
Morphologically complex	• Compound words • Affix-root structure • Latin/Greek derivation • Rule-based generalizations • Foreign language spelling patterns	• caretaker, playfellow • undoing, refilled • circle, circus, circular • stuff, fill, pass, liked, happily, running • chaise, buffet, beautiful	Another 10% of so-called "irregular" words are explained.
Odd, truly unpredictable spellings	• Leftovers from our Anglo/ Saxon heritage	• of, aunt, does	Approximately 4% of words in our language.

Source: This table was created by Kathryn Grace in 2001 and is based on the work of Louisa Cook Moats in *Speech to Print: Language Essentials for Teachers* (2000) and a study by Hanna, Hanna, Hodges, & Rudorf (1966) of the 17,000 most commonly used words.

Getting Started With Phoneme-Grapheme Mapping

Phonics and Spelling Through Phoneme-Grapheme Mapping provides lessons for a wide range of reading and spelling skill levels. It is organized by syllable type, with lessons that provide simple to more complex word items; therefore, any one lesson can be adapted for young to adult students through word item selection— simpler words for younger students and more complex words for more capable students. The lessons can be taught in sequence as presented in the manual, or they can be presented randomly as needed to support learners in the acquisition or strengthening of a particular phoneme-grapheme relationship. Make sure that students know the syllable types represented by the lessons you choose. Each lesson follows an organized and consistent format:

- **Tutorial.** Most lessons begin with a teacher tutorial. Many of the presented concepts may be unfamiliar; a quick refresher may be in order. Take time to familiarize yourself with the lesson's sound/symbol concepts and unique mapping procedures. The tutorials are clearly written and simply referenced with bullets and highlighted points for your quick reference.

- **Teach.** Some lessons provide explicit guidelines for teaching students the lesson concept.

- **Mapping Procedure.** Each lesson illustrates phoneme-grapheme mapping of the target spelling concept. Target concepts are highlighted in gray in each lesson. Sometimes syllable types are shaded, as in the case of concepts involving open syllables.

- **Word List.** Comprehensive word lists supply many word options for you to choose from when compiling word lists for students. If you are a primary teacher, select one-syllable words for use at the beginning of lessons and progress to multisyllabic word choices as each concept becomes solidified.

Prerequisite Skills for Students

Students who have been exposed to a regular phonological awareness regimen and are beginning to make associations between sounds and their corresponding spellings are ready for phoneme-grapheme mapping. Students benefit from phoneme-grapheme mapping when they are able to:

1. Orally segment words containing up to three phonemes: "Tell me the sounds in *wave*."

2. Auditorily blend three phonemes: "/c/ /ŭ/ /p/. What word?"

3. Delete initial, final, and medial sounds in orally presented words: "Say *cat* without the /c/. Say *mate* without the /t/. Say *break* without the /r/."

4. Accurately recognize and produce letter sounds: (Students see flash cards.) "Tell me the sounds of these letters."

5. Distinguish between and among short vowel sounds: "*Cop. Cap.* Which word has /ŏ/? Which word has /ă/?"

Phonics Expectations by Grade Level

Use these general guidelines (Grace, 1992) to plan appropriate phoneme-grapheme lessons for students in grades K–8. For example, most first grade students benefit from lessons that teach the bulleted items under "First Grade" below.

Kindergarten

- Attaining concepts of sentence, word, letter sound.
- Letter naming, sound correspondence, letter writing, hearing initial sounds in words.
- Writing one's name; recognizing names of others.
- Beginning phonics instruction; initial and final consonants with two vowels (short *a* and *o*).

First Grade

- All letter/sound correspondence for single consonants, blends, digraphs.
- Short vowels; consonant-vowel-consonant (CVC); closed, open, and silent -*e* syllables.
- Using syllables to sound out longer words.

Second Grade

- Vowel teams, *r*-controlled vowels.
- Structural analysis skills (base words, common prefixes and suffixes).
- Vowel team, *r*-controlled syllables, consonant -*le*.

Third Grade and Up

- Knowledge of all six syllable types.
- Multisyllabic word practice.
- Increased word item complexity and structural analysis.
- Relating syllabication skills to unfamiliar content and text.

Adolescents

- Adolescents and adults who can't read the newspaper continue to have difficulties with vowels and multisyllabic words.

Matching Lessons to Student Skill Levels

This book provides lessons for a wide range of reading and spelling skill levels. It is organized by syllable type, with lessons that provide simple to more complex word items. Therefore, it can be adapted for young to adult learners. Find your students' skill levels on Table 2 to help you plan the most appropriate lessons.

Remember: Oral segmentation skills and alphabetic knowledge are important precursors to using phoneme-grapheme mapping. Therefore, these skills are not included in Table 2.

Table 2 is organized by four skill level phases borrowed from the work of L. Ehri (1996), which includes approximate corresponding grade levels. An emergent, or logographic, phase is not included in this instructional blueprint because pre-requisite skills for phoneme-grapheme mapping include accurate recognition and production of letter sounds and a readiness to distinguish between and among short vowel sounds.

Find your students' approximate skill levels using the descriptions of the four stages below and then refer to Table 2 for lesson planning. Units and lesson numbers are listed after each key concept in the table.

Early Alphabetic. Kindergarten and early first grade. Phonics instruction begins during this time. Students improve their knowledge of initial and final consonants and begin to include one or two vowels accurately in their decoding and spelling.

Transitional/Late Alphabetic. Grades one and two. Students are learning all letter/sound correspondences for single consonants, blends, and digraphs. They are ready to learn the short vowels, CVC patterns, the six syllable types, base words, and common prefixes and suffixes. These students begin to use syllables to sound out longer words before transitioning to the mature alphabetic phase.

Mature Alphabetic. Grades three and four. Students know the six syllable types and are introduced to the majority of phonics principles through these six basic syllable types. They are also introduced to "a few good spelling rules" (Unit 8) to help them manipulate more complex suffixes. The continuum provides direction for teaching students who are beginning to mix and match syllable types to read and spell accurately.

Multisyllabic/Orthographic. Grade four through adult. Students learn more complicated phonics principles, such as syllabic consonant -*m,* vowels as placeholders, more complex spelling rules, and common exceptions, as well as a variety of more complex affixes and word derivations. They become adept at recognizing and manipulating the six basic syllable types in multisyllabic words.

Table 2 Word Analysis Stages			
	Early Alphabetic	**Transitional/Late Alphabetic**	**Mature Alphabetic**	**Multisyllabic/Orthographic**

	Early Alphabetic	**Transitional/Late Alphabetic**	**Mature Alphabetic**	**Multisyllabic/Orthographic**
Syllables	Auditory Blending, Unit 1	Closed Syllables, Unit 1	The -ve Rule, 3:6	Closed Syllables in Multisyllabic Words, 1:29
		Open Syllables, 2:1	Consonant -le Syllable, Unit 5	Syllabic Consonant -m, 1:30
		The Silent -e Syllable, Unit 3	Vowel Team Syllables, Unit 6	Combined Syllable Types, 3:4
		Closed/Silent -e Syllables, 3:1	Vowel r Syllables, Unit 7	
Vowels	Short vowels 1:1	Short Vowels, 1:1	y as a Vowel, 1:2	Schwa, 1:3
		One-Syllable Silent e Words, 3:2	Vowels as Placeholders for Soft c and g, 1:18	Busy Silent -e and Past Tense -ed, 3:5
		Vowels Preceded by Consonant w, 1:4	Vowel r and Silent -e Patterns, 3:3	When Vowel y Replaces Vowel i, 3:7
				Versatile Vowel i, 2:2
		Long Vowel a, 6:1	Long Vowel u as /y/ /$\overline{oo}$/ 6:5	
		Long Vowel e, 6:2	Long Vowel u as /$\overline{oo}$/ 6:6	
		Long Vowel i, 6:3	Three Sounds of ea, 6:7	
		Long Vowel o, 6:4	Vowel Diphthongs, 6:8 oi/oy and ou/ow	
			Vowel Teams au and aw, 6:9	
			Two Sounds of oo, 6:10	
		r-Controlled ar, 7:1	r-Controlled er, 7:3	r-Controlled Vowels and Consonant w, 7:6
		r-Controlled or, 7:2	r-Controlled ir, 7:4	
			r-Controlled ur, 7:5	
Consonants	m, l, s, and t, 1:5	Initial y and z, 1:9	Soft c and g, 1:17	ch as /sh/, 1:13
	p, h, f, and c, 1:6	Consonant Oddities qu, 1:10	ch as /k/, 1:13	Double Consonants in the Middle of Words, 1:28
	n, b, r, and j, 1:7	Consonant Oddities x, 1:11	Silent Consonant Patterns, 1:31	
	v, w, k, Hard g, 1:8			
	Consonant d, 1:8			
Consonant Blends	Blending While Decoding, Unit 1	Initial Blends, 1:20	Consonant Three-Letter Blends, 1:22	The Syllabic Consonant -m, 1:29
		Final Blends, 1:21	Digraph Blends, 1:24	
		Blends That Appear at the Beginning and End of Syllables, 1:23	Blend Oddities, 1:25	
Digraphs		Digraphs (sh, ch, th, wh, ph), 1:11	ch or tch for /ch/, 1:14 k or ck for /k/, 1:16	ch as /ch/ and /sh/, 1:12
Word Relatives		-ild, -ind, -old, -olt, -ost, 1:26	-ald, -alk, -all, -alt, 1:26	
		-ald, -alk, -all, -alt, 1:27		
Affixes	Plural s, 4:2	Inflectional Suffixes, Unit 4	Common Affixes 4:1	Common Derivational Suffixes, 4:5
	Affixo, 4:1	Inflectional Suffix -ed, 4:4 Affixo, 4:1	Common Prefixes, Unit 4 Affixo, 4:1	Rebellious Suffixes, i.e., -tion, -sion, -ition, 4:10 Affixo, 4:7
Spelling Rules		-ff, -ll, -ss, and -zz, 1:15	ch or tch for /ch/, 1:14	
		The -ve Rule, 3:6	-ge or -dge for /j/, 1:19	Accent or Stress, 8:2
		Silent -e Rule, 8:4	Doubling Rule With Single-Syllable Base Words, 8:1	Doubling Rule for Words of Two or More Syllables, 8:3
			Change the y to i Rule, 8:5	

Planning for Phoneme-Grapheme Lessons

Groups and Schedule

Phoneme-Grapheme mapping works best in small groups but can be used successfully in whole-class settings when enough time, practice, and immediate feedback are provided. Plan for three days of instruction per week with phoneme-grapheme mapping. The most time (25–30 minutes) is needed on the introductory day; less time (15–20 minutes) is needed on two additional days that week.

Materials

Phonics and Spelling Through Phoneme-Grapheme Mapping. The lessons in this book are organized by phoneme-grapheme concept. The teacher tutorials (**TEACH** sections) offer teaching tips and lists of concept words accompany the lessons. Explicit mapping procedures are provided for each newly introduced phoneme-grapheme pair.

Six to Ten Square Tiles for Each Student to Manipulate. The number of tiles depends on the number of phonemes in the concept words because each tile stands for just one sound. Once students develop one-to-one correspondence between the tile and the sound the tile represents, they can use a separate but consistent color (e.g., red) to represent a vowel sound. This is especially useful when teaching the concept of a syllable because each syllable has just one vowel sound; therefore, it has just one vowel tile (e.g., red tile). Using a predetermined color to represent a vowel sound is also an excellent way of helping students differentiate between open and closed syllables as highlighted in the following examples, where the vowel sound is shown in the gray shading.

A vowel is followed by a consonant in a closed syllable. The vowel sound is short.

A vowel is found at the end of an open syllable. The vowel sound is long.

Phoneme-Grapheme Mapping Paper. One sheet for each student in the group (see Appendix B).

Pencils. Provide plain and colored pencils.

Document Camera

Dedicated Computer Projection System

Interactive Whiteboards

Smart TV

If using a document camera, projection system or interactive whiteboard, copy or digitize the phoneme-grapheme mapping grid.

You will also need transparent tiles for the document camera and digitized boxes in two different colors (red for vowels and yellow for consonants) for your interactive whiteboard.

Step-by-Step Process

Each phoneme-grapheme mapping lesson follows a step-by-step process over three days. Read through the following steps to develop familiarity with the phoneme-grapheme lesson. Then read through the scripted lesson that follows for a more comprehensive picture of an entire phoneme-grapheme lesson. The lesson procedure is synthesized in Appendix A. You can duplicate and laminate the list of steps in Appendix A for use while teaching until the lesson process becomes automatic.

Day One: Teach Concept and Segment Sounds. Compile lesson word list. Choose words appropriate to students' reading levels. Provide students with colored tiles.

1. *TEACH:* Teach the new sound, spelling concept, and pattern.

2. *SEGMENT:* Instruct students to use colored tiles to segment dictated words into phonemes, or sounds. Tell students the tiles always represent sounds— *not* letters—in these lessons.

3. *CHECK:* Check each word immediately by having students touch and say each sound. Circulate among the group to ensure that the students are matching the appropriate sound to each tile.

Day Two: Read Words; Find, Circle, and Say Target Sound. Provide each student a list of the words used on Day One.

1. *READ:* Instruct students to independently read the list silently. Then lead the group to read the words chorally.

2. *FIND AND CIRCLE THE SOUND:*

    a. Instruct students to find, point to, and say the target sound or phoneme. "Say the sound."

    b. Instruct students to find, circle, and say the letter(s) for the target grapheme in each word. "Say the letter(s)." Instruct younger students to say the *sounds* when circling the letters.

Day Three: Introduce Phoneme-Grapheme Mapping. Provide tiles and phoneme-grapheme mapping paper. Prepare Day One word list for dictation.

1. **SEGMENT:** Dictate word. Students say each sound and position one tile in each grid square for each sound, or phoneme, that is heard. (Be sure students understand that the number of grid squares covered by the tiles equals the number of sounds in a word, *not* the number of letters.)

2. **SAY SOUND AND GRAPHEME:**

   a. Point to the first tile. Say, " What do you hear?" Students say the sound, *not the letter.*

   b. Ask, "What do you write?" Students say grapheme, move the tile up, and write the grapheme in the square.

   c. Repeat a and b for each sound/spelling until the whole word is written. When the word is completely written, students should have the exact spelling of the word on the paper, with the letters distributed across the boxes based on their phoneme-grapheme correspondences.

3. **REPEAT:** Repeat the process with the remainder of the lesson's words.

4. **REVIEW:** Instruct students to restate in their own words the sound/spelling relationship from the lesson. Ask them if they can think of any other words not on their list that might have this special relationship, and have them try to list some on a separate piece of paper. This will enable you to see to what degree students are making connections to their own vocabulary.

   (A step-by-step guide for you to laminate and use in daily instruction can be found in Appendix A.)

Sample Lesson

The following dialogue between students and their teacher illustrates the four steps of the phoneme-grapheme lesson. Each new lesson begins with explicit teaching about a target sound and its associated spelling or a spelling concept.

Day One: Teach Concept and Segment Sounds.

TEACH	Teach the new sound, spelling concept, and pattern.

Teacher: Today we are going to learn about digraphs. A digraph is two letters that spell one sound. *Di-* at the beginning of *digraph* means *two*, and *-graph* in the second syllable of *digraph* means *written down*. The one sound represented by a digraph is a unique sound to the letters used in the digraph. For example, today we will learn about the digraph **sh** (*says letter names and writes digraph on the board*). This digraph is spelled with **s** and **h**, but when we say the sound we don't hear /s/ or /h/. Instead, we hear a completely new sound that is unlike /s/ or /h/. Remember, there is one sound for these two letters together: /sh/. Say it with me.

Teacher and students: /sh/

Teacher: (*Hands out six to ten colored tiles to each student.*) Get ready to segment the sounds in some dictated words that have digraphs. Line up your tiles on the table in front of you like this (*lines up transparent tiles on the overhead*).

SEGMENT: Instruct students to use colored tiles to segment dictated words into phonemes, or sounds. Tell students the tiles always represent sounds—*not* letters—in these lessons.

Teacher: Listen while I say a word and you segment the word into its phonemes. *Shop.*

Students: (*pull down one tile for each sound*) /sh/ /ŏ/ /p/.

CHECK: Check each word immediately by having students touch and say each sound. Circulate among the group to ensure that the students are matching the appropriate sound to each tile.

Teacher: Touch each tile and say the sounds with me.

Teacher and students: /sh/ /ŏ/ /p/.

Teacher: Push your tiles up. Here's the next word: *crash*. Pull down one tile for each sound you hear. Good. Touch each tile and say the sounds with me (*circulates to check each individual's phoneme segmentation*).

Teacher and students: /c/ /r/ /ă/ /sh/. (*Teacher reads the remainder of the digraph words; students* **segment** *the sounds independently and then* **check** *immediately as a group with the teacher.*)

Day Two: Read Words; Find, Circle, and Say Target Sound

Teacher provides each student a list of the words used on Day One.

READ: Instruct students to independently read the list silently. Then lead the group to read the words chorally.

Teacher: Here is a list of the words that we just segmented with our tiles. Please read them to yourselves. Raise your hand if you need help reading any of the words (*provides time for students to read the words*). Now let's read them together one at a time and find the digraphs. Put your finger on the first word; say the word.

Teacher and students: *Shop.*

FIND AND CIRCLE THE SOUND:

    a. Instruct students to find, point to, and say the target sound or phoneme. "Say the sound."

Teacher: Find /sh/. Point to it. Say the sound. *(Teacher models the procedure on the overhead.)*

Students: *(Point to* **sh***)* /sh/.

    b. Instruct students to find, circle, and say the letter(s) for the target grapheme in each word. "Say the letter(s)." Instruct younger students to say the *sounds* when circling the letters.

Teacher: Circle the letters that spell /sh/. Say the letter names. *(Teacher models this on the overhead.)*

Students: *Point to* **sh** *in* shop, *and circle the letters* **sh**.

Teacher: *(Leads students through the Find and Circle process for each word.)*

Day Three: Introduce Phoneme/Grapheme Mapping

Teacher: *(Provides phoneme-grapheme mapping paper and tiles.)*We have spent some time moving tiles to show the number of sounds in our words. We have also read the words as a group. We are now ready to see how the sounds in these words match up to the letters we use to represent those sounds. What do you notice about this grid paper I have given you?

Students: There are little squares on the paper.

Teacher: Yes, and read the title at the top.

Students: Phoneme-Grapheme Mapping (or Sound/Spelling Boxes—Primary Paper).

Teacher: Listen: *phoneme, telephone*. Do you hear a similar word part in these words?

Students: *Phone*.

Teacher: Yes. What do you think that word part, *phon(e),* means?

Students: Something you hear?

Teacher: Yes, *phon(e)* means *sound*. There are lots of words that have this word part *phon(e)*: *pho<u>n</u>ics, micro<u>phone</u>, mega<u>phone</u>,* and *sym<u>phony</u>*. What same word part do you hear in the two words *gra<u>pheme</u>* and *auto<u>graph</u>*?

Students: *Graph*.

Teacher: Right. What do you think *graph* means? *(Students contribute their ideas.)* *Graph* means something that is recorded in print. Graph is in the words *gra<u>ph</u>ics, bio<u>graph</u>y, tele<u>graph</u>,* and *photo<u>graph</u>*. These words are used to describe something that is recorded visually—like your autograph, or your written name, that is recorded on paper for others to see. Today, we are going to work with the sounds (phonemes) and letter combinations (graphemes) in words using this phoneme-grapheme paper to record what you hear *and* see!

SEGMENT: Dictate word. Students say each sound and position one tile in each grid square for each sound, or phoneme, that is heard. (Be sure students understand that the number of grid squares covered by the tiles equals the number of sounds in a word, *not* the number of letters.)

SAY SOUND AND GRAPHEME:

   a. Point to the first tile. Say, " What do you hear?" Students say the sound, *not the letter.*

   b. Ask, "What do you write?" Students say grapheme, move the tile up, and write the grapheme in the square.

Teacher: Line up your sound tiles above the first row of boxes like this *(models the process on the overhead).* I'll say a word and you segment all of the sounds in the word. Use your tiles. Each box on the grid represents one sound. Place each tile in its own square. One sound. One tile. One square. First word: *shut.*

Students: /sh/ /ŭ/ /t/ *(touch and move tiles into the sound boxes, one sound per box in the first row on the grid).*

Teacher: *(points to the first square/tile on the overhead)* What do you hear?

Students: /sh/.

Teacher: What do you write?

Students: s, h *(say letter names).*

Teacher: Move the tile up and write the grapheme *sh* in the square.

   c. Repeat a and b for each sound/spelling until the whole word is written. When the word is completely written, students should have the exact spelling of the word on the paper, with the letters distributed across the boxes based on their phoneme-grapheme correspondences.

Teacher: *(points to the second square)* What sound?

Students: /ŭ/.

Teacher: What do you write?

Students: u *(say letter name).*

Teacher: Move the tile up and write the grapheme *u* in the square. *(Points to the third square.)* What sound (phoneme)?

Students: /t/.

Teacher: What do you write?

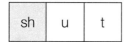

Students: *t (say letter name).*

Teacher: Move the tile up and write the grapheme *t* in the square.

REPEAT: Repeat the process with the remainder of the lesson's words.

Teacher: *Dish.*

Students: *(place one tile in each square on the next row) /d/ /i/ /sh/.*

Teacher: *(points to the first square)* What do you hear? /d/. What do you write? *d.*

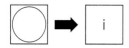

Teacher: *(points to the second square)* What do you hear? /i/.
What do you write? *i.*

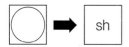

Teacher: *(points to the third square)* What do you hear? /sh/.
What do you write? *s, h.*

PHONEME-GRAPHEME MAPPING

Following is a completed phoneme-grapheme mapping grid for this lesson. Notice that words are selected to demonstrate both initial and final positions of the
sound/spelling concept /sh/. Blends are represented as separate speech sounds.
This process provides the opportunity for students to strengthen the basic phoneme-grapheme skill—one sound per box, one grapheme per box, even though
some sounds are spelled with more than one letter.

sh	u	t	
d	i	sh	
c	r	a	sh
b	l	u	sh

REVIEW: Instruct students to restate in their own words the sound/spelling relationship from the lesson.

Teacher: Great job segmenting words with digraphs and writing the graphemes for those sounds! Look at all of the words you spelled and can read! Now, tell me in your own words about the special sound and spelling you have learned.

Students: We learned that /sh/ is one sound but we use two letters to spell that one sound. That's why we only use three sound boxes on the phoneme-grapheme mapping paper. Even though *shut* has four letters, *s* and *h* go together in one sound box. It's a digraph. One sound, but two letters spell that sound.

Teacher: Can you think of any other words that have the digraph /sh/?

Students: *brush, shin, dishpan.*

Teacher: You are brilliant students!

Teaching Syllables

As students begin to learn about sounds and blending, they should also start to learn about syllables. Research has established that orally segmenting words into syllables generally precedes oral segmentation of words into sounds. The latter is a well-known precursor to decoding and encoding and is the primary focus of this text.

Good readers are often defined as those who can read multisyllabic words with relative ease and comprehension; therefore, it is imperative to teach students about syllables as a component of early reading instruction. First grade is not too soon to begin this instruction. Understanding of closed and open syllables as well as silent-*e* syllables is easily attainable for most students by the end of first grade. (Closed and open syllables together make up almost 75 percent of English syllables; Stonback 1992.) Access to these syllable types allows students to read more than 50 percent of the words they encounter.

Early Instruction

Clapping syllables is an effective way to reinforce the parts of spoken words. However, young students often do not clearly understand that the *written* word can be segmented and that segmentation can be used as an aid to pronunciation. Students need explicit instruction in *listening* for, *clapping* out, and *visually segmenting* words into syllables for both reading and writing. These practice routines need to be used on an ongoing basis during reading and spelling lessons.

Auditory Blending

Phoneme-grapheme mapping requires that students are able to auditorily blend. This means that when given the auditory (not visual) information /l/ /ee/ /f/, students are able to blend the sounds together and say the word *leaf*. Teaching auditory blending initially takes place at the syllable level (*pic-nic = picnic*), and then at the onset rime level (*b-ird = bird*), and finally at the complete phoneme segmentation level (/m/ /oo/ /n/ = *moon*). Include auditory blending exercises at the syllable and onset rime levels in daily word work routines with young students. Once students are capable at this level, move to the complete phoneme segmentation level for practice.

Blending While Decoding

When students know the sounds for at least one vowel and two or three consonants, you can begin teaching them how to blend sounds into simple words *while decoding*. This can be a really exciting time!

Here's one way to begin instruction in blending while decoding:

- Call the vowels (*a, e, i, o, u*) **singers** because they make a sound that keeps on going, like a musical note. Start with the sound of the letter *a* as it sounds in the word *apple*.

- Start with continuing consonants like *m, s,* or *n* that make sounds that can be prolonged and that can be combined with *a* to make the sound of recognizable words.

- Teach students to blend the vowel and the consonant together to make a word, as in *at*. Then build on that blending skill by adding a consonant at the beginning of the word, as in *bat, rat, fat, sat*.

- If the student meets with frustration at this point, let him/her know you will both try again at a later time. You will probably need to back up on the phonological awareness continuum to phoneme segmentation and/or deletion before you try again to blend letter sounds into words.

Knowing syllable patterns enables students to read and spell longer words in chunks rather than letter by letter, and it helps them decide whether or not suffixes have been added to the base word. Identifying syllable types allows readers to know whether a vowel is short, long, *r*-controlled, a schwa, or a diphthong. Syllable types provide clues to the vowel sounds in words so that we pronounce the vowels correctly in visually similar words such as these:

| slop | slope | sloped | slopped |

This book is arranged according to the six syllable types common in English spelling. Each unit is developed around one of the syllable types:

closed	open	silent -*e*
vowel team	*r*-controlled	consonant -*le*

Unit 1 covers closed syllables. Before you present the first lesson on short vowels, teach students about syllables.

Present each of the syllable tips below. Accompany instruction with word samples that illustrate the concepts.

- A **syllable** is a part of a word with a vowel sound that makes a beat or a clap when you say the word. The number of syllables in a word is generally equal to the number of *vowel sounds* (not vowel letters) in a word:

ran	one vowel letter, one vowel sound, one syllable
rain	two vowel letters, one vowel sound (*ai* represents /ā/), one syllable
concrete	three vowel letters, two vowel sounds (the *e* is silent), two syllables

- A syllable can sometimes be just one letter, as in <u>a</u>-*go*, <u>o</u>-*pen*, <u>e</u>-*go*, etc.
- A word can sometimes be a syllable itself, as with *in, at, pin, sit.*
- A syllable may be part of a longer word (*At-lan-tic*).
- When *u* appears after a *q* in a word, do not count the *u* as a vowel (e.g., *quit*). (*qu* is a letter team corresponding to two phonemes: /k//w/.)

Syllable Sorts

Syllable sorts are an effective way to ascertain whether your students have internalized how syllables work. Because the vowel sound is the key component of any syllable, it makes sense to teach students to pay particular attention to the vowel pattern in specific syllables and, ultimately, in whole words.

The Syllable Writing Grid and Syllable Sorting Grid (see Appendix B) are effective tools for instruction, practice, and review of syllable concepts. Students segment their words into syllables and determine the syllable types and vowel sounds using these forms. Through application of these segmentation and sorting procedures, students quickly see if they have segmented a syllable or not, because they see that a syllable has to have at least one vowel to create a vowel sound.

Using the Syllable Writing Grid

1. Provide students with words that are representative of the syllable types and spellings to which they have been previously introduced.

2. Provide each student a copy of the Syllable Writing Grid form (from Appendix B).

3. Demonstrate how to segment and write each syllable of a word in the boxes. First, second, third, and other syllables are written in order on the grid across a row. See the following examples of student work.

Syllable Writing Grid

Scott	Clark				
Az	tecs				
Ham	mock				
Sung	Dynasty	nas	ty		
John	Cab	ot			
Baf	fin	Isle	tand		
In	ca				
Cape	Ver	de			
Bar	ce	lo	na		
Hud	son	Riv	er		
gar	lic				
Per	u				
Rob	ert	Scott			
Her	nan	do	de	So	to
Green	Land				
foot	hold				
silk	roads				
Red	Sea				
Spain					
Gi	bral	tar	Strait		
Meri	Wether	Lew	is		

Using the Syllable Sorting Grid

1. Provide each student a copy of the Syllable Sorting Grid (from Appendix B).

2. Provide words for students to sort. Compile a list that is representative of the syllable types and spellings that have been taught and may need review.

3. Read the words together. Segment them into syllables and instruct the students to color the vowel within each syllable orange. The orange vowels serve as a focal point for deciding which vowel pattern is represented in the word. For example, a vowel team is usually signaled by two vowels together. If there is a syllable with a vowel before the consonant with a final orange *e*, a silent -*e* syllable is visible (with some exceptions: *house, mouse, cause,* etc.).

4. The words can then be cut apart into their component syllables and sorted onto the Syllable Sorting Grid. See an example of a student's work on the following page.

The explicit guidance students receive through this sorting and classification process helps bring their knowledge of syllables to a more automatic level that is useful when reading and spelling multisyllabic words.

Syllable Sorting Grid

Name: _____ Date: _____

Closed syllables
These syllables have a vowel followed by one or more consonants. The vowel sound is short and spelled with one letter.

Scott Az tecs hold
ham Rob Red Dynasty
John eral Cabot En Lew
Baf fin land silk
Hud nan land son lic is

Schwa Closed Syllables:

mock

Open syllables
These syllables end in a single vowel. The vowel sound is long, or sounds like the vowel's name.

lo na ca de ce
do So to
Gi

Schwa Open Syllables:

de
s

Silent -e syllables
These syllables have one vowel, followed by one consonant and a final e. The first vowel is long. The e is silent.

Cape
isle

Schwa Silent -e Syllables:

Vowel team syllables
These syllables contain teams of letters that come together to make a distinct vowel sound (ou as in out, oi as in oil, eigh as in eight.) Sometimes they can be a vowel team pair, as in team and boat.

Green foot roads
Sea Spain Strait

Schwa Vowel Team Syllables:

r-controlled syllables
These syllables contain a vowel followed by an r. The r controls the sound of the vowel.

ar   or   er   ir   ur

Clark Ver Bour
River gor Per bert
Meri wether

Schwa r-Controlled Syllables:

Consonant -le syllables
These syllables end in a consonant followed by -le, as in the -ble in table. The le sounds like /ul/.

Schwa Silent -e Syllables:

All consonants -le syllables have a schwa vowel, so they are placed in the main syllable box above.

Periodic Review of Previously Taught Concepts Is Very Important!

Periodically review skills that you have taught via mapping of multisyllabic words. Follow these guidelines to plan review lessons:

- Plan to include review words in every lesson. For example, when planning the word list for the week's lesson, add a few words to map from previous lessons. Choose words that will provide the most review (i.e., multisyllable words).

- Plan for review. Every three to four weeks, compile word lists from several lessons for review. Follow the lesson steps. Ask students to state the spelling concept after they map a word.

- Choose words that do not have a one-to-one correspondence between sounds and letters. In other words, include words that contain digraphs, consonant oddities, silent *e*, and the soft *c* and *g* principles. This will let you know if students' thinking has become metacognitive when working with more complex spelling patterns.

- Instruct students to color the blends in their words green and the digraphs blue to assess understanding and application of the phonics vocabulary.

- When students map multisyllabic words, do not have them skip a sound box between syllables. As words become more complex, they will not always break evenly between boxes. In fact, syllables may even share boxes, as in the following two examples:

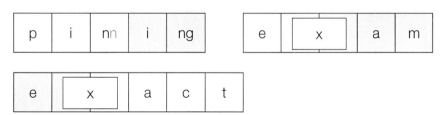

- For this reason, instruct students to draw dotted lines between the syllable breaks or to color each syllable within a word a different color as above and below:

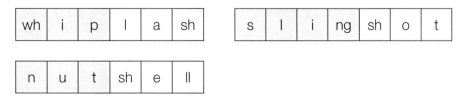

A Note From the Author

The basic principle of teaching *Phonics and Spelling Through Phoneme-Grapheme Mapping* is:

> **The number of sounds in a word is not always equal to the number of letters needed to spell the word.**

Throughout this program, this principle is demonstrated by showing students how to map the intricate relationships between sounds and print. Some sound mappings have their own particular rules that will require explicit modeling. If students receive explicit instruction and practice, phoneme-grapheme mapping can make a difference in their independent reading and writing skills. Concrete manipulatives linked to graphic mapping strategies can help your students build a bridge between their understanding of the sounds they hear and the letters they write. Only then will this process become truly automatic and internalized.

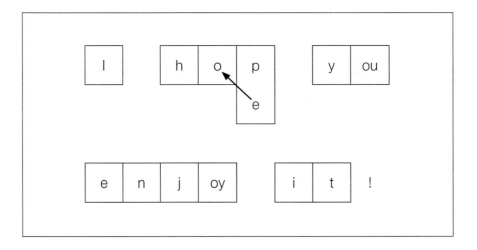

— Unit 1 —

Closed Syllables

Introduction to Short Vowel Syllables

A **closed syllable** is a syllable that ends with one or more consonants and has only one vowel that is almost always short (*at, bit*). The consonants serve as a gate that closes off the end of the syllable and keeps its short vowel sound intact. It is important that students be exposed to two-, four-, and five-letter closed syllables and not just regular CVC words (as is often taught in the primary grades). Otherwise, students might assume that a closed syllable always comprises three letters. The following examples demonstrate otherwise.

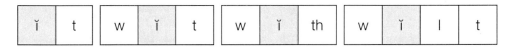

Two or more consonant letters can follow the short vowel in a closed syllable (*latch, sack, stiff, ball, ledge*). This spelling convention provides extra protection for the short vowel in these single-syllable words. Thus, if a vowel suffix (*-ed, -ing, -er*) is added to these words, the short vowel remains sheltered and the base word does not look like it has a long vowel.

If a closed syllable is connected to another syllable that begins with a consonant, two consonant letters will separate the syllables. This pattern is easy to spot in words with twin consonants such as *better, tennis,* and *follow*. However, the generalization is also true when the two consonants are different, as in *helmet* and *whisper*. The VCCV sandwich that is made in this relationship of unlike consonants is also a syllable generalization worth teaching to students early.

Closed syllables comprise just under 50 percent of the syllables in running text. Therefore, it is imperative that students learn to discriminate between and among short vowel sounds as early as possible, at least by the end of first grade. (Suggestions for teaching short vowels are included in this text.)

Often struggling high school and adult readers do not know their short vowel sounds but merely use the visual configuration or beginnings and ends of words along with context to predict a word's pronunciation. This inefficient method of word recognition generally takes its toll on fluency as the text becomes more complicated and lengthy. This results in an increased amount of time necessary to complete reading assignments as well as a growing sense of frustration on the part of the reader.

Teaching Short Vowels

Prior to teaching Lesson 1:1, ensure that students are ready for the mapping procedure. They should be able to differentiate between and among the short vowel sounds. Provide multiple practice opportunities to determine when they are ready. This can be done using the short vowel key words in Table 3 and the activities that follow. Once students can differentiate the vowel sounds, they are ready for Lesson 1:1, Short Vowels. When using key words for short vowel phonemes, avoid nasalized sounds (*n, m*), *r*-controlled vowels (e.g., *ar, or, er, ir, ur*), and vowels distorted by the consonant that follows the vowel.

Table 3 Key Words for Short Vowels

Vowel	Key Word	Words to Avoid
short *a*	apple, at	ant, bag, air
short *e*	Ed, edge, echo	egg, elephant
short *i*	itch, it, icky	igloo, Indian, ink
short *o*	octopus, ox	on, off
short *u*	up, us	umbrella, uncle

It is particularly helpful to provide students with picture cue cards to help them discriminate between and among the five short vowel sounds. A blackline master of the short vowel cue cards is provided in Appendix B. Introduce the short vowel sounds one at a time in the following order: short *a*, short *o*, short *i*, short *u*, and finally short *e*.

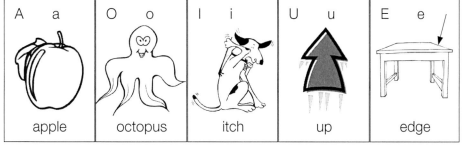

Short Vowel Cue Cards.

To help students discriminate between and among these very important vowel sounds, play matching games with the vowel cue cards.

Activities

Learn the Cue Words

Have students practice segmenting the initial vowel sound from the remaining phonemes in the key word by dragging or pulling the initial sound to their mouth and swallowing (or whispering) the remaining phonemes behind their covered mouths. Doing so allows students to clearly articulate, isolate, and hear the initial short vowel sound. The students affectionately refer to this activity as pulling or stretching the short vowels.

If students have daily practice articulating vowels, first with the short vowel cue cards and then with their eyes closed to see if they can visualize the short vowel cues, it helps make the process of discriminating short vowels easier.

> *apple* would become /ă/ .... *pple* (swallowed)
>
> *octopus* would become /ŏ/ .... *ctopus* (swallowed)
>
> *itch* would become /ĭ/ .... *tch* (swallowed)
>
> *up* would become /ŭ/ .... *p* (swallowed)
>
> *edge* would become /ĕ/ .... *dge* (swallowed)

Short Vowel Bingo

Once the students are able to articulate the five short vowel sounds, have them practice discriminating between and among them. Create a simple bingo game using the short vowel cue cards (Appendix B) on a bingo board and six to ten bingo chips or markers. Instruct students to listen for a given vowel sound in the words presented. When students hear the target sound, they cover the cue card representing that sound. Follow a sequential, cumulative path by adding another sound each day. This should be done over several days, depending on how successful your students are with each vowel sound that is added. The purpose of the activity is to build student awareness of the differences between these very important vowels.

Short /a/ and /o/. Each student begins with a vowel cue card. (See Appendix B.) The students only discriminate between short *a* and short *o* at first, so cover the pictures for short *e, i,* and *u* with small sticky-notes. Using the Short Vowel Word List (Table 4), dictate words that have the short vowel sound in the initial position, because it is more difficult for students to discriminate between short vowels when the vowels are found in the middle of words. Dictate the words randomly. Ask the students to put a bingo chip over the picture that represents the initial sound in the word you dictate. Once students show some proficiency with the task, add nonsense words so that you are sure they are not doing the activity by merely using their visual memory to reconstruct the spellings.

Add /i/. After the students are discriminating between short *a* and short *o*, uncover the short *i* picture on the short vowel cue card. Now, randomly dictate short *a*, *o*, and *i* words (Table 4) to see if the students can accurately discriminate among these three sounds.

Add /u/. Uncover the short *u* picture cue and dictate short *u* words from Table 4, as well as words for the previous three vowels.

Add /e/. Lastly, uncover the short *e* picture cue and dictate short *e* words from Table 4 as well as words for the previous four short vowels.

This activity should be repeated daily until the students are able to isolate and say the five short vowel sounds when prompted with a short vowel word. Instruct students to visualize the short vowel cues in their head and retrieve the sounds on their own.

Table 4   Short Vowel Word List for Bingo
(Vowels are in the initial position.)

Short *a*	Short *o*	Short *i*	Short *u*	Short *e*
apple	ox	it	up	Ed
Adam	octopus	itch	us	Eddy
add	otter	Ichabod	*ug*	echo
Abby	ostrich	is	*uck*	edge
act	odd	if	*ush*	Evan
ask	octagon	icky	*udge*	*eck*
ash	*ob*	*ip*	*ub*	*ep*
at	*og*	*ix*	*ut*	*et*
ack	*ock*	*ick*	*uzz*	*eb*

More words can be created by simply deleting the initial consonant in basic CVC words (see italic "words" in Table 4). Remember, though, to avoid words with nasalized sounds after the vowel (*in* and *an*), as well as *r*-controlled vowels (*arm*) and those vowels distorted by consonants, such as *g*, *l*, and sometimes *f* (*egg, elf*).

Short Vowel Picture Sort

This activity will help students associate short vowel phonemes in both the initial and medial positions. Therefore, phoneme deletion is an important prerequisite skill for this task. The basic premise of all sorting tasks is to help students compare and contrast word elements by separating the picture examples that go with a particular stimulus sound from those that do not. It is important that you review the names of the pictures with the students before they begin the sort and ensure they are able to pronounce the picture cue names.

To prepare for this activity:

- Photocopy and laminate enough sets of the five short vowel picture mats (see Appendix B) for each student or pair of students.

- Cut the laminated pictures on each sheet apart and place them in envelopes according to their short vowel sound. On the outside of the envelope, glue a picture of the key word for each of the short vowels represented by the pictures in the envelope. For example, place the 12 short *a* pictures in an envelope with a picture of the apple cue glued to the front. Do the same for each of the remaining short vowels, always gluing on the front of the envelope the picture prompts that were introduced at the beginning of the short vowel unit in this book. Each student or pair of students should have five envelopes of short vowel pictures labeled with their corresponding short vowel cue on the outside of the envelope.

To start this activity:

1. Have students compare and contrast only two of the short vowel sounds (short *a* and short *o*). Have them empty the short *a* and short *o* envelopes on to their desk and mix them up. Then have students turn their envelopes over displaying the short vowel picture cue for each vowel sound at the top of their desk. (These envelopes will serve as their sorting column headers for this entire activity.)

2. If this is the first time students have done a sorting activity, you may need to model the process for the entire class or a small group. Select one picture from the short *a* or *o* picture piles and name it for the students. Have students try to isolate the short vowel by deleting the initial consonant(s) if necessary. Help them to match the isolated sound to one of the vowel cue pictures on their envelopes. Repeat this procedure for six to eight of the 24 pictures in this two-vowel sort.

3. When you think students understand the procedure, have them select a picture from their pile and name it. They should then try to isolate its corresponding short vowel sound and place the picture under the correct header. For example, the picture of a bat will be placed under the short *a* envelope header, while the picture of an otter will be placed under the short *o* envelope header.

4. Once students are able to correctly discriminate between short *a* and *o*, add short *i* pictures to the sorting activity and help students to discriminate between and among short *a*, *o*, and *i*.

5. When students are able to differentiate between these three short vowel sounds, add short vowel *u* pictures to the sorting activity and help them to discriminate between and among 4/5 short vowel sounds presented thus far.

6. After several days or weeks (depending on the age and skill level of your students), you should be able to add the short *e* pictures to the vowel sort.

7. After students are able to successfully short among the five short vowel sounds, you can extend this activity by having them find pictures in magazines that represent the five short vowel sounds and asking them to glue them on a large classroom wall chart (see the example below) that has the five short vowel cues as headers for the five columns.

A a	O o	I i	U u	E e
apple	octopus	itch	up	edge

The following list will help you select additional pictures from other sources for this activity. In multisyllabic words, students match the vowel sound in the first syllable.

a	o	i	u	e
astronaut	octopus	itch	up	edge
ax	ox	sick	tub	echo
alligator	otter	pin	cub	Ed
apple	mop	pig	sun	pet
rat	soccer	wig	cup	peg
mad	fox	six	pup	ten
sad	dog	lip	bus	jet
mat	rod	zip	tux	net
gas	dolphin	bib	mud	vet
fan	log	hip	jug	bed
cat	frog	rib	gum	Eskimo
pan	ostrich	fin	umbrella	wet
hat	box	stick	submarine	web
bag	clock	dig	mug	men
nap	blocks	kid	rut	hen
saxophone	golf	sit	bug	wren
clap	top	mix	hug	pen
trap	lobster	brick	rug	keg

Short Vowels

TUTORIAL Vowels are a group of *speech sounds* that are found in all English syllables. (Some syllables are spelled with syllabic consonants, as in *chasm* and *rhythm*.) A vowel forms the nucleus of a syllable, and consonants are formed around that vowel sound. Vowels are made with an open mouth, and you can say them for as long as you can breathe—that is why they are called **continuants.** Opera singers often sing short vowels when practicing their scales. Short vowels comprise the majority of vowel sounds found in the early grades because they are found in closed syllables (VC and CVC) words. They are also frequent in multisyllabic words. Closed syllables (those containing short vowels) are the most commonly occurring syllable type in English.

TEACH

"Vowels are a group of speech sounds that are found in all English syllables. Vowels are made with an open mouth, and you can say them for as long as you can breathe. Say *paaaaaaaaaaaaaaaat*." Instruct students to say it with you. Do the same with *sock, bug,* and *jet,* holding the vowel as long as the breath lasts.

"Closed syllables have one vowel letter, and it makes the short sound like on our cue cards. When we look at the word, the vowel is closed in at the end of the word (or syllable) by one or more consonants." Show and discuss with students *pat, sock, bug,* and *jet.* Instruct students to tell you the characteristics of a closed syllable.

On Day One, when segmenting the sounds of words with tiles, instruct students to place an orange tile where they think they hear a vowel sound, even if they are not yet able to discriminate the correct one. This activity establishes the principle early that each word contains a vowel sound.

Note: Depending on the students' skill levels, phoneme-grapheme mapping lessons with the Short Vowel, Closed-Syllable Word List that follows may take several weeks—one week for each of the short vowel sounds and then a week or two working on words with a combination of the short vowel sounds. Start with short *a* words, then move on to those containing short *o.* Next, work on short *i* and short *u* words, leaving short *e* until last. Short *e* is the most difficult short vowel to discriminate. Mapping procedures are presented for each short vowel in the word list.

Short Vowel, Closed-Syllable Word List													
Short *a*			**Short *o***		**Short *i***		**Short *u***		**Short *e***	
[a] [t]			[g] [o] [t]		[i] [t]		[r] [u] [b]		[f] [e] [d]	
lap	hag	map	cot	mop	bib	Tim	cub	bun	web	jet
yam	lag	nap	dot	pop	fib	fin	rub	fun	bed	let
van	nag	yap	got	top	rib	pin	sub	gun	fed	met
ran	sag	cab	hot	cod	bid	sin	tub	nun	led	net
fan	tag	jab	jot	nod	did	tin	bud	run	red	pet
pan	cat	wax	lot	rod	hid	win	mud	sun	Ted	set
fat	hat	ax	not	pod	kid	dip	suds	cup	beg	vet
tan	mat	fax	pot	sod	lid	hip	bug	hup	leg	wet
pat	pat	lax	rot	bog	rid	lip	dug	pup	Meg	yet
tap	rat	lap	tot	cog	Sid	nip	hug	bus	peg	den
rap	sat	yap	cob	dog	big	rip	jug	tux	hem	hex
at	bad	can	dob	fog	dig	sip	lug		hen	rex
bat	dad	fan	fob	hog	fig	tip	mug		men	sex
ham	had	man	lob	log	jig	yip	pug		pen	
pal	mad	pan	mob	tog	pig	zip	rut		ten	
map	pad	ran	rob	mom	rig	bit	tug		yen	
nap	sad	gas	sob	con	wig	fit	bum		pep	
zap	yak	tax	bop	don	dim	hit	gum		yes	
bag	cap	sax	cop	non	him	kit	hum		bet	
sap	rag	max	hop	box	rim	lit	sum		get	
tap	ham		fox	pox	quit	pit				
lap	yap		lox		sit	if				
					six	fix				
					mix	it				

Phoneme-Grapheme Mapping
(A Method for Bridging Sound to Print)

Name: _____ Date: _____

j	o	b		g	o	ng			
g	o	t		b	l	o	tch		
j	o	t		p	o	n	d		
b	o	g							
p	o	d							
sh	o	p							
ch	o	p							
l	o	ck							
m	o	th							
wh	o	p							
s	l	o	p						
b	o	n	k						

Note: This sample demonstrates a student's mapping of short vowel *o* within single syllable words containing blends and digraphs (Grades 2 and 3).

Phoneme-Grapheme Mapping
(A Method for Bridging Sound to Print)

Name: _____   Date: _____

i	f				g	i	f	t
h	i	m			l	i	f	t
m	i	ss			m	i	l	k
m	i	⨉			m	i	n	k
s	i	⨉			g	i	v̶ (✓)
f	i	⨉			l	i	v̶ (✓)
th	i	s	p	i	c	n	i	c
sh	i	f	t		l	i	t	t	le
sh	i	n	m	i	l	k	i	ng
i	s	sh	i	f	t	l	e	ss
Wh	i	m	sh	i	n	p	a	d
Ph	i	l	m	i	⨉	i	ng

Note: This sample demonstrates a student's mapping of short vowel *i* within the context of reviewing the following concepts: consonant *x*, digraphs, blends, *f-l-s* rule, and the mapping of final consonant *v*. Note that when *x* represents two sounds (/k/ and /s/), it is mapped in two boxes. For more about mapping *x*, see Lesson 1:11. Also note that the mapping of "little" is incorrect; there is only one /t/ sound in the word.

y as a Vowel

TUTORIAL The letter *y* is very versatile. It represents the consonant sound /y/ when it comes at the beginning of a word or syllable as in *yes* and *yo-yo*. It represents the vowel sounds /ī/, /ē/, and /ĭ/ as in *why*, *baby*, and *gym*.

TEACH

Teach *y* as a vowel. Ask students to segment the sounds in *by*. Ask them to say the last sound, /ī/. Tell them that the long /ī/ is spelled with a *y* at the end of one-syllable words.

Ask students to segment the sounds in *baby*. Ask them to say the last sound, /ē/. When *y* follows a consonant at the end of a word with more than one syllable, it stands for the long sound of *e*.

Teach the two sound/spelling concepts that follow. Teach the more complex uses of *y* as a vowel if students are reading multisyllable words.

MAPPING PROCEDURE

When *y* is used as a vowel, it makes a single vowel sound, so its letter is placed in one box (as demonstrated on the following page).

y as a Vowel Word List	
When *y* follows a consonant at the end of one-syllable words, it usually sounds like long *i*.	**When *y* follows a consonant at the end of multisyllabic words, it stands for the long sound of *e*.**

	At the End of Nouns			At the End of Adjectives		At the End of Multisyllabic Verbs
wh ȳ	c i t ȳ			sh ow ȳ		t i d ȳ
fly	by	baby	dandy	fifty	angry	grassy	bury
why	fry	forty	county	sixty	chewy	gloomy	tidy
ply	my	taffy	bunny	gravy	creamy	silly	tarry
shy	pry	city	puppy	dandy	grumpy	sticky	hurry
sly	sky	copy	thirty	dairy	silly	stormy	carry
spy	spry	body	dandy	family	bossy	needy	study
thy	sty	ivy	county	daddy	chilly	empty	worry
wry	guy	lady	library	puppy	hairy		
		belly	derby	penny	showy		
		daisy	twenty	bully	sketchy		
		ferry	eighty	derby	lazy		
		ivory	enemy	army	dirty		
		candy	artery	county	dizzy		

More Complex Uses of *y* as a Vowel Word List	
TEACH When *y* comes at the end of a two-syllable word and the accent is on the last syllable, it makes the sound of long *i*.	**TEACH** When used before another vowel, *y* makes the sound of long *e*.

a	pp	l	ȳ

e	m	b	r	ȳ	o

apply	reply	embryo
comply	deny	halcyon
imply	supply	presbyopia

When used to make the suffix *-ify*, /ĭ/ becomes a schwa (ə) vowel.*

g	l	or	ĭ	f	ȳ

dignify	specify	beautify
glorify	amplify	certify
lassify	dignify	diversify
electrify	fortify	gratify
horrify	identify	intensify
justify	magnify	modify
mortify	mystify	notify
personify	qualify	ratify
rectify	satisfy	signify
simplify	solidify	testify
unify	dehumidify	disqualify

* For more about the schwa, see Lesson 1:3.

1:3

Schwa

TUTORIAL The schwa is an upper-level concept—students must be reading and spelling multisyllable words. The **schwa** (ə), which is sometimes called a neutral vowel or a murmur vowel, is an unstressed vowel sound, such as the first sound in *around* or the last vowel sound in *custom*. Any of the single vowel spellings may represent the schwa under specific circumstances. The schwa seems particularly common in unstressed syllables of the proper names for the fifty states, as in *Al-a̱-bam-a̱, Ok-la̱-ho-ma̱, Del-a̱-ware,* and in common first names, such as *San-dra̱, Don-na̱,* and *A-lex-a̱.*

Although some programs give generalizations for the schwa, they can be cumbersome and not very useful. For decoding a known word, the schwa is not necessary. Words that contain the schwa may usually be decoded successfully if the reader tries the short sound of the vowel. Since the schwa often appears in syllables after adding a suffix, understanding the schwa becomes more necessary when learning roots, prefixes, and suffixes for spelling.

Although *a* appears to be the most frequently used vowel to represent the schwa, any of the five vowel letters can spell a schwa. And the schwa can occur in any syllable type. However, the vowel sound heard in a consonant *-le* syllable type is always a schwa.

TEACH

"The schwa vowel is found in an unaccented syllable." Ask students to find the unaccented syllable in several words from the Schwa Word List that follows. Model how to hold the lips together and say the word inside of the mouth. The unaccented syllable is one in which the voice drops out, or falls down. Isolate and say the vowel sound in the unaccented syllables. Show students the word's spelling. Explain that knowing which letter to use to spell the schwa takes a lot of practice, as we have to create a visual memory of the spelling of many words with schwa. Show students the schwa symbol (ə). Help them find words in the dictionary that contain a schwa. The pronunciation can be found beside the word entry (e.g., ago [ə • go]). Then demonstrate how to wrap text with it (procedure follows). This aspect of phoneme-grapheme mapping helps students recall the spelling of the schwa in words.

MAPPING PROCEDURE

When mapping a schwa, half-wrap the schwa symbol, leaving the straight edge to lie under the vowel spelling, as with the word *totem*. Teach students how to do this on the second day of instruction. A student phoneme-grapheme mapping follows the Schwa Word List.

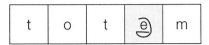

Schwa Word List			
a as Schwa (ə)			*e* as Schwa (ə)
In the initial position	**In the medial position**	**In the final position**	
a g o	o v a l	y ō g a	t o t e m
ago	rival · local	umbrella	kitten · problem
awake	central · oval	vanilla	mitten · system
about	capital · nasal	comma	planet · puppet
alone	vocal · moral	quota	totem · locket
amaze	choral · naval	scuba	closet · angel
alive	coastal · mortal	Atlanta	comet · funnel
atomic	colossal · mental	Sandra	channel · jewel
amid	digital · vocal	delta	dozen · panel
Alaska	disloyal · pelican	vista	basket · pocket
awhile	dismal · available	gala	hyphen · rebel
along	federal · principal	yoga	panel · easel
acute	final · several	stanza	novel · colonel
amid	carnival · signal	harmonica	sentence · nickel
away	formal · skeletal	opera	siren · shovel
adrift	frugal · spinal	retina	warden · sequel
alike	general · spiral	extra	problem · squirrel
asleep	global · Mexican	formula	Salem · rocket
awoke	herbal · verbal	tuba	agency · silence
aside	identical · Roman	rotunda	science · towel
atop	universal		moment

Schwa Word List (continued)		
i as Schwa	*o* as Schwa	*u* as Schwa
ē v ⓘ l	a t ⓞ m	f ō c ⓤ s

animal	audible	button	capsule
April	credible	cotton	chorus
basil	horrible	carton	cactus
devil	illegible	piston	callus
evil	impossible	apron	campus
fossil	incredible	method	circus
pencil	responsible	beckon	fungus
pupil	possible	carbon	census
stencil	terrible	jargon	focus
tonsil	visible	lemon	minus
utensil	legibility	patron	mucus
service	vanity	atom	sinus
fertile	hesitate	custom	Uranus
missile	compliment	random	Venus
destiny	cabinet	ransom	focus
dignity	apricot	seldom	lotus
resident	domino	venom	litmus
vanity	difficult	second	album
multiply	cavity	freedom	forum
obligate	continent	kingdom	minimum
mobilize	gravity	Boston	bonus
antidote	estimate	lesson	discuss
president	indirect	person	
magnitude	sensitive	awesome	
flexibility	investigate	handsome	
eligibility			

Phoneme-Grapheme Mapping
(A Method for Bridging Sound to Print)

Name: _____ Date: _____

ⓐ	g	ō					
ⓐ	b	ou	t				
r	ī	v	ⓐ	l			
c	e	n	t	r	ⓐ	l	
l	ō	c	ⓐ	l			
m	e	n	t	ⓐ	l		
A	t	l	a	n	t	ⓐ	
v	i	s	t	ⓐ			
c	ⓐ	m	ⓔ	t			
d	ⓐ	z	ⓔ	n			
s	y	s	t	ⓔ	m		

Note: This sample demonstrates a student's understanding of schwa (ə) as found in the initial, medial, and final position of multisyllabic words.

Vowels Preceded by Consonant w

TUTORIAL When the vowel letters *a* or *o* are preceded by *w* in a word or syllable, the sound of the vowel may be other than the short or long vowel sound generally associated with that letter. This generalization helps explain why many common words in which *w* is followed by *a* or *o* do not contain their expected short vowel sound.

TEACH	When you see the vowel letters *a* or *o* after a *w* in a word or syllable, the sound may not be the short or long sound usually made by *a* or *o*.

Vowels With *W* Word List	
With *wa*	**With *wo***
want	wolf
want	woman
waddle	wolfish
wash	wolverine
water	wolves
wad	womb
wander	won
wasp	wonder
watch	wonderful
schwa	
swab	
swap	
swat	
swan	
swallow	

UNDERSTANDING CONSONANTS

TUTORIAL Consonants are a class of speech sounds that are not vowels. They are formed with either complete obstruction or partial obstruction of the air flow through the mouth.

Table 5 The Six Types of Consonants			
Type of Consonant	**Description**	**Examples**	
		Voiceless	**Voiced**
Stop	This consonant sound is produced with a complete obstruction of air.	/p/ as in *stop* /t/ as in *pot* /k/ as in *kiss, stack*	/b/ as in *bat* /d/ as in *dip* /g/ as in *got*
Nasal	This consonant sound is produced through the nose.	/m/ as in *map* /n/ as in *nap* /ng/ as in *wing*	
Fricative	This type of consonant is produced by partially obstructing the air flow. Friction is created and you hear a slight hissing noise.	/f/ as in *fit* soft /th/ as in *both* /s/ as in *sap* /sh/ as in *ship*	/v/ as in *vet* hard /th/ as in *bother* /z/ as in *buzz* /zh/ as in *vision*
Affricate	This type of consonant is made with a complete obstruction of air followed by friction that creates a slight hissing noise.	/ch/ as in *chase*	/j/ as in *jug* /j/ as in *gist*
Glide	This type of consonant is almost like a vowel in its pronunciation.	/wh/ as in *where* and *which* /h/ as in *hat* and *who*	/w/ as in *wig* and *quick* /y/ as in *you*
Liquid	This type of consonant is a group that includes *l* and *r*.	/l/ as in *lady* /r/ as in *race* and *ringer*	

There are six types of consonants based on their method of production (see Table 5). Helping students discover where and how these sounds are made in the mouth is key to helping them differentiate between and among sounds. These distinctions lead to more accurate sound/letter correspondences.

In English, eight pairs of consonants are made in the same position in the mouth. These related sounds are in boldface in Table 5. They differ only in whether they are voiced or unvoiced. A **voiced sound** is made in your throat and can be felt by placing your hand gently over your voice box when you speak or by covering your ears as you say the sound. Because students' spelling errors often reflect a lack of understanding of how voicing affects specific consonants, it is important to instruct students about voiced and unvoiced consonants when making phoneme-grapheme connections.

Table 6 includes articulatory clues for the consonant sound to help you guide students through tactile discovery of how these sounds are created and whether they are voiced and unvoiced. Other phonological awareness programs provide activities to help students discover the articulatory gestures specific to each consonant.

Table 6	Consonant Phonemes by Place and Manner of Articulation						
	Lips	**Teeth/ Lips**	**Tongue/ Teeth**	**Ridge/ Teeth**	**Roof of Mouth**	**Back of Throat**	**Glottis**
Stops Unvoiced	/p/			/t/		/k/	
Voiced	/b/			/d/		/g/	
Nasals	/m/			/n/		/ng/	
Fricatives Unvoiced		/f/	/th/	/s/ /z/	/sh/		
Voiced		/v/	/th/		/zh/		
Affricates Unvoiced					/ch/		
Voiced					/j/		
Glides Unvoiced					/y/	/wh/	/h/
Voiced						/w/	
Liquids				/l/			
				/r/			

From _Language Essentials for Teachers of Reading and Spelling (LETRS)_, Module 2, by Louisa Cook Moats, Sopris West, 2005.

MAPPING PROCEDURE

Teach the consonant sounds using the articulatory process provided in Table 6. Depending on how limited or advanced students' reading and spelling skills are, present up to four sounds during the one-week lesson. Follow the sequence as it is presented in Table 2.

Table 6 includes articulatory clues for each consonant sound to help you guide students through tactile discovery of how and where these sounds are created and whether they are voiced or unvoiced. In addition, the consonant lessons include a TEACH box that gives specific language for you to use to help students explore how and where each consonant sound is made. These articulatory gestures, or tactile cues, are invaluable in helping students develop the phonological awareness skills they will need to become proficient readers and spellers.

Consonants m, l, s, and t

TUTORIAL Please review the general tutorial information for consonants on pages 42–44 before teaching this lesson. Articulatory gestures, or tactile cues, are given in each consonant box below.

MAPPING PROCEDURE

The consonants *m*, *l*, *s*, and *t* contain one sound (or phoneme), so students place one letter (or grapheme) in each box to illustrate their one-to-one correspondence, as shown below.

Consonants *m, l, s,* and *t* Word List			
m = /m/	**l = /l/**	**s = /s/**	**t = /t/**
TEACH "Firmly close your two lips together and force the sound through your nose." **It is a voiced nasal sound.**	**TEACH** "Push your flattened tongue against the upper gum ridge behind your teeth. The sound leaks from the sides of your tongue." **It is a voiced sound that takes on the shape of the sounds around it.**	**TEACH** "Place your tongue tip behind your upper or lower teeth. A hissing sound will be made as long as you continue the breath." **It is an unvoiced sound made like its voiced partner /z/.**	**TEACH** "Raise your tongue to the upper gum ridge behind your teeth and push out the air while you quickly drop your tongue." **It is an unvoiced sound made like its voiced partner /d/.**
`m` `a` `t`	`l` `o` `t`	`s` `a` `t`	`i` `t`

m = /m/		l = /l/		s = /s/		t = /t/	
man	men	lap	led	sad	suds	it	top
map	ham	lip	less	sag	sum	tab	tot
met	him	let	list	Sam	sun	tad	tub
mat	Tim	lot	lob	sap	so	tag	tug
me	Sam	lab	lock	sat	see	tam	pet
my	Pam	lad	loft	set	say	tan	hot
make	sum	lag	log	Sid	us	tap	hit
much	am	lass	left	sin	this	tat	hat
many	seem	lid	loss	sip	yes	Tim	hut
may		leg	lump	sis	sod	tin	let
must		lick	limp	sit	sub	tip	met
made		lit		sob		pet	pot
						ten	

1:6

Consonants p, f, h, and c

TUTORIAL Please review the general tutorial information for consonants on pages 42–44 before teaching this lesson. Articulatory gestures, or tactile cues, are given in each consonant box below.

MAPPING PROCEDURE

The consonants p, f, h, and c are one sound (or phoneme), so students place one letter (or grapheme) in each box to illustrate their one-to-one correspondence.

Consonants *p, f, h,* and *c* Word List			
p = /p/	*f* = /f/	*h* = /h/	*c* =/k/
TEACH "Put your lips together and pop out the air." **It is an unvoiced sound made like its voiced partner /b/.**	**TEACH** "Press your lower lip against your upper teeth. A stream of air will be forced out the narrow space between them. You can continue this sound as long as the breath." **It is an unvoiced sound made like its voiced partner /v/.**	**TEACH** "Open your mouth slightly and allow a very gentle flow of air to escape from your throat area. The sound can be continued as long as your breath." **It is an unvoiced sound.**	**TEACH** "Firmly raise the back of your tongue to the back of the roof of your mouth. Then quickly drop the tongue and the air will be forced out." **It is an unvoiced sound made like its voiced partner /g/.**
p o p	i f	h i p	c o p
pad dip	fad fish	had hug	cab call
pal lip	fan cliff	hag hum	cad cam
Pam nip	fat stuff	Hal hut	can cut
pan rip	fed off	ham he	cap
pat sip	fib	hat how	cat
pen lap	fig	hem hub	cob
pet top	fin	hen hot	cod
pig cop	fit	hid hop	cog
pin hop	fob	him	con
pit mop	fog	hip	cop
pod tip	fun	his	cot
pot hip	if	hit	cub
pub pup		hog	cup

Consonants n, b, r, and j

TUTORIAL Please review the general tutorial information for consonants on pages 42–44 before teaching this lesson. Articulatory gestures, or tactile cues, are given in each consonant box below.

MAPPING PROCEDURE

The consonants *n*, *b*, *r*, and *j* are of one sound (or phoneme), so students place one letter (or grapheme) in each box to illustrate the one-to-one correspondence that exists between what is heard and what is written.

Consonants *n, b, r,* and *j* Word List			
n = /n/	**b = /b/**	**r = /r/**	**j = /j/**
TEACH "Open your mouth slightly and raise your tongue, but not its tip, until it touches the upper gum ridge behind your teeth. Force the sound out through your nose. This sound can be continued until you run out of breath." **It is a voiced, nasal sound. You cannot make this sound if you plug your nose.**	**TEACH** "Place your lips together and pop out air." **It is a voiced sound made likes its unvoiced partner /p/.**	**TEACH** "Raise the tip of your tongue slightly. Its sides should lightly touch your upper molars. The sound will come out of your throat and over your tongue." **It is a voiced sound.**	**TEACH** "Press your tongue against the roof of your mouth as if making the /d/ sound. Then flatten your tongue and bring it slightly back. A stream of air will be forced over the top of the tongue while your lips are partly rounded. Since the air is pushed out, the sound cannot be continued." **It is a voiced sound made like its voiced partner /ch/.**
n a b	b u n	r o b	j a b

n = /n/			b = /b/			r = /r/			j = /j/		
nab	nut	ten	bad	big	bin	rag	rob	rest	jab	job	jaw
nag	van	pin	bag	bit	rob	ram	rod	ride	jag	jog	July
Nan	hen	fun	bam	Bob	rub	ran	Ron	rock	jam	jock	June
nap	man	gun	ban	bog	rib	rap	rot	for	Jan	jot	jacket
Ned	pan	run	bat	bop	tab	rat	rub	her	jazz	jug	joy
net	ran	bun	bed	bug	tub	red	rug	year	Jed	just	jar
nip	tan	nun	beg	bum	bib	rev	rum	rig	Jen	jut	jig
nod	men	not	Ben	bun	bid	rib	run	rip	jet	jump	Jim
non	den		bet	bus	but	rid	rut	read	jib		

1:8

Consonants *v*, *g*, *w*, and *k*

TUTORIAL Please review the general tutorial information for consonants on pages 42–44 before teaching this lesson. Articulatory gestures, or tactile cues, are given in each consonant box below.

MAPPING PROCEDURE

The consonants *v*, *g*, *w*, and *k* each represent one sound (or phoneme), so students place one letter (or grapheme) in each box to illustrate their one-to-one correspondence.

Consonants *v*, *g*, *w*, and *k* Word List			
v = /v/	*g* = /g/	*w* = /w/	*k* = /k/
TEACH "Press your lower lip against your upper teeth. Force a stream of air out the narrow space between your lip and teeth and continue the sound as long as the breath. A mild vibration will be felt on your lower lip." **It is a voiced sound made like its unvoiced partner /f/.**	**TEACH** "Firmly raise the back of your tongue to the back of the roof of your mouth." **It is a voiced sound made like its unvoiced partner /k/.**	**TEACH** "Round your lips in a puckered position, and then relax them as you begin to voice the sound." **It is a voiced sound that assumes its second shape from the vowel that follows it.**	**TEACH** "Firmly raise the back of your tongue to the back of the roof of your mouth. Quickly drop your tongue and the sound will be forced out." **It is an unvoiced sound made like its voiced partner /g/.**

| v | a | n | | g | a | g | | w | i | g | | k | i | d |

van	very	*have*	gab	girl	good	wag	with	win	kid	king	look
vat	verb	*give*	gap	get	gum	web	work	wit	Kim	keep	book
vet	vent	*move*	gag	go	fog	wed	word	won	kin	kitten	cook
vim		*live*	gal	gun	lag	well	week	we	Kip	kick	bank
vote		*above*	gas	game	leg	west	world		kit	walk	milk
vest		*love*	gob	bog	pig	wet	wave		kiss	work	speak
vase		*twelve**	god	dog	log	went	way		keg	mark	kill
			gave	big	bag	wig			kelp	kind	
			got	egg	fig	will			Ken	key	

*No words in the English language end in the consonant letter *v*. Therefore, a final silent *e* is placed after the *v* for protection. (See word list and mapping procedure in Lesson 3:6.)

Consonants d, Initial y, and z

TUTORIAL Please review the general tutorial information for consonants on pages 42–44 before teaching this lesson. Articulatory gestures, or tactile cues, are given in each consonant box below.

MAPPING PROCEDURE

The consonants *d*, initial *y*, and *z* represent of one sound (or phoneme), so students place one letter (or grapheme) in each box to illustrate the one-to-one correspondence that exists between what is heard and what is written.

Consonants *d*, Initial *y*, and *z* Word List		
d = /d/	**Initial y = /y/**	**z = /z/**
TEACH "Raise your tongue so it touches the upper gum ridge behind your teeth. Then push out air while you quickly drop your tongue." **It is a voiced sound made like its unvoiced partner /t/.**	**TEACH** "Press your tongue against the roof of your mouth as in producing /d/, and then slightly draw it back. A stream of air will be forced over your tongue, while you partially round your lips." **It is a voiced glide that is made similarly to a voiced /g/ and the first phoneme in the long vowel *u* [y oo].** Students often confuse *u* and *y* when either is heard in the initial position of a word. Note that when y is at the beginning of a syllable, it makes a consonant and not a vowel sound.	**TEACH** "Place the tip of your tongue behind your upper or lower teeth. A buzzing sound will be created." **It is a voiced sound made like its unvoiced partner /s/.**

		One-Syllable Words	**Multisyllable Words**		
	d | i | g	y | e | s	y | e | ll | ow		z | i | p
dab	dub	yes	yam	yellow	yucca	zip	quiz
dad	dud	yell	yale	yoga	Yukon	zap	whiz
dog	dug	yet	yew	yahoo	Yuma	zest	buzz
end	red	yam	yea	youth	**In Medial**	zinc	fizz
hid	duck	yen	yurt	yonder	**Position**	zoo	jazz
den	do	you	yeah	yourself	canyon	zap	fuzz
dent	day	yak	yew	yogurt	beyond	zone	zebra
did	done	yap	yarn	Yankee	papaya	zigzag	gaze
dig	door	yip	yank	yesterday	backyard	zipper	prize
dim	bed	youth		Yiddish	lawyer	zoom	
din	and	yon		yodel	barnyard	zeal	
dip	had	yard					

Consonant Oddities: qu

TUTORIAL Moats (2000) has deemed *qu* and *x* **consonant oddities.** Unlike the consonants we have previously studied, they do not follow the regular one-to-one relationship between a consonant and its sound.

In our written language, *q* is never seen without a *u* following it, so it makes sense to treat them as a consonant partnership. However, that partnership varies as to the number of phonemes created. For example, most of the time *qu* represents the two phonemes /k/ and /w/, as in *queen, quit,* and *quilt.* Therefore, it takes two closely linked boxes to make this phoneme-grapheme relationship apparent, as demonstrated in the *qu* Word List that follows.

In a much smaller group of words, of French origin, *qu* plus *e* can represent the single phoneme /k/. When this is the case, the *que* grapheme is placed in one sound box instead of two, as in the third column of the *qu* Word List.

TEACH

"The consonant letter *q* is a partner letter and won't go anywhere without his friend *u*. That is why you will always see them side by side in words. The speech sounds *qu* makes most often are /k/ /w/. Say the sounds in *quit:* /k/ /w/ /i/ /t/." Instruct students to say the sounds they hear at the beginning of *quit.* Ask students how to spell those sounds.

MAPPING PROCEDURE

Show students how to map *qu, /k/ /w/*—over two boxes, the q and u close together and circled (or looped, just as friends and/or partners join arms). In a very few words, *qu* is followed by *e*, as in *antique*. The sound in this case is /k/, so the letters *que* go together in one box and no looping is necessary.

Consonant Oddities: *qu* Word List

qu = /kw/

Initial *qu-* Words		Medial *qu-* Words	Final *-que* = /k/
q u i t		e q u i p	t or que
quit	question	squeeze	antique
quilt	quality	squirm	clique
quiz	quiver	liquid	critique
quiet	quadruple	equal	mosque
queen	quartet	equator	Mozambique
quest	quartz	sequence	mystique
quack	quart	frequent	oblique
quill	quarry	squirrel	opaque
quad	quarter	squid	physique
quake	quaver	squint	plaque
quick	query	squeal	technique
quite	Quaker	equip	torque
quail	quantum	equipment	unique
quote	qualify	square	picturesque
quaint	quarterback	require	grotesque
quaff	quarterly	equation	
quell	quahog	equivalent	
quench	quotient	squash	
quick	quibble	earthquake	
quite		squeak	
quote		inquire	
quint			
quirk			

Consonant Oddities: x

TUTORIAL The consonant *x* is troublesome because it is the only grapheme in our language that represents two phonemes—/k/ and /s/ or /g/ and /z/. Yet, alphabet charts across the nation continue to depict *X ray* or *xylophone* for this consonant oddity. It is best to teach this oddball consonant using a key word such as *ax*. Instruct your students to delete the first phoneme in the word, leaving the final two, which will give the two sounds (/k/ and /s/) embedded in the consonant *x*. That relationship is shown in the *x* Word List that follows. The *x* crosses two boxes to demonstrate that its single-letter grapheme *(x)* comprises two sounds, or phonemes.

TEACH

"*X* is the only letter that represents two sounds! Say *ax*. Say it again without the /a/." Students should say /k//s/ together like a kissing sound. Explain to them that we coarticulate the sounds so closely that it is hard to pull them apart. Show them how to map the word *ax*, crossing the *x* across two sound boxes because there are two sounds for *x*.

"Say *exam*." Help students isolate the /g/ and /z/ sounds for *x* in this word. *X* can stand for /k//s/ or /g//z/. In a very few words, *x* is /z/, as in *Xerox*.

MAPPING PROCEDURE

In unaccented syllables, when *x* is paired with *e* to become the prefix *ex-,* the *x* takes on two different phonemes, /g/ and /z/, as in the word *exact*. It also happens that if the base word or root that you are combining with *x* begins with a vowel or a silent *h*, the *x* is pronounced /egz/. Students still map the *x* across two boxes to show that it has two consonant phonemes instead of one.

In a very small number of words, *x* is found in the initial position, where it produces an initial /z/ sound. When this is the case, the *x* is placed in one sound box to show this single-consonant phoneme at work.

Consonant Oddities: *x* Word List			
x = /k/ /s/		*x* = /g/ /z/ in an Unaccented Syllable	*x* = /z/ as an Initial Consonant
a x ‖ e x i t	e x a m	x er o x
lax fix	exit excess expand	**TEACH** The vowel after the *x* is accented.	xerox
hex nix	six except expedite		xylophone
lox Tex	sixty exclaim expend	exact	xenon
vex ax	excel exodus expose	exam	xylem
wax fax	axis expense excuse	exist	xenophobia
sex max	oxen except exhale	examine	
next tax	exit expel extreme	example	
mix	extra expert expire	exhort	
box	exile explore explain	exhume	
fox	index export explicit	exist	
ox	relax expose explode	exult	
sox	taxes express exploit	exhaust	
six	text extend exhale	exhibit	
ox	extract exclaim	exhilarate	
	exclude	exotic	
	excite	exude	
	excerpt	exaggerate	

Phoneme-Grapheme Mapping
(A Method for Bridging Sound to Print)

Name: _____   Date: _____

H	e	✕						
W	a	✕						
N	e	✕	t					
e	✕	p	er	t				
e	✕	h	ā	le				
t	e	✕	t					
e	✕	a	M					
e	✕	i	t					
e	✕	i	s	t				
X	ȳ	l	ō	ph	ō	ne		

Note: This student shows her understanding of consonant *x*. Note how she differentiates between consonant *x* when it has two phonemes, as in *wax*, and when it has one phoneme, as in *xylophone*. She also demonstrates an understanding of open syllables as shown by the long vowel marker (a horizontal line) over the open and silent *e* vowels.

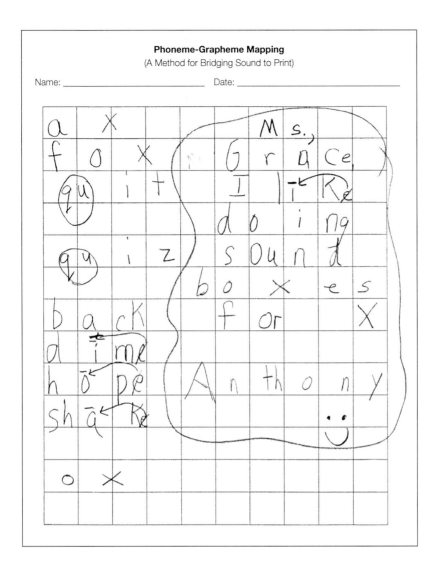

Phoneme-Grapheme Mapping
(A Method for Bridging Sound to Print)

Name: _____ Date: _____

Note: In this review mapping exercise, the student demonstrates his understanding of *x*, *qu*, *k/ck*, and silent *-e*. He also expresses his satisfaction for phoneme-grapheme mapping in his note to me.

Digraphs
(sh, ch, th, wh, ph, and ng)

TUTORIAL **Consonant digraphs** are two consonant letters that, when put together, stand for a sound that is entirely different from either of the letters alone. Most of the digraphs end in the letter *h* such as **ch**, **sh**, **th**, **ph**, and **wh**.

However, one commonly used digraph in early elementary grades is *ng*. Yet, many teachers tend to teach *ng* as a suffix ending prior to discussing the two phonemes in this well-used word ending. This can lead to the following misspellings: *saing* for *sang*, *raing* for *rang* and *siing* for *sing*. Unless this delicate relationship is explicitly taught, students may erroneously believe that it is the *ing* creating the /ng/ rather than the /ng/ having its identity separate from the *i*.

TEACH

"A consonant digraph is two letters that when put together stand for one sound. *Di-* at the beginning of *digraph* means two. There are two letters in a digraph. The one sound represented by a digraph is a unique sound to the letters used in the digraph." Teach students the digraphs one at a time. Show students the digraph spellings and teach them the sounds as described in the Digraph Word List that follows. Digraph lessons could last several weeks. Teach students the mapping procedure on Day Two. One box for one sound means that there are two letters in one box when a word has a digraph.

MAPPING PROCEDURE

Since digraphs have just one sound, the two-letter grapheme representation is placed in one box. See the examples in the word list that follows.

Digraph Word List			
sh	**ch**	**soft th** (unvoiced)	**hard th** (voiced)
TEACH "Raise the tongue into a flattened position and draw it back slightly. Force a stream of breath over the top of the tongue while your lips are partly rounded. You can continue the sound as long as your breath." **It is an unvoiced sound.**	**TEACH** "Press the tongue against the roof of the mouth and flatten it. Then draw it back and push a stream of breath over your tongue while your lips are partly rounded. The force of air cannot be continued." **It is an unvoiced sound made much like its voiced partner /j/.**	**TEACH** "Place the tip of your tongue between your upper and lower front teeth. Force air gently out so your tongue is slightly cooled when you make this sound, which can be continued." **It is an unvoiced sound made much like its voiced partner, hard /th/.**	**TEACH** "Place the tip of your tongue between your upper and lower front teeth. Force air gently out so your tongue is slightly tickled by the sound's vibration." **It is a voiced sound made much like its unvoiced partner, soft /th/.**
a · sh	ch · u · m	th · i · n	th · a · t

sh		ch		soft th		hard th	
ship	clash	chum	such	thin	bath	than	either
shop	crash	chop	lunch	thud	math	that	neither
shelf	dash	chest	crunch	third	path	them	farther
splash	flash	champ	bunch	theft	tenth	then	father
shack	mash	chill	ranch	thump	bathtub	this	feather
shaft	rash	chip	branch	thug	fifth	thus	gather
shell	sash	chimp	munch	thong	sloth	there	heather
shed	smash	chess	punch	thank	with	their	lathe
shift	trash	chat	clench	thick	within	they're	northern
shin	fresh	chap	drench	thing	rath	bathe	rather
shock	dish	chug	trench	think	hath	another	scathe
shot	fish	chant	clinch	thong	south	brother	seethe
shut	wish	chub	rich	theme	oath	clothe	sheathe
shim	blush	chaff	flinch	thermal	sixth	either	slither
flush	brush	check	inch	thermos	mouth	loathe	smooth
gush	crush	chin	pinch	thirst	teeth	clothing	soothe
hush	rush	chomp	much	thunder			teethe
mush	ash		hunch	thorn			tether

Digraph Word List (continued)			
wh	***ph = /f/***	***-ng ***	**suffix *-ing***
TEACH "Round your lips into a puckered position and then relax them as you begin to voice the sound. It assumes its second shape from the vowel that follows it." **It is an unvoiced sound that is made much like its voiced partner /w/. In American English, *wh* is often pronounced /w/.**	**TEACH** "Press your lower lip against your upper teeth. A stream of air will be forced out the narrow space between them. You can continue this sound as long as the breath." **It is an unvoiced sound made like its voiced partner /v/.**	**TEACH** "Raise the back of your tongue until it makes contact with your lowered soft palate near the roof of your mouth. Force the sound through your nose." **It is a voiced nasal sound.** *Also see "When a Single *n* Sounds Like /ng/" on the following page.	**TEACH** "Raise the back of your tongue high to the front of your mouth to formulate the short *i* sound. Then allow your tongue to make contact with the lowered soft palate near the roof of your mouth and force the sound through your nose." **It combines two sounds: a vowel and a voiced nasal sound.**

`wh` `e` `n`	`ph` `l` `o` `x`		`s` `i` `ng` `i` `ng`

wham	wheat	phase	phosphorus	sang	gong		adding
wheel	whether	phew	photogenic	sing	tongs		holding
which	whew	phlox	photograph	ring	fling		helping
whiff	whey	phantom	graphics	rang	flung		ending
whim	which	photo	phrase	twang	prong		sending
when	whiffle	physics	physical	hang	thong		landing
whack	while	phone	physics	gang	nothing		spending
whip	whimper	Phil	physique	swung	tang		fixing
whir	whimsical	pharaoh	alpha	wing	king		twisting
whiz	whine	symphony	alphabet	sung	sting		painting
whoa	whinny	telephone	cellophane	hung	zing		rushing
why	whittle	sphinx	diphthong	lung	length		swinging
whale	whirl	Philippines	dolphin	bring	strength		bringing
wharf	whisk	phlegm	graph	sting	bong		hanging
what	whiskers	phoneme	lymph	fling	rung		singing
whatever	whopper	phonics	orphan	bang	stung		ringing
wheat	whisper	phonetics	pamphlet	thing	long		heating
wheeze	whistle	phonograph	atmosphere	swing	wrong		clinging
whence	white	philosophy	sphere	spring	song		stinging
where		phosphate		sling	tongs		painting

Phoneme-Grapheme Mapping
(A Method for Bridging Sound to Print)

Name: Becca   Date: _____

Ch	a	ll	e	n	ge				
ch	a	m	p	i	o	n			
ch	a	nn	e	l					
ch	a	n	t						
ch	i	m	n	ey					
ch	oi	ce							
ch	u	n	k						
F	r	e	n	ch					
M	ar	ch							
Q	u	e	n	ch					

Note: This mapping exercise demonstrates the student's understanding of digraphs in both the initial and final position.

TEACH

In some words, the digraph /ng/ is spelled with just the letter *n*. This occurs when the next sound is /k/ spelled *c* or *k* or hard /g/ spelled as a *g*. Young spellers often include the ng in their spellings (i.e., *thingk*, *thank*). A symbol such as ⬚*ngk*⬚ in their word study notebook alerts them that such a sequence does not exist in our language.

When a Single *n* Sounds Like /ng/ Word List

As in words where the letter *n* precedes the sound of hard *c,* as in /k/	As in words where the letter *n* precedes the sound of hard *g,* as in /g/
	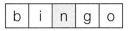
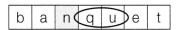	
In the words below, the single grapheme *n* is making the sound of the digraph **ng**. Therefore, the letter remains in a single box, as it represents a single sound. Written phonetically, *banquet* looks like this:	In the words below, the single grapheme *n* is making the sound of the digraph **ng.** The *g* that follows the single *n* makes the hard sound of /g/. Written phonetically, *bingo* looks like this:
/b/ /a/ /ng/ /k/ /w/ /e/ /t/	/b/ /i/ /ng/ /g/ /o/

bank	blink	chunk	uncle	banquet	linger	lingo	tingle
sank	brink	drunk	wink	dunk	hunger	tango	shingle
tank	clink	flunk	sunk	hunk	longer	bongo	mingle
yank	drink	plunk	sunken	junk	mongoose	fungus	jingle
blank	shrink	shrunk	sink	bonkers	mongrel	hungry	jangle
clank	slink	skunk	punk	bunkers	amongst	language	tangle
rank	stink	spunk	thank	hunky	Mongolia	languish	angle
crank	think	stunk	link	lanky	monger	linguist	bangle
drank	bonk	trunk	mink	linkage	congregate	anger	bungle
flank	honk	ankle	pink		angry	anguish	mangle
plank	monk	uncle	rink		angler	angular	strangle
prank	konk	donkey	Wonka		Anglo	bungalow	
shank	tonka	monkey	bunk		angora	kangaroo	
						congress	

ch as /k/ and ch as /sh/

TUTORIAL Older students benefit from knowing that **ch** makes two other sounds. Students have previously learned that **ch** is a digraph and represents the single sound of /ch/.

- **ch** can stand for the single consonant sound of /k/ in words derived from the Greek language.

- **ch** can also stand for the sound /sh/, especially in words borrowed from or influenced by French.

Introduce **ch** = /k/ prior to the digraph sound of /sh/. Several words in educational settings (e.g., *school, chorus, Chris, echo, schedule.*) contain the "**ch** as /k/" sound.

TEACH

"The digraph **ch** can represent two other sounds: /k/ and /sh/. Words influenced by Greek use the *ch* spelling for /k/, and words influenced by French use the *ch* spelling for /sh/."

MAPPING PROCEDURE

Since both letters of **ch** continue to stand for a single sound, either /k/ or /sh/, the letters *c* and *h* are both placed in one sound box as shown below.

s	ch	oo	l

ch	e	f

ch as /k/ and *ch* as /sh/ Word List					
ch as /k/			**ch as /sh/**		
e | *ch* | o			ch | i | c		
ch | or | u | s			ch | i | ff | o | n		
One-Syllable Words	**Two-Syllable Words**	**Three- and Four-Syllable Words**	**One-Syllable Words**	**Two-Syllable Words**	**Three-Syllable Words**
ache	echo	character	cache	brochure	chandelier
school	chorus	orchestra	Cher	chagrin	chanterelle
chord	chaos	technical	chute	chalet	Charlemagne
scheme	anchor	anarchy	chef	chamois	chauvinist
synch	scholar	architect	chic	champagne	Chevrolet
Chris	chemist	chameleon	gauche	Charlotte	Chicago
	orchid	chlorinate		chassis	Michigan
	schedule	psychology		chateau	nonchalant
	monarch	mechanical		chiffon	
	chronic	chromosome		Chopin	
	chlorine	technology		chivalry	
	archive	synchronize		machine	
	Christmas			chenille	
	epoch				
	chasm*				

*This word has the syllabic consonant *m;* see Lesson 1:30.

Phoneme-Grapheme Mapping
(A Method for Bridging Sound to Print)

Name: Danielle   Date:

A	che							
S	ch	oo	l					
ch	or	d						
S	ch	ē	me					
E	ch	ō						
Ch	or	ŭ	s					
ch	ā	ŏ	s					
ch	ū	te						
ch	ĕ	f						
ch	i	c						
m	a	ch	ī	ne				

This map contrasts the two less frequently used sounds of *ch* as /k/ and /sh/. Note, however, that at least four of the selected words (*school*, *chorus*, *ache*, and *machine*) are frequently found in elementary texts.

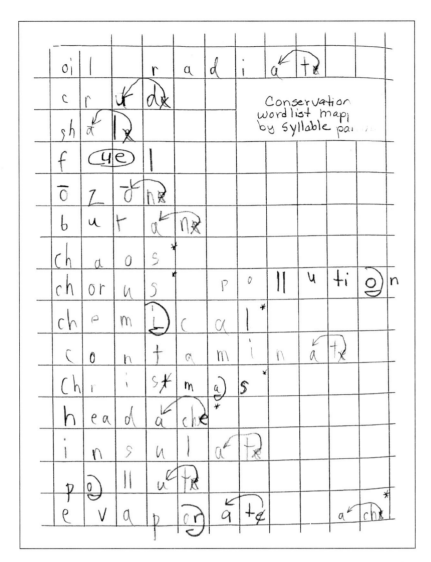

Note: This map of theme-related words for a unit on conservation demonstrates the need for students to understand the silent *e* syllable and *ch* as /k/ when reading content area and scientific vocabulary. Also, notice the frequency of the silent *e* syllable as a final syllable in multisyllabic words.

When Do You Use ch or tch to Spell /ch/?

TUTORIAL The sound /ch/ can be spelled with a digraph **ch** or a trigraph **tch**. There are specific generalizations that can help students know which spelling to use when they hear the sound /ch/ in a word.

TEACH

Provide a list of several words with the two spellings of /ch/. Instruct students to cut the words apart and sort the words by /ch/ spelling. Lead a discussion to help them discover when to use **ch** and when to use **tch**. Explain the generalizations presented below.

Use **ch** to represent /ch/:

- At the beginning of a word, as in *chap*
- After a consonant, as in *punch*
- After two vowels, as in *beach*

Use **tch** to represent /ch/:

- At the end of word or syllable if there is a single short vowel directly before it (*stitch, stretch, latch*)

MAPPING PROCEDURE

Since the digraph *ch* and trigraph **tch** both represent one sound, the graphemes are mapped in one box.

ch and *tch* Word List			
ch as /ch/			*tch* as /ch/
⬚*ch*⬚ ur ⬚ch⬚		c ⬚oa⬚ ⬚ch⬚	c a ⬚tch⬚
At the Beginning of a Word	**After a Consonant**	**After Two Vowels**	**At the End of a Word or Syllable (if there is a single short vowel directly before it)**
chain chirp	bench	beach	batch scratch
chair chitchat	birch	beech	bewitch sketch
chalk choice	branch	bleach	blotch snatch
challenge choke	brunch	breach	butcher snitch
chamber chop	bunch	breech	catch splotch
champ churn	church	broach	clutch stitch
chance chore	cinch	coach	crotch stretch
chip chose	clench	couch	crutch stretcher
champion chuckle	crunch	crouch	ditch swatch
change chug	drench	grouch	dutch switch
channel chum	finch	leach	etch thatch
chant chunk	clinch	leech	fetch twitch
chap church	French	mooch	glitch vetch
chaplain churn	gulch	pooch	hatch watch
chapter	hunch	pouch	hatchet witch
chare	launch	preach	hitch wretch
chart	lunch	reach	hutch
chat	lurch	roach	itch
cheap	lynch	slouch	ketchup
cheat	march	speech	kitchen
check	mulch	teach	latch
cheek	munch	touch	match
chase	parch	vouch	notch
child	perch		patch
chin	pinch		pitch
chimney	porch		pitcher
	punch		ratchet
	quench		satchel
	ranch		scotch

Phoneme-Grapheme Mapping
(A Method for Bridging Sound to Print)

Name: _____   Date: _____

a	s	k						
l	a	n	d					
f	a	s	t					
th	a	t						
p	a	s	t					
ch	a	t						
b	a	tch						
m	a	tch						
r	a	n	ch					
b	r	a	n	ch				
c	a	tch						
c	r	u	n	ch				

Note: By circling the preceding vowel in words that end in the final sound of /ch/, students can easily see that a short vowel directly precedes the -*tch* spelling whereas a consonant comes between the preceding short vowel and sound of /ch/.

-ff, -ll, -ss (and -zz)

TUTORIAL The letters *l, f, s,* and *z* are almost always doubled when they come at the end of a one-syllable word and are preceded by one short vowel. Some teachers refer to this phenomenon as the FLS (floss) rule, as it gives students a handy mnemonic to help them remember most of the rule. This generalization also occurs in a much smaller group of final /z/ words.

> **TEACH**
>
> "The letters *l, f, s,* and *z* are almost always doubled when they come at the end of a one-syllable word and are preceded by one short vowel. We call this the **floss rule**—double the *f, l,* and *s* (and sometimes *z*) at the end of one-syllable short vowel words."

MAPPING PROCEDURE

Because these distinct consonants do not create more than one sound, the two letters are placed within the same box as demonstrated below.

-ff, -ll, -ss (and -zz) Word List			
-ff	**-ll**	**-ss**	**-zz**
o | ff	i | ll	p | a | ss	j | a | zz
off puff	bill skill	bass gloss	jazz
stiff scuff	fill spill	pass loss	buzz
stuff gruff	grill still	class moss	fuzz
staff cuff	ill bell	glass fuss	fizz
Jeff if	hill cell	less toss	razz
miff **Exception**	kill fell	dress cuss	**Exceptions**
cliff of	pill smell	mess muss	Oz, quiz
sniff	till spell	press mass	
bluff	will swell	hiss sass	
	well tell	kiss miss	
	Exceptions	**Exceptions**	
	pal, gal	yes, as, is, was, has, his	

Phoneme-Grapheme Mapping
(A Method for Bridging Sound to Print)

Name: _____   Date: _____

c	r	u	n	ch		t	r	u	ck
ch	u	m			s	t	u	n	t
c	r	u	sh		sh	r	u	n	k
s	t	u	ff						
b	r	u	n	ch					
th	u	d							
m	a	ss							
m	u	ff							
b	u	fl							
f	u	ss	y						
s	t	r	u	m					
s	t	r	u	ng					

This short *u* map reviews blends, digraphs (including the mapping of *ng*), the double *f, l, s* rule, and the *y* suffix that makes the phoneme /e/.

When Do You Use k or ck to Represent /k/?

TUTORIAL The spellings of /k/ are dependent on the position of the sound in a word and the vowels around it.

TEACH

Use *k* to represent /k/:

- At the beginning of a word as in *kit, kangaroo, karate*
- After a consonant as in *bunk*
- After a vowel team as in *speak*
- After a long vowel sound as in *bike*

Use *ck* to represent /k/:

- At the end of word or syllable when there is an accented short vowel spelled with a single letter directly before it *(stick, track, locket)*

MAPPING PROCEDURE

Map the *k* and *ck* as illustrated in the *k* and *ck* Word List that follows. A more complete introduction and practice of soft *c* and soft *g* is in lesson 1:17.

k and *ck* Word List				
k as /k/				*ck* as /k/
At the Beginning of a Word (when *k* is followed by an *i* or *e*) k ey	**After a Consonant** i n k	**After a Vowel Team** oa k	**After a Long Vowel Sound** l ī k e	**At the End of a Word or Syllable (when there is a single short vowel directly before it)** s a ck
keel	ink	dusk	leak	bake	back	lick
keep	thank	sink	beak	mike	beckon	lock
keg	blink	pink	sneak	woke	black	luck
kelp	stink	tank	squeak	smoke	block	mock
kennel	twinkle	market	freak	stroke	brick	neck
kept	sprinkle	basket	croak	snake	buck	pack
kerchief	market	blanket	cheek	shake	hammock	dock
kerosene	basket	chunk	spook	strike	heck	peck
key	blanket	drink	bleak	quake	jack	ick
kick	chunk	brisk	hawk	spike	kick	pluck
kid	drink	milk	shook	bike	knack	prick
kidney	brisk	plank	tweak	lake	lack	puck
kill	milk	plunk	look	stake	check	smack
kiln	plank	spark	squeak	rake	chick	quick
kilometer	stink	shrunk	hook	take	chuck	rack
kilowatt	plunk	shrink	meek	poke	deck	shock
kind	spark	park	week	broke	quack	sick
kindle	shrunk	work	fleet	like	shack	struck
kite	shrink	task	peak	hike	duck	ticket
king	park	bank	peek	make	flack	thick
kingdom	work	mask	weak	fake	fleck	sock
kink	bank	bulk	cook	stake	flick	track
kin	mask	dusk	tweek	gawk	flock	trick
kiss	bulk	stink			frock	truck
		sink			hack	whack
		pink			sack	speck
		tank				stack
At the Beginning of a Word (when *k* is followed by *a, o,* or *u*)						stuck
						slick
koala (Australian)		kumquat (Chinese)		kudos (Greek)		slack
kangaroo (Australian)		kowtow (Chinese)		kurta (Indian)		rock
karate (Japanese)		kosher (Yiddish)				

"Why do we need an initial _k_ in words? Why not just use _c_ instead? As you have learned, the most common spelling of /k/ is the hard _c_ when it is followed by any letter except an _e, i,_ or _y._ If that's the case, why do we need the letter _k_ anyway?

"We need _k_ to stand in front of an _e, i,_ or _y_ if we want to preserve the hard sound. Imagine how _keep_ would sound if it was spelled _ceep?_ It would then need to be pronounced /sēp/, as the soft sound would have been created by the use of _c_ instead of _k_.

"If we use _c_ partnered with the vowels _a ,o,_ and _u_ to represent the hard sound of /k/, then why do we need to use a _k_ to do the same job? If you study the eight words at the bottom of the _k_ as /k/ Word List, you will find the answer."

Soft c and Soft g

TUTORIAL The sounds of hard *c* and hard *g* were introduced and reinforced when students worked with initial consonants. Now the time has come to let students know these two letters also stand for two *different* sounds that are called **soft sounds.** The concept of alternate spellings and sounds for *c* and *g* can be taught together in one lesson or in separate lessons, depending on students' abilities and whether they have previously been introduced to the concepts.

TEACH

Soft c. Tell students that the letter *c* can stand for two sounds, /k/ and /s/. Direct students to experiment with the different feeling the stop (hard) sound /k/ makes in their mouth compared to the hissing (soft) /s/ sound. Note that the letter *c* stands for each sound. Help students generate some words that begin with the hard and soft sounds of *c*. (The labels are somewhat arbitrary.)

c<u>a</u>t   c<u>u</u>t   c<u>o</u>t   versus   c<u>e</u>nt   c<u>i</u>ty   c<u>y</u>cle

Now ask the students to look at the vowels that come after the *c* in each word. Which sequences represent the soft sound of *c*? (Answer: *ce, ci,* and *cy.*)

Soft g. Repeat the above process for hard *g* = /g/ and soft *g* = /j/. Direct students to experiment with the feeling the stop (hard) sound /g/ makes in their mouth and voice box (throat) compared with the affricate (soft) /j/ sound, which also requires the voice box. Once again, help them generate some words that begin with hard and soft *g*. Note that *g* stands for each sound.

g<u>a</u>p   g<u>u</u>m   g<u>o</u>t   versus   g<u>e</u>m   g<u>i</u>ant   g<u>y</u>m

Now ask the students to look at the vowels that come after the *g* in each word. Which vowels create the soft sound of *g* most of the time? (Answer: *ge, gi,* and *gy,* but *get, give,* and *gift* are notable exceptions.)

Once young students have been taught each of the sounds of *c* and *g*, teach them the following song about the soft sounds of *c* and *g*.

TEACH Use this catchy song (to the tune of "Old McDonald") to help students understand when *c* and *g* make the soft sound.

There are three letters that soften *c* -

> e... i
>> e... i
>>> ...y

The same three often soften *g*

> e... i
>> e... i
>>> ...y

With a /s/ /s/ here and a /j/ /j/ there
Here a /s/... there a /j/... everywhere a /s/ /j/.

> Note the very important addition of the word *often* in the second verse. This helps students to learn there are a few exceptions to soft *g*.

The words to this song were the original creation of Kathryn Grace in 1983.

MAPPING PROCEDURE

Instruct students to loop the soft *c* or *g* with the *e, i,* or *y* that follows it. This demonstrates the influence the vowel has on the softening of these sounds. Do not have students loop the *a,* o, and *u* vowels that follow a *c* or *g*; they are the typical sounds for those letters and occur much more frequently than the soft sounds.

Sound of Soft *c* Word List				
In the Initial Position			In the Final Position	
ce-	*ci-*	*cy-*	*-ce*	*-cy*
c e ll	c ī t e	c y s t	r ā c e	l ā c y
cell	cider	cyst	ace	price	fancy
cent	cigar	cycle	brace	prince	lacy
center	cinch	cyanide	dance	race	Tracy
Cecil	cinder	cyclone	dice	rice	Stacy
cedar	circle	cyclops	face	sauce	
ceiling	circus	cylinder	fence	since	
celebrate	city	cynic	fleece	slice	
celery	civic	cypress	force	space	
cellar	cinema		France	spice	
cellophane	cinnamon		glance	splice	
Celtics	cipher		grace	spruce	
cement	circa		chance	stance	
cemetery	circuit		hence	thence	
censor	circular		ice	trace	
census	circulate		juice	trance	
cereal	circumference		lace	truce	
ceremony	circumstance		lance	twice	
certain	cirrus		mice	vice	
cesspool	citadel		mince	voice	
	citation		nice	whence	
	cite		niece	wince	
	citizen		notice	advance	
	citrus		place	advice	
	civil		once	balance	
			pace	bounce	

Sound of Soft *g* Word List

In the Initial Position			In the Medial or Final Position	
ge-	*gi-*	*gy-*	*-ge*	*-gy*
g e m	g i n	g y m	a g e	e n er g y

gem	giblet	gym	large	energy
giant	gigantic	gymnasium	large	prodigy
gentle	gin	gymnast	age	synergy
germ	ginger	gypsum	cage	strategy
gerbil	giraffe	gypsy	page	
genius	gist	gyrate	rage	
gesture	gibber	gyration	age	
Gemini	gibberish	gyro	strange	
germ	Gibraltar	gyroscope	angel	
gender	gigolo	**Exception**	barge	
gene	Gillette	gynecology	change	
genealogy	ginseng		voyage	
general	Gerard		leakage	
generator			manage	
generic	**Exceptions**		garbage	
generous	gift		message	
genetics	give		package	
genial	giggle		postage	
Exceptions	girl		shortage	
gear	girth		tragedy	
geek	gimp		vegetable	
geese	gingham		damage	
geisha	ginkgo		village	
get	gimmick		savage	
	gizmo		percent-	
	gizzard		age	
			cringe	
			grunge	
			range	
			hinge	

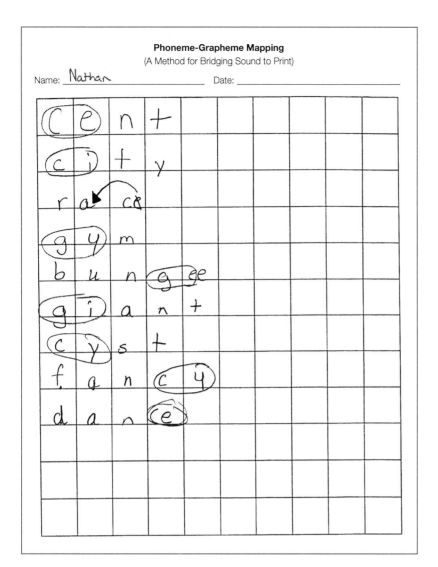

Phoneme-Grapheme Mapping
(A Method for Bridging Sound to Print)

Name: Nathan   Date:

c	e	n	t						
c	i	t	y						
r	a	ce							
g	y	m							
b	u	n	g ge						
g	i	a	n	t					
c	y	s	t						
f	a	n	c	y					
d	a	n	ce						

Note: Some students erroneously think that a final *e* always represents a silent -*e* syllable pattern. Therefore, it is important to have them map words where the final *e* is present simply to soften the preceding *c* or *g*.

Using the Vowels as Placeholders for Soft c and Soft g

TUTORIAL Once students understand that the vowels *e, i,* and *y* soften *c* and *g* most of the time, you can introduce the concept that the other three vowels (*a, o,* and *u*) can be used as placeholders to preserve the hard sound of the *c* and *g.* For example, if the *u* was not positioned after the *g* in the word *guess,* the reader would see *gess.* Then, the reader would erroneously apply the soft *g* rule and pronounce the word as /jĕs/. The same would be true for the longer word *biscuit.* If the *u* was not holding its place next to the *c,* the word would be *biscit* and would be pronounced /bĭs sĭt/.

By having students map some of these words that contain placeholder vowels, they are once again asked to become metacognitive about the application of the soft *c* and soft *g* principle. When you are working with older students and adults who have a more sophisticated understanding of this principle, you can use sample words in which these placeholders occur in the middle of the word.

TEACH "Now that you know the roles of *i, e,* and *y* with *c* and *g,* you are ready to learn about important roles of the other vowels, *a, o,* and *u.* In a few words, *a, o,* and *u* are placeholders that help *c* and *g* keep their hard sounds." Present the words *guest* and *biscuit* for discussion about the vowel positions and sounds of *c* and *g.*

MAPPING PROCEDURE

Place the vowel that is acting as a placeholder in the same box as the *g* or *c* and cross out the unnecessary vowel as shown below.

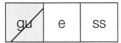

Vowels as Placeholders Word List		
guy	guild	biscuit
guess	guillotine	
guest	disguise	
guide	guerrilla	
guilt	guidance	
guilty	guernsey	
guinea		
guitar		

In the case of the word *accident,* the two *c*'s are put in separate boxes because the first *c* represents a hard *c* and the second *c* combines with the *i* to create the soft sound of *c*.

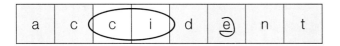

a	c	c	i	d	e	n	t

Phoneme-Grapheme Mapping
(A Method for Bridging Sound to Print)

Name: _Danielle_____   Date: _____

gu	e	s	t						
gu	e	ss							
gu	ar	d							
b	i	s	cu	i	t				
gu	y								
gu	i	de							
gu	i	t	ar						
gu	i	l	t						
gu	i	l	t	y					
gu	i	d	a	n	ce				

When Do You Use -ge or -dge to Represent /j/?

TUTORIAL There are specific positions and conventions for using the spellings *-ge* and *-dge* for /j/ at the ends of words. Once students have mapped the soft sound of *g* with basic words, introduce them to the spellings *-ge* and *-dge*. Remember, the letter *j* cannot be used to end a word. At the ends of words, *-ge* represents one sound /j/, as in *urge*. The spelling *-dge* also represents one sound.

Use *-ge* to represent /j/ at the ends of words:

- After a consonant, as in *sponge*
- After a long vowel sound, as in *cage*
- After an unaccented schwa, as in *village*

Use *-dge* to represent /j/ at the ends of words or syllables:

- If there is a single, accented, short vowel directly before it (*badge, dodge, ridge*)

MAPPING PROCEDURE

Map *-ge* and *-dge* as one sound unit. See the examples in the *-ge* and *-dge* Word List that follows.

-ge and *-dge* Word List			
-ge as /j/			*-dge* as /j/
After a Consonant	**After a Long Vowel Sound**	**After an Unaccented Schwa**	**At the End of a Word or Syllable (if there is a single, accented short vowel directly before it)**
angel	age	college	badge judge
barge	huge	spillage	badger trudge
change	oblige	courage	bridge ledge
-ge as /j/			*-dge* as /j/
bulge	page		budge ledger
cringe	cage		budget lodge
forge	stage		dodge Madge
hinge	rage		dredge midget
indulge	wage		drudge pledge
large	rampage		edge wedge
Marge			fidget ridge
merge			fledge sledge
plunge			fridge sludge
serge			fudge smudge
splurge			gadget **Exceptions**
surge			grudge knowledge
twinge			hedge porridge
urge			hodgepodge
verge			nudge

TEACH

1. During spelling dictations, instruct students to draw a box anytime they hear the sound of /j/ at the end of a syllable or base word.

2. After the word is dictated, ask them to color the preceding vowel (<u>not</u> <u>vowels</u>) orange. If the immediately preceding **single** vowel is **short**, then the students know they must use **dge** instead of **ge** to spell the sound of /j/ and write it in the box they had previously left blank.

Dictate *page*	Dictate *bulge*	Dictate *budge*
p a ☐	b ŭ l ☐	b ŭ ☐
ge	**ge**	**dge**
	Note that there is a consonant *between* the short vowel /ŭ/ and the sound of /j/. That's why *ge* and not *dge* is used.	

Phoneme-Grapheme Mapping
(A Method for Bridging Sound to Print)

Name: _Stephanie_   Date: _____

INTRODUCE CONSONANT BLENDS

Two or more consonant letters may stand for a blend, as in c̲l̲ock, s̲w̲im, and s̲p̲l̲it. Unlike digraphs, **blends** retain their individual sounds within the word. Some consonants are easier to hear in blends than others. Start with sound when introducing this complex concept.

For example, ask students to close their eyes and concentrate on how many movements are being made in their mouths when they say /sp/. They can feel their mouths change position as they move from the /s/ to the /p/, from one consonant sound in the blend to the other. Contrast this with digraphs. Students feel only one continuous movement when making a digraph phoneme.

This method helps form a bridge between the sounds students hear and/or feel and the number of sound boxes they must use when mapping words containing blends. In other words, if they feel and/or hear two sounds, they cover two sound boxes. If they hear just one sound, as in a digraph, they merely cover one.

Some consonant blends are easier to discriminate and blend than others. Consonant blends can come at the beginning or at the end of words, as well as in medial positions. However, some blends are more prevalent in specific positions. Table 7 displays the blends in ascending order of difficulty within each position.

Table 7 Consonant Blends		
Blends that appear at both the beginning and end of a syllable	**Blends that appear at the beginning of a syllable**	**Blends that only appear at the end of a syllable**
-st- as in s̲t̲op and we̲s̲t	*bl- cl- fl- gl- pl- sl-*	*-ft*
-sp- as in s̲p̲ot and clas̲p̲	*sc- sl- sn- sw- tw-*	*-nd -nk -nt -nk*
-sk- as in s̲k̲ate and whis̲k̲	*br- cr- dr- fr- gr- pr- tr-*	*-ld -lk -lt*

Sometimes it is helpful to have students color the blends after they have mapped their words. Instruct the students to use a green crayon and color the boxes lightly. This is just another way to help solidify the concept that when each phoneme (sound) in the blend is heard, it retains the same number of graphemes (letters) as in the blend.

1:20

Initial Blends

Begin consonant blend instruction with words that have blends in the initial position. Choose a variety of words from the Blend Word Lists to use in the phoneme-grapheme lessons.

TEACH

Instruct students to say /sp/. Ask them how many sounds they feel. (Two sounds.) Ask them to say /sh/ and tell how many sounds they feel. (One sound.) "/sp/ is a consonant blend; **sh** is one sound spelled with a digraph. When we read and spell words with consonant blends, each consonant retains its individual sound even though we blend those sounds together really fast. Consonant blends can come at the beginnings and endings of words."

MAPPING PROCEDURE

Map consonant blends by placing one letter in each box to indicate that both sounds are heard. Students may be instructed to color the blends a specific color to indicate their knowledge.

Initial *l* Blends Word List

bl-		cl-		fl-		gl-		pl-	
b l a t		c l i p		f l y		g l ee		p l ay	
black	blink	cloth	close	flat	fled	glad	glove	plan	plain
blank	blue	club	closet	fly	flip	glum	glade	plank	play
blame	blot	clap	claw	flit	flit	glance	glee	plod	ploy
blast	bloom	clip	clear	flap	flub	gland	glide	plop	plant
blat	blast	clan	clean	flag	float	glass	gleam	plink	plot
blue	blew	cliff	clasp	flap	fleet	gloss	glitter	plum	plunk
blond	bliss	click	cloud	flow	floss	glen	glider	plug	plane
blend	blow	clack	clog	flog	flock	glib	glue	ply	pluck
bled	blanket	cluck	class	flop	flower	globe	glaze	plus	
blip	bleach	clock		flush	flash	glow			

Initial *s-* Blends Word List

sc-		sl-		sn-		sw-	
s c a n		s l u sh		s n a ck		s w e ll	
scab	scout	slab	slob	snack	snuff	swab	swan
scale	scallop	slam	slop	snag	snug	swag	swift
scam	scarf	slap	slash	snap	snuck	swam	sway
scan	**scr-**	slat	slosh	snatch	snow	swell	swine
scat	scratch	sled	slush	sneak	snarl	swept	swoop
scoff	scramble	slept	slot	snicker	snail	sweat	swindle
scone	scream	slick	slow	sniff	snoop	swim	swarm
scoop	screw	slid	slum	snip	snorkel	sweater	swear
score	scram	slim	slug	snub	snort	sweep	swat
scare		slip	slice	sneeze	snout	switch	swirl
scud		slit		snooze	snowman	swung	swish
scum				snob	sniper	sweet	

Initial *r-* Blends Word List

br-		*cr-*		*dr-*		*fr-*	
b r o th		c r a b		d r i ll		f r i n ge	

br-		*cr-*		*dr-*		*fr-*	
brick	brush	crab	cress	drab	dredge	franc	frizz
brag	brink	crack	crest	draft	dregs	Frank	frock
bran	brisk	craft	crib	drag	drench	frantic	frog
branch	bronze	crag	crick	dragon	dress	fresh	frolic
brand	broth	cram	cricket	dram	drift	fret	from
brash	brother	cramp	crimp	drama	drill	frigid	frond
brat	brunch	crank	crimson	dramatic	drink	frill	front
bred	brunt	crash	cringe	drastic	drip	fringe	frost
brick	brig	crass	crisp	drat	drub	frisk	froth
bridge	brim	credit	critic	drum	drudge	fragment	
brandish	britches	crept	crock	drunk	drug		

More Complex *br-* Blends and **More Complex** *fr-* Blends follow.

More Complex *br-* Blends		*cr-* cont.		*dr-* cont.		More Complex *fr-* Blends	
brace	brave	crook	crop	drank	droll	fraction	frosty
bracelet	brazen	cross	crud			fragrance	frizzle
brain	breach	crunch	crypt			fragrant	frugal
brake	breakfast	crutch	crux	**More Complex** *dr-* Blends		frail	frontier
bramble	break	crescent	crumb	drake	drain	frame	frown
brandy	breathe	crumpet		drone	drape	frazzle	frozen
breath	breeze	**More Complex** *cr-* Blends		drool	drawl	fray	fruit
brigade	broiler	cradle	crazy	dread	droop	freak	frustrate
bristle	broke	cranberry	cream	dream	drown	freckle	friction
brocade	brook	crane	creek	dreary	drowsy	free	friend
brochure	broom	cranny	creepy	drew	dry	freeze	fracas
brown	bronco	crate	crinkle	dribble	draw	freight	fraught
bruise	bronze	crave	croak	drive	drawer	frenzy	
brute	broccoli	crayfish	crocodile	drizzle	drawl	frequent	
brawl	brigade	crayon	crow	drier	driver	fracture	
brawn	bright	crouch	crevice	drive	dromedary	fragile	
bray	brilliant	crawl	crinkle	drivel	drone	franchise	
breadth	brine	creak	cripple	drowse	drool	fraternal	
breathe	brittle	creation	crumple	dropper	druid	fraud	
breech	broach	creature	crumble	drought	dryad	freedom	
breed	brought	creel	croup	drove	dresser	fright	
brevity	broad	creep	crown	dryly		fritter	
bridle	browse	cremate	crusade			frivolous	
		crescent					

More Initial *r-* Blend Words

gr-		*pr-*	
Closed Syllables	**More Complex *gr-* Blends**	**Closed Syllables**	**More Complex *pr-* Blends**
g | r | i | <u>d</u>	g | r | u | (dge)	p | r | e | ss	p | r | ea | ch

grab	grid	grew	greet	greed	press	practice	prize
graft	grill	ground	grouch	grove	prank	pray	problem
gram	grim	grow	grapple	grade	prick	preach	proceed
grand	grin	grain	griddle	grime	prim	prefer	program
grant	grip	grape	groove	gripe	prince	pretend	prism
graph	grit	grave	grumble	group	princess	price	proof
graphic	grog	gravy	grizzly	groan	print	pride	prose
grasp	gross	gray	grocer	groin	prompt	prickle	proud
grass	grudge	great	groom	grieve	prong	pretty	prowl
grunt	gruff	green	ground		prop	prime	prune

Initial Consonant Blend *tr-* Word List

Closed Syllable *tr-* Blends			**More Complex *tr-* Blends**				
t | r | u | ck			t | r | ō | ph | ȳ				
track	trend	trudge	tractor	treason	trillion	trouble	trooper
tract	tress	trump	trade	treat	trio	trough	trophy
traffic	trick	trumpet	trail	treaty	tripe	trounce	tropical
tragic	trim	trunk	train	tree	triple	trout	tried
tramp	trip	truss	trait	tremble	tripod	true	trifle
trance	trod	trust	trample	tremor	trite	truly	trigger
transit	troll	tryst	transfer	trestle	triumph	trundle	trawler
transmit	tropic	trek	trapeze	triangle	trolley	truth	tray
trap	trot	trench	trashy	tribe	trombone	try	tread
trash	truck	trivet	travel	tribute	troop		

Initial Consonant Blend *tw-* Word List

t	w	i	s	t		t	w	i	n	ge		Medial Position
twig	twine	twang	twenty	twitter	twin							between
twist	tweed	twentieth	twelve	twitch	twinkle							entwine
twang	twilight	tweet	twirl	twinge	twice							untwist
twill	twit	twelfth	twilight	twiddle	twister							
tweak	tweezers			twinkling								

Final Blends

"Many consonant blends are found at the ends of words. The words we will be mapping in this lesson will have these consonant blends. Let's see how many there are!"

MAPPING PROCEDURE

The sounds in consonant blends are separate sounds, therefore each letter is mapped in its own box as shown in the examples in the word list.

Final Blends Word List				
Final -ft blend	**Final -pt blend**	**Final -n blends**		
-ft	*-pt*	*-nd*	*-nk*	*-nt*
l e f t	a p t	a n d	i n k	a n t
lift	apt	and	bank	ant
theft	abrupt	band	hank	rant
graft	adapt	hand	rank	hint
loft	adept	land	sank	lint
drift	adopt	sand	tank	mint
thrift	apt	bind	yank	pint
thrifty	erupt	kind	blink	stint
rift	except	find	blank	tint
draft	inept	hind	wink	bent
adrift	kept	mind	link	dent
aft	opt	rind	sink	lent
aloft	prompt	end	think	vent
cleft	rapt	bend	kink	scant
daft	slept	fend	mink	rent
deft	swept	lend	rink	sent
shift	wept	mend	junk	tent
soft	disrupt	brand	bunk	went
	accept	round	clunk	grant
	corrupt	fond	drink	flint
	interrupt	pound	lank	pant
				event

-ft	-pt	-nd	-nk	-nt
left		blend	dunk	faint
heft		bland	hunk	paint
shaft		blind	punk	taint
swift		blond	skunk	saint
shift		gland	pink	font
gift		spend	thank	haunt
craft		stand	honk	bunt
sift		brand	bonk	hunt
raft		grand	sunk	punt
tuft		send	drunk	runt
waft		sound	drank	stunt
weft		bond	flunk	spent
		refund	drink	meant
		behind	ink	plant
		fund	shrink	print
		found	shrank	blunt
		friend	crank	cent
		grind		extent
		hound		grunt
		mound		indent
		stand		shunt
				invent

Final Blends Word List (continued)								
-ld				**-lk**		**-lt**		
bald	mild	bold	gold	milk	milky	tilt	bolt	belt
scald	wild	cold	mold	silk	silky	kilt	colt	felt
held	scold	fold	sold	bilk	elk	stilt	jolt	melt
meld	mild	hold	told	bulk	hulk	silt	molt	pelt
old	wild	scold	smolder	skulk	sulky	salt	volt	wilt
		boulder	shoulder			vault	tilt	silt
						malt	kilt	stilt

I always begin with sound when I am introducing a new phonics concept. I use the wood or plastic blocks on the first day of each lesson so students can have a concrete manipulative to help them ascertain the correct number of sounds they hear in each word. The number of blocks are then easily transferable to the phoneme-grapheme mapping paper. However, after the students become proficient at identifying the number of sounds in a word, they may no longer need to manipulate the blocks. When students are ready to leave the blocks behind, they will begin to place small dots at the bottom of their sound boxes to indicate how many of them should be filled with a grapheme to match each phoneme (sound) they hear in a particular word.

Phoneme-Grapheme Mapping
(A Method for Bridging Sound to Print)

Name: _____ Date: _____

l	e	f	t						
y	e	l	p						
l	e	n	d						
s	w	e	l l						
ch	e	s	t						
r	e	n	t						
s	w	e	p	t					
b	l	e	n	d					
b	e	s	t						
ch	e	s	t						
sh	r	e	d						
th	e	m							
sh	e	l	f						
wh	e	n							

Note: This student shaded both his initial and final blends. He also used dots to mark the number of sounds he heard in each word. These steps usually occur when a student is ready to leave the concrete manipulatives behind.

Consonant Three-Letter Blends

TEACH

"Sometimes three consonants will come together to form a consonant cluster referred to as a **three-letter blend**. You should be able to feel three movements in your mouth if you articulate the blend slowly. Say *spr*. You can hear the three sounds, too. Because we can feel and hear the individual consonants in the three-letter blends, they will be put into separate boxes."

MAPPING PROCEDURE

Each letter in a three-letter blend represents a single sound; therefore, each letter is mapped in its own box, as in the examples shown in the word list.

Three-Letter Blend Word List			
scr-	*spl-*	*spr-*	*str-*
s c r a p	s p l i t	s p r ȳ	s t r ay
scram	splash	sprain	straddle · strum
scramble	splat	sprang	strain · strung
scrap	splatter	sprawl	straight · strut
scrape	spleen	spray	strand · abstract
scratch	splendid	spread	strange · restrain
scrawl	splendor	spree	stranger · streak
scream	splice	sprig	strangle · obstruct
screen	splint	sprightly	strap · instruct
screw	splinter	spring	stride · strategy
scribe	split	sprinkle	straw · stroke
scrimp	splotch	sprite	streamer · struck
scrimmage	splurge	sprint	stream · stricken
scrip	splutter	sprocket	street · strident
scrod		spruce	strength · unstrung
scroll		sprout	stress · stroll
scrounge		sprung	stretcher · stroller
scrub		spry	stretch · strong
scruff			strict · strove
scribble			

Blends That Appear at the Beginning and End of Syllables

The consonant blends in this lesson are found at the beginnings and endings of words. Introduce this concept to students and choose a mix of the two for students to segment and map.

MAPPING PROCEDURE

Each letter in a consonant blend represents a single sound; therefore each letter is mapped in its own box, as shown in the examples in the word list.

Blends Word List: Initial and Ending of Syllables					
st			*sp*		*sk*
s | t | o | p			c | l | a | s | p		s | k | i | t
Initial	Final		Initial	Final	Initial	Final

Initial		Final		Initial		Final	Initial	Final
stop	stiff	best	mist	spit	spud	clasp	skit	musk
step	stun	bust	most	spot	spun	crisp	sky	mask
still	stamp	cast	must	spam	space	gasp	skull	ask
stick	stat	cost	past	spank		grasp	skew	desk
stab	stay	dust	rest	spat		wasp	skirt	task
stub	stem	fast	rust	speck		lisp	skim	brisk
staff	stink	fest	test	sped		wisp	skin	husk
stag	stack	gust	vast	spell			skeet	dusk
stand	stuff	gist	vest	spent			ski	tusk
stall	stunk	host	west	spend			skeleton	bask
stump	stint	last	zest	span			skillet	cask
stuck	stunt	lost	pest	spill			skill	
		mast		spin			skate	

Digraph Blends

Sometimes a digraph and a single consonant combine to make a **digraph blend,** as in **shr** and **thr**. Two sounds are heard in these combinations: the digraph comprising two letters and the single consonant sound. Therefore, it is mapped in two boxes.

MAPPING PROCEDURE

When mapping a digraph blend, remember that the digraph represents one sound and is mapped in one box. The third consonant is mapped in another. (See examples in the word list.)

Digraph Blend Word List					
shr-			*thr-*		
sh | r | i | ll			th | r | o | ng		
shred	shrine	shroff	thrall	threshold	thrive
shrink	shrew	shrove	thrash	threw	throat
shrill	shrubby	shrubbery	thread	thrift	throb
shrimp	shrug	shrinkage	threat	thrill	throne
shrub	shrewd	shrivel	three	thrust	throng
shrunk	shriek	shroud	thresh	thrush	throttle
shrank			throw	thresher	through
			thrush	thrave	thruway

Blend Oddities

TEACH

There are a couple of three-letter combinations that do not seem to follow the true definition of a three-letter blend. *Squ-* represents three consonant sounds: /s/ /k/ /w/. The letter *u* stands for /w/ as it does in plain *qu*. *Chr* represents two consonant sounds: /k/ and /r/. Words in which *ch* stands for /k/ are from Greek.

MAPPING PROCEDURE

When a word has a blend with *qu,* the sounds represented by *qu* are separate sounds /k/ /w/ and are mapped in two boxes. When a blend has /k/ spelled with *ch,* the *ch* is mapped in one box. (See examples in the word list.)

Blend Oddities Word List					
squ-			**chr-**		
s q u i n t			ch r o n i c		
squint	squash	squishy	Christmas	chrism	chronometry
squall	squeak	squelch	chrome	chrisom	chrysalis
squat	squeal	squid	chromite	christen	chrysanthemum
squab	squeamish	squiggle	chromo	Christian	Chrysler
squad	squeeze	squeegee	Christina	Christianity	chrysolite
squalid	squib	squill	Christopher	chromoplasm	
squalor	squish	squinch	chrom	chromosome	
squander	squire	squirrel	chroma	chronic	
square	squirm	squirt	chromate	chronograph	
squaw	squawk		chromatic	chronology	

Phoneme-Grapheme Mapping
(A Method for Bridging Sound to Print)

Name: _____   Date: _____

sh	r	i	ll						
sh	r	a	n	K					
th	r	i	ll						
th	r	a	sh						
s	qu	i	sh						
s	qu	ea	K						
ch	r	o	m						
sh	r	i	m	P					

Note: This map shows how a student was able to differentiate between digraph blends (two boxes) and three-letter blends (three boxes).

Word Relatives
-ild, -ind, -old, -olt, and -ost

TUTORIAL There are several one-syllable words that share the same vowel sound and final consonant(s), which we group together for reading and spelling. These word relatives are exceptions to the closed syllable rule because their vowel sound is not short.

TEACH

"We have learned that a closed syllable has one vowel letter, a short vowel sound, and one or more consonants at the end of it. There are families of words that look like closed syllables, but the vowel does not make a short sound. We will learn these word relatives in this lesson. When you see the vowels *i* and *o* in one-syllable words that end in *-ld, -nd,* and *-st,* the vowel is usually long." Show students the words *child, find,* and *most.* Instruct students to tell you about the word relatives. Instruct them to tell you other words that will fit in the word families: *child, mild, wild, find, wind, mind, most, ghost,* and *host.*

MAPPING PROCEDURE

These word relatives should be mapped according to their phoneme-grapheme relationships with vowels. Each letter in the Word Relative Word List that follows represents a separate sound, so each letter is mapped in its own box.

Word Relative Word List			
-ild as /ild/	**-ind as /ind/**		
m | i | l | d	b | l | i | n | d		
mild	bind	rind	find	mind
child	blind	remind	grind	kind
wild	hind	behind	wind (the verb)	

Word Relatives Word List (continued)							
-old as /old/				**-ost** as /ost/		**-olt** as /olt/	
f o l d				h o s t		j o l t	
old	gold	mold	unfold	host	almost	bolt	molt
cold	hold	sold	behold	most	inmost	colt	dolt
fold	scold	uphold	enfold	post	utmost	holt	volt
told	bold	untold	retold	ghost		jolt	

Word Relatives -ald, -alk, -all, and -alt

"When *a* is followed by either the sound /l/ or a silent *l* in single-syllable words, the *a* is pronounced /aw/. The *a* followed by *l* appears in many words, and we refer to them as **word relatives**. Sometimes *l* is sounded and sometimes it is silent."

MAPPING PROCEDURE

The word relatives *-ald*, *-alk*, *-all*, and *-alt* should be mapped according to their phoneme-grapheme relationships with vowels. Each letter in the Word Relative Word List that follows represents a separate sound, so each letter is mapped in its own box.

Word Relatives Word List					
-ald as /awld/	**-all** as /awl/			**-alt** as /awlt/	

-ald	-all			-alt
b a l d	s t a ll			s a l t
bald	all	hall	wall	halt
scald	ball	mall	small	malt
	call	pall	thrall	salt
	fall	stall	scall	
	gall	tall	hall	

Double Consonants in the Middle of Words

TUTORIAL In the middle of two-syllable words, you often see two of the same consonants written for one sound (e.g., *button, mitten, ribbon*). Generally the second consonant is there to ensure that the reader knows the preceding vowel is short. For example, if you take away the first *t* in *button,* the reader might think it an open syllable and read the word as /bū/ /ton/.

Additionally, in a one-syllable base word, the final consonant is sometimes doubled when a vowel suffix is added.

TEACH

"In the middle of two-syllable words, we often see doubled consonants. These two consonants stand for one sound." Show students the words *button, mitten,* and *ribbon* to illustrate the two consonants. Segment the sounds in these words to illustrate that the double consonants stand for one sound. Tell students that there are two consonants because, without the second consonant, the vowel would be long. Say the words with a long vowel in the first syllable: /bū/ /ton/, /mī/ /ten/, and /rī/ /bon/. The consonant protects the short vowel sound.

MAPPING PROCEDURE

Both concepts—the juncture of two syllables and the addition of an ending to a base word—are mapped by placing the twin consonants in the same box. (See the examples in the word list that follows.)

Double Consonant in the Middle Word List					
In the medial position of words		*-le**	**When following the doubling rule**		
t e nn i s			r u nn i ng		
tennis	attic	*huddle*	pinned	running	robbed
sudden	button	*riddle*	planned	sitting	thinnest
puppet	bottom	*fiddle*	banned	wagging	banner
gossip	funnel	*kettle*	stepped	stepping	jabbed
blossom	possum	*hobble*	tapping	hemmed	slipper
collect	rabbit	*gobble*	flapped	flapping	flapper
common	follow	*settle*	tagged	tagging	batter
bonnet	shallow	*battle*	jammed	slamming	slammer
coffin	shimmer	*dribble*	madder	maddest	shopping
ribbon	differ	*bubble*	daddy	grabbing	sadden
kitten	wallet	*rattle*	saddest	digging	sipping
mitten	buffalo	*kettle*	rammed	fanning	sledding
lesson	muffin	*whittle*	gladden	trimming	snobby
Dennis	sudden	*bottle*	plotting	swimming	dotting
happen	juggle	*little*	sloppy	quitting	soggy
mammal	collar	*topple*	biggest	buggy	mugger
gallon	traffic	*ripple*	flatten	nippy	flapped

*The italicized words end in a consonant *-le* syllable, which is more completely discussed in Lesson 5:1. They are listed here because many words ending in consonant *-le* have a doubled consonant before the final syllable. Do not use these words as examples of double consonants unless you have already taught the consonant *-le* syllable pattern. For a complete explanation of the doubling rule, please see lesson 8:1.

1:29

Closed Syllables in Multisyllabic Words

TUTORIAL Once students understand the concept of a closed syllable in single-syllable words, they are ready to begin reading closed syllables in multisyllabic words. In this way, primary students are exposed to multisyllabic words at an earlier stage of literacy. For example, if they can read the single closed-syllable words *cat* and *nip*, then they are ready to put them together to read *catnip*.

Compound words are generally a student's first introduction to words of more than one syllable. Generally, these are readily grasped because they easily describe nouns in their everyday life, like *dishpan, backpack,* and *bathtub*. This lesson provides lists of compound words that only have closed syllables.

Most students need the concept of polysyllable words taught explicitly. Do not assume that students will automatically apply what they learned about reading and spelling one-syllable words to words having more than one syllable. Writing syllables on index cards and having students physically manipulate them to make multisyllabic words is an excellent method for teaching the building of multisyllabic words.

As soon as multisyllable words are introduced, the schwa will be heard in many unaccented syllables. Acknowledge this reality, as in *puppet*. Students may need to adjust pronunciation after decoding to make the word "sound normal."

TEACH

Tell students that they can read many little words and are ready to read some big words. Show students an index card with *cat* written on it. Instruct them to read it. Show them a card with *nip,* and instruct them to read it. Put the two cards together to make one word. Ask students to read the new "big" word—*catnip*. Say the word together and clap the syllables. Two syllables. Explain that they will be mapping words that have two, three, or four syllables.

MAPPING PROCEDURE

The mapping process is the same as for single-syllable closed syllables except in the case of words containing twin consonants between the two syllables. Since the extra consonant is only there to prevent the reader from reading the word as an open syllable and producing a long vowel sound, the twin letters are placed in one box. The double consonant does not stand for two sounds. Both letters represent the individual consonant sound that the single consonant represents. See Lesson 1:28 for a more complete list of double-consonant words.

It is often helpful to have students color each syllable a different color after they have successfully mapped a word. This will mean coloring each of the twin letters a separate color when they are broken into two syllables (i.e., when a word is split between the double letters). However, since the double letters make one sound, they are placed in the same box, as demonstrated in the following word list.

Two-Syllable Words with Closed Syllables			
Compound Words		**Twin-Consonant Words**	**VCCV Words Without Twin Consonants**
w | i | th | i | n		k | i | tt | e | n	u | n | t | i | l
hatbox	craftsman	kitten	napkin	ostrich
backpack	dishpan	puppet	bandit	husband
himself	eggshell	blossom	cactus	problem
bandbox	farmland	ribbon	riblet	subtract
hatrack	football	tennis	candid	trumpet
catnip	footstep	gallop	frantic	publish
bathtub	hilltop	gossip	tendon	humbug
blacksmith	freshman	tunnel	hectic	nutmeg
buckskin	headdress	cotton	velvet	hundred
cannot	hopscotch	muffin	selfish	subject
catfish	inland	coffin	picnic	until
pickpocket	bedrock	lesson	pilgrim	public
offspring	shipwreck	attic	infect	splendid
scrapbox	bellhop	address	signal	dentist
sunfish	locksmith	channel	kidnap	magnet
sunset	crabgrass	happen	children	discuss
upland	jackrabbit	annex	contest	quintet
windmill	redhot	kennel	convict	enchant
within	muskrat	Dennis	goblin	mascot
backstretch		mitten	consent	pumpkin
		bonnet	optic	sandwich
		sudden	conquest	pretzel
			contact	basket
			wisdom	chipmunk
			conquest	goblet
			bandit	metric
			index	object
				plastic

Phoneme-Grapheme Mapping
(A Method for Bridging Sound to Print)

Name: _____ Date: _____

s	p	r	i	n	T				
s	t	r	a	n	d				
s	p	r	a	ng					
s	t	r	u	ck					
s	t	r	u	n g					
✷ p	u	ff	b	a	ll				
✷ b	a	th	m	a	t				
✷ sh	e	ll	f	i	sh				
✷ d	i	sh	p	a	n		✷ = compound		
✷ wh	i	p	l	a	sh		words		
i	n	d	e	✕					
u	n	z	i	p					
p	u	b	l	i	c				
l	i	m	i	t					
t	o	p	i	c					

Note: This mapping exercise introduces closed two-syllable words in the context of reviewing previously taught concepts. My word selection is always based on what should be reviewed and what should be introduced. Then I plan the list accordingly.

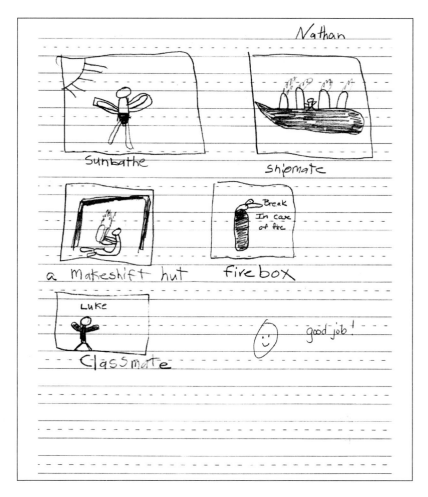

Note: Compound words are often fun examples of closed and silent -*e* syllables. As a short break from mapping, students enjoy drawing and labeling pictures of their compound words.

Three- and Four-Syllable Words with Closed Syllables Word List				
q u i n t u p l e t				
Atlantic	continent	fantastic	establish	Wisconsin
subtraction	segmented	climatic	recommend	badminton
misspelling	successful	accident	bulletin	insistent
basketball	enrichment	intellect	extinguish	kidnapping
pedestal	enchantment	contraption	continent	fantastic
problematic	suddenly	splendidly	magnetize	quintuplet
contestant	represent	publisher	discussing	individual
contacted		continental	kindergarten	introduce
consonant		tornado	beginning	excellence

The Syllabic Consonant m (an Advanced Concept)

TUTORIAL The consonant *m* can sometimes represent a whole spoken syllable–a vowel and a consonant articulated together. This only happens when the /m/ is unaccented and in the final syllable, as in *rhythm* and words with *-asm* and *-ism.* This occurrence is unique: all other syllables in English require a vowel letter. Even the syllabic consonants (/l/ as in *lit-tle* and /r/ as in *but-ter*) are spelled with a vowel letter plus the consonant. Syllabic consonant *m* is addressed here because there are a few of these words (such as *rhythm*, *spasm*, and *chasm*) that come up in elementary school. Understanding the concept of a syllabic consonant is necessary to address these words because teachers frequently tell students, "Every syllable has to have a vowel letter." As you can see, there is an exception to this generalization.

TEACH

"Say *rhythm*. Say the syllables in *rhythm*." (Rhyth-m.) "What is the second syllable?" (-/m/.) "It is spelled without a vowel! There is a hidden vowel sound, but it is not represented in the written syllable. Do you hear the slight /u/? Say the separate syllables in *rhyth-m* again. There are a few words with these syllabic consonants in our language, which we will study in this lesson. The important thing to remember about these words is that there is no vowel letter in the final syllable—the *m* is the syllabic consonant."

MAPPING PROCEDURE

Students map the syllabic -*m* by placing it in one box and shading the box to show that there is a syllable break that occurs before the final *m*. As previously suggested, this will also work if you have students color each syllable in a word a different color, choosing a specific color to represent the syllabic consonant -*m*.

Syllabic Consonant -*m* Word List		
Syllabic -*m*	**Syllabic -*m* within the suffix -*ism*** (which means a theory, doctrine, or condition)	
ch | a | s | m	r | ē | a | l | i | s | m	

Syllabic -*m*	Syllabic -*m* within the suffix -*ism*		
prism	activism	favoritism	negativism
rhythm	absenteeism	feminism	ostracism
spasm	tourism	feudalism	pantheism
sarcasm	Americanism	humanism	professionalism
enthusiasm	animalism	humanitarianism	patriotism
chasm	autism	hyperthyroidism	pragmatism
	baptism	commercialism	polytheism
	barbarism	imperialism	realism
	catechism	impressionism	rheumatism
	idealism	individualism	skepticism
	communism	journalism	symbolism
	conservatism	lyricism	synergism
	criticism	magnetism	socialism
	cynicism	mannerism	territorialism
	defeatism	materialism	terrorism
	exorcism	mechanism	electromagnetism
	alcoholism	metabolism	traditionalism
	embolism	monotheism	tribalism
	emotionalism	mysticism	vandalism
	expressionism	nationalism	voluntarism

Silent Consonant Patterns

TEACH "Two consonant letters may represent the sound of only one of the consonants. The remaining consonant is silent. These grapheme pairs usually occur in either the initial or final positions of words."

MAPPING PROCEDURE

Silent consonant patterns are mapped by placing the grapheme pair in one box and crossing out the silent letter, as shown in the word lists that follow.

Silent Consonant Word List

kn- = /n/	wr- = /r/	-mb = /m/	sc- = /s/
knap	wrath	climb	scene
knack	wrap	comb	scenery
knapsack	wreath	crumb	scenic
knead	wrest	lamb	scepter
knee	wren	limb	sciatic
kneel	write	numb	science
knew	written	plumb	scintillating
knickers	writer	plumber	scion
knife	wrist	thumb	scissors
knight	wretch	succumb	scythe
knit	wriggle	tomb	
knob	wrong	womb	
knock	wrote	bomb	
knoll	wrung		
knot	wry		
know			
known			

This word list offers final silent consonants/graphemes that are less commonly found in elementary vocabularies. In the past, both of the letters of many of these were sounded as individual phonemes. For example, in Middle English *gnat* was once pronounced /g/ /n/ /a/ /t/.

Silent Consonant Word List (continued)		
gh- = /g/	***gn- = /n/***	***-bt = /t/***
g̸h̸ o s t	g̸n̸ a t	d ou b̸t̸
ghost	gnat	doubt
spaghetti	gnarl	debt
aghast	gnash	subtle
sorghum	gnome	
ghoul		

The silent letter patterns that follow are taught more frequently because they occur in many words found in elementary school vocabularies. However, students will come across other silent letter patterns, especially in upper-grade science and literature vocabulary. Some of these are listed in the following word list.

-ld = /d/	***-lf = /f/***	***-lm = /m/***
c ou l̸d	h a̸l f	c a̸l m
could	half	calm
would	calf	balm
should	behalf	psalm
		becalm

Silent Consonant Word List: Upper Grades		
-mn = /n/	**pn- = /n/**	**pt- = /t/**
h | y | m̸n̸	p̸n̸ | eu | m | ō | n | ī | a	p̸t̸ | o | m | ai | n̸e̸
hymn	pneumonia	ptomaine
damn	pneumatic	pterodactyl
solemn		ptosis
autumn		
column		
mnemonic		

Sometimes a letter may be silent in one form of a word but may be heard in another. This is especially true of base words ending in -mn.

Examples: hymn —► hymnal

autumn —► autumnal

column —► columnist

solemn —► solemnity

Silent Consonant Word List: Upper Grades (continued)		
sw- = /s/	**rh- = /r/**	**wh- = /h/**
s̸w̸ | or | d	r̸h̸ | ȳ | m / e	w̸h̸ | ō | l / e
sword	rhyme	who
answer	rhythm	whom
	rhubarb	whoever
	rhombus	whole
	Rhine	whose
	rhetoric	wholesome
	rheumatism	

— Unit 2 —

Open Syllables

Introduction to Open Syllables

The open syllable is the second of the six syllable types introduced in *Phoneme-Grapheme Mapping*. An *open syllable* ends with a single vowel letter. The vowel says its own name (or has a long sound). Examples of open syllables as a component of a two-syllable word include *ma-ple*, *mo-tel*, and *cre-ate*. An open syllable can be just one letter if that letter is a vowel: *i, a, o-pen*. Understanding open syllables helps spellers know whether to double consonants and helps readers determine the vowel sound.

Open Syllables

Tell students that they are going to learn a new syllable type. They already know about closed syllables. Instruct them to tell you the characteristics of a closed syllable. The vowel in an open syllable is spelled with one vowel, too, but it is not closed in with a consonant, and it makes the long sound, or says its name. Write the characteristics of an open syllable on the board. Contrast the open syllable with the closed syllable. Show students the words *robot*, *focus,* and *create*. Illustrate the syllable division, determine the vowel sound, and show students that the vowel is open at the end of the syllable; there is no consonant following it in the syllable.

MAPPING PROCEDURE

Because an open syllable contains a single vowel, that letter is placed alone in its box. Do not have students leave spaces between syllables when using the phoneme-grapheme mapping procedure. Instruct students to demonstrate their understanding of an open syllable by shading the boxes that contain open syllables a specific color, such as yellow. They can also place a horizontal line above the final vowel in the syllable to show that it makes the long sound or its letter name.

Open-Syllable Word List		
Words Containing Two Open Syllables ē g ō	**Words Containing One Open and One Closed Syllable** f ō c u s	**Words Containing One Open and One Silent *e* Syllable** r ē t ā k

crazy	July	vacant	virus	beside	became
lady	ego	simply	final	recline	refine
polo	photo	decal	tulip	behave	retake
tiny	pony	naval	total	decide	reuse
navy	ivy	pilot	foggy	beware	decode
hifi	holy	copy	Jell-O	before	refuse
tidy	zero	robot	study	locate	retune
duty	baby	humid	bonus	reduce	deflate
hobo	Cy	matron	hello		create
truly	puny	haven	empty		
veto	silo	focus	riot		
bonus		propel	duet		
		apron	diet		
		student	totem		
		motel	tulip		
		minus	holly		
		dusty	pansy		
		began	basin		
		begin	omit		

Phoneme-Grapheme Mapping
(A Method for Bridging Sound to Print)

Name: _Anthony_   Date: _____

b	e								
sh	y								
f	l	u							
p	r	y							
wh	y								
b	e	h	i	n	d				
s	t	u	d	e	n	t			
r	e	s	p	e	c	t			
s	i	l	e	n	t				
r	e	f	u	n	d				
d	o	n	a	te					
d	e	f	i	ne					
u	n	i	te						
r	e	t	i	re					
r	e	qu	i	re					

Note: This open syllable map once again connects previously taught concepts with new instruction. For this particular lesson, the silent -*e* syllable was taught prior to the open syllable.

2:2

Versatile Vowel i

TUTORIAL This lesson is divided into four parts. Each part presents a generalization in which the vowel *i* makes the long *e* sound. It is recommended that the lesson parts be taught on separate days.

<table>
<tr>
<td>TEACH</td>
<td>"The vowel *i* can make the short sound, as heard initially in the word *itch*, or it can make the long sound—the name of its letter—/ī/ as in *ice*. The vowel *i* can also make the sound of long *e*, /ē/, when in various positions in a word and within predictable letter combinations. When this occurs, the *i* is placed in its own box because it represents the single phoneme /e/."</td>
</tr>
</table>

<table>
<tr>
<td>TEACH PART 1</td>
<td>The vowel *i* is pronounced /ē/ when *i* is followed by a different vowel sound in a suffix.</td>
</tr>
</table>

MAPPING PROCEDURE

The letter *i* is written in one box. Predictable letter combinations can also be shaded during initial instruction so that students have a visual sense of two vowels following each other. (See examples in the word list.)

Versatile Vowel *i* Word List			

c	o̲	m	ē	d	ī	a̲	n

-iate		-ian		-ient	-ial
abbreviate	mediate	amphibian	utopian	disobedient	bacterial
affiliate	opiate	barbarian	valedictorian	disorient	serial
alleviate	radiate	collegian	vegetarian	expedient	bronchial
appropriate	expatriate	comedian	Indian	gradient	burial
asphyxiate	repudiate	custodian	Italian	transient	centennial
conciliate	retaliate	equestrian	Iranian	ingredient	ceremonial
defoliate	associate	librarian	Romanian	nutrient	territorial
disaffiliate	gladiate	humanitarian	Serbian	obedient	editorial
expropriate	humiliate	median	Austrian	orient	tutorial
foliate	infuriate	meridian	Colombian	recipient	perennial
	ingratiate	radian	ruffian	salient	pictorial
		Rotarian	thespian		

When *i* Is Followed by a Different Vowel Sound in a Suffix			

i	n	s	i	g	n	ī	a̲

-ior	-ia			-iance	-ience
interior	hernia	Albania	Siberia	ambiance	audience
exterior	cafeteria	Arabia	gardenia	deviance	obedience
inferior	insignia	Austria	magnolia	radiance	expedience
superior	insomnia	Bosnia	memorabilia	variance	experience
	mafia	Colombia	trivia		lenience
	malaria	India	zinnia		recipience

Versatile Vowel *i* Word List (continued)			
When *i* Is Followed by a Different Vowel Sound in a Suffix			

s	t	ū	d	ī	͡ou	s

-ium	*-ious*		*-ient*	*-iator*
aquarium	previous	serious	disorient	aviator
atrium	curious	studious	expedient	gladiator
auditorium	devious	tedious	ingredient	mediator
condominium	envious	various	lenient	radiator
cranium	furious	victorious	nutrient	retaliator
medium	glorious	copious	obedient	alleviator
stadium	mysterious	previous	percipient	
geranium	injurious	dubious	recipient	
gymnasium	obvious	harmonious	salient	

i	d	ī	͡o	t

-iot	*-iac*		*-atric*
idiot	cardiac	maniac	pediatric
chariot	hemophiliac	Pontiac	cardiatric
	hypochondriac	pyromaniac	geriatric
	insomniac	zodiac	

TEACH PART 2 When *i* is before **que** or **gue**, the *i* is pronounced /ē/. These are French spellings borrowed by English.

MAPPING PROCEDURE

Place the **que** or **gue** in one box since the trigraph produces just one phoneme in each word: **que** = /k/ and **gue** = /g/.

Versatile Vowel *i* (Part 2) Word List		
When *i* Is Before *que*		When *i* Is Before *gue*

a	n	t	ī	que

f	ā	t	ī	gue

When *i* Is Before *que*		When *i* Is Before *gue*
antique	physique	fatigue
clique	technique	intrigue
critique	unique	colleague
oblique	mystique	league

TEACH PART 3

When a final *y* that is pronounced /ē/ is changed to *i* before a suffix is added, the *i* keeps the original /ē/ sound. However, when *y* is pronounced like /ī/, keep the long *i* (/ī/) sound (*fly, flies*).

MAPPING PROCEDURE

The *i* is placed in its own box. Note that when the plural suffix *-es* is added, both the *e* and *s* are placed in one box. Have students cross out the *e* because it is not heard. The final *s* sounds like /z/.

Versatile Vowel *i* (Part 3) Word List
When a final *y*, pronounced /ē/, is changed to *i* before a suffix is added, the *i* keeps the original /ē/ sound.
However, when *y* is pronounced like *i*, keep the long *i* (/ī/) sound (*fly flies*).

c	ō	z	ī	er		c	i	t	ī	es

sleepier	sunniest	crazier	cities	hardiness
sleepiest	sunnier	ladies	stingiest	uglier
prettiest	funnier	tragedies	studious	rockiness
happiest	shinier	families	ugliness	groceries

TEACH PART 4

Teach these three principles:

1. When a verb that is more than one syllable ends with *y* (e.g., carry), the *y* is changed to *i* to form the third person singular (e.g., carries), but the *i* retains the long *e* sound.

2. Usually a final *i* is pronounced /ē/.

3. Letter *i* is pronounced /ē/ in French, Spanish, and Italian words.

MAPPING PROCEDURE

The *i* is placed in its own box. Note that when the third-person singular suffix *-es* is added to a verb, it is placed in one box. The *e* is crossed out because you do not hear it. The final *s* sounds like /z/.

Versatile Vowel *i* (Part 4) Word List		
When forming a third-person singular verb from a verb ending in *y* that is more than one syllable, change the *y* to an *i*. The *i* retains its long e sound.	**Usually a final *i* is pronounced /ē/.**	**Letter *i* is pronounced /ē/ in words of French, Spanish, and Italian origin.**
c o p i es	M i a m i	p i zz a
carries accompanies hurries pities studies rallies worries caddies buries copies curries dallies	broccoli pastrami Hawaii ravioli Hindi Suzuki martini Tahiti mi macaroni ravioli Da Vinci	pizza cliché fiancée *amigo* *merci* *fiesta*

Unit 3

The Silent -e Syllable

Introduction to the Silent -e Syllable

Introduction to long vowels is generally done by first teaching the silent *e* generalization, fondly referred to by many teachers as the "magic *e* rule."

When there is a one-syllable word with one vowel followed by a single consonant sound and then a final *e*, the first vowel is usually long and the final *e* is silent. In this way, the magic silence of the *e* allows the voice of the first vowel to be heard. Be aware that a single consonant sound can be represented by two letters if a digraph is involved, as in the words *bathe, ache,* and *clothe.*

The first step in teaching this very useful generalization is to pair closed one-syllable words (CVC) with their corresponding one-syllable silent -*e* partners (CVC*e*), as in the following pairs:

mad/made	rob/robe	bath/bathe
pin/pine	pet/Pete	cut/cute*

Instruct students to voice the short vowel sound of the closed syllables and the long vowel sound of the silent -*e* syllables. Work with students to discriminate between the short and long vowel sounds and to use the *name* of the vowel letter as a sound in words with silent -*e* syllables.

*Two sound patterns are represented by long *u*. They are /yo͞o/ as in *use* and /oo/ as in *rule*. When initially teaching the *uCe* pattern, it is less confusing to present long *u* words that are pronounced with the phoneme /yo͞o/ (*cute, mule, fume*), because that is the sound that aligns with the name of the vowel letter *u*.

Contrast Closed and Silent -e Syllables

TUTORIAL It is important to teach silent -e syllables and then contrast closed-syllable words with the silent -e syllable words. Students will see that the silent -e words use the same number of boxes as their closed-syllable partners. However the extra letter (e) in the last box works to magically create a different sound. Students will begin to see how additional letters in a word generally have important jobs to do. If the letters are omitted, they will get a completely different word.

TEACH

Show students the word *mad* and ask them to read it. Place a separate card with an *e* on it at the end of *mad*. Ask students to tell you what you did. (Placed an *e* at the end.) Tell students about the magic e, whose job it is to stay very quiet but change the sound of the vowel in the middle. This magic e makes the other vowel friend say its name.

"What is the name of the vowel in *mad*?" (*a*.) "So read the new word–*made*." Repeat this process with *pin–pine, cut–cute.* Tell students that they just learned the silent-e syllable type. Repeat the characteristics of the silent -e syllable.

MAPPING PROCEDURE

1. Place the silent *e* in the same box as the final consonant because it makes no sound of its own.

2. Drop the silent *e* to the base of the sound box. (It makes sense to teach this from the outset because students will eventually need to map words in which the final *e* is dropped when a vowel suffix is added.)

3. Draw a slash line through the final *e*.

4. Draw an arrow from the silent *e* to the preceding vowel and mark the vowel with a line to show that it is a long, rather than a short, vowel sound.

Closed and Silent -e Contrasts Word List

h	o	p		h	ō	p

VC or CVC	VCe	VC or CVC	VCe	VC or CVC	VCe
hat	hate	bit	bite	shad	shade
Sam	same	kit	kite	fad	fade
can	cane	rob	robe	mad	made
cap	cape	rod	rode	tam	tame
tap	tape	hop	hope	rag	rage
hid	hide	mop	mope	wag	wage
rid	ride	not	note	flam	flame
Tim	time	shin	shine	sham	shame
fin	fine	slid	slide	man	mane
pin	pine	slim	slime	pan	pane
win	wine	strip	stripe	plan	plane
rip	ripe	glob	globe	van	vane
scrap	scrape	fat	fate	mat	mate
rat	rate	us	use	stat	state
Sid	side	dim	dime	spin	spine
twin	twine	grip	gripe	writ	write
bath	bathe	cloth	clothe	tub	tube
cub	cube	cop	cope	pop	pope
dot	dote	not	note	pal	pale
pet	Pete	fad	fade	pip	pipe
rid	ride	din	dine	cod	code
con	cone	slop	slope	crud	crude
dud	dude	plum	plume		

TEACH

Help students solidify the concept of changing a closed syllable to a silent e syllable through the addition of an e by helping them write *Word Problems* as shown in the attached student sample.

Word Problems

cut ⊕ e = cute

hug ⊕ e = huge

sham ⊕ e = shame

quit ⊕ e = quite

scrap ⊕ e = scrape

strip ⊕ e = stripe

sanbath ⊕ e = sanbathe

shipmat ⊕ e = shipmate

classmat ⊕ e = classmate

Note: Have students create "word problems" for those closed syllable words that make a real word when a silent e is added. Students can also do "Reverse Word Problems" by starting with a silent e word and subtracting the e to make a closed syllable word. Students also enjoy illustrating their new words.

One-Syllable Silent e Words Arranged by Vowel Sound

TEACH Depending on student reading levels, work through the word lists in this lesson one by one, or work with a combination of words representing a variety of vowels.

MAPPING PROCEDURE

For an explanation of soft *c* and *g* and mapping instructions for these patterns, please see Lesson 1:17. Use the mapping examples in the following word lists as a guide.

Silent -e Syllables With *a* Word List					*a* With Soft *c*	*a* With Soft *g*
blade	rake	blame	vane	late	ace	age
fade	sake	came	cape	mate	face	cage
grade	shake	flame	scrape	plate	grace	page
made	snake	frame	shape	rate	lace	rage
shade	stake	game	tape	skate	pace	stage
spade	take	lame	base	state	place	wage
trade	wake	name	case	brave	race	
wade	gale	same	chase	cave	space	
bake	male	shame	vase	gave	trace	
brake	pale	tame	crate	grave		
cake	sale	cane	date	shave		
fake	tale	crane	fate	save		
flake	scale	lane	gate	slave		
lake	stale	mane	grate	wave		
make	whale	plane	hate	pane		

Silent -*e* Syllables With *e* and *i* Word List

e	*i*				*i* With Soft *c*
eve	bribe	dike	slime	pipe	dice
Steve	tribe	hike	time	ripe	lice
Pete	bride	like	dine	stripe	mice
	glide	spike	fine	wipe	nice
	hide	strike	line	rise	price
	pride	file	mine	wise	rice
	ride	mile	nine	bite	slice
	side	pile	pine	kite	spice
	slide	smile	snipe	white	twice
	stride	tile	spine	write	ice
	tide	while	swine	dive	
	wide	chime	twine	drive	
	life	crime	vine	five	
	wife	dime	wine	hive	
	bike	lime	gripe	live	

Silent -*e* Syllables With *o* Word List

globe	hole	zone	cove	smoke	cone	rose	broke	whole
robe	mole	hope	drove	spoke	lone	those	choke	dome
code	pole	rope	grove	stroke	stone	note	chose	
rode	stole	slope	stove	woke	tone	vote	close	
poke	bone	nose	joke	home	hose	pose		

TEACH

The long *u* sound can be pronounced /o͞o/ as in *tune* or with the hidden sound of *y*, /y/ /o͞o/, as in *cute.* Contrast the two words in discussions with students. Show them how to box the *u* over two sound boxes when they hear the hidden sound of *y*, /y/ /o͞o/. For complete teaching instructions on long vowel *u*, see lessons 6:5 and 6:6.

Silent -*e* Syllables With *u* Word List	
***u* as /y/ + /o͞o/** **Two Phonemes/** **Two Sound Boxes**	***u* as /o͞o/** **One Phoneme/** **One Sound Box**

***u* as /y/ + /o͞o/**		***u* as /o͞o/**		
cube	huge	crude	dune	induce
mule	fume	dude	June	spruce
yule	mute	rude	prune	truce
fuse	July	duke	tune	Bruce
use	refuse	rule	flute	
cute	consume	plume	tube	
cure	muse	brute	Luke	
bugle	volume			

Phoneme-Grapheme Mapping
(A Method for Bridging Sound to Print)

Name: _____   Date: _____

Note: This map demonstrates a student's emerging knowledge of the silent -*e* syllable. There is still some confusion about the long *u* sound when it makes the phonemes /y/ and /o͞o/, as in *cute*.

3:3 Vowel r and Silent e Patterns

TUTORIAL Many words have a single vowel followed by the /r/ phoneme and then a silent *e*. Some programs teach these as a variation of an *r*-controlled vowel. *Phoneme-Grapheme Mapping* instructs students to map these as two separate phonemes, consisting of the long vowel sound followed by the single /r/ and a final silent *e*. Although *or* and *ore* do sound exactly alike, instruct students to map *ore* like a silent *e* pattern for purposes of consistency.

TEACH In some silent -*e* syllables, you will find a single vowel followed by the /r/ phoneme and then a silent *e* (e.g., *flare*). The magic *e* still works its magic and makes the vowel say its name.

MAPPING PROCEDURE

Place the silent *e* in the same box as the final consonant because it makes no sound of its own. Drop the silent *e* to the base of the sound box and slash through it. Then, draw an arrow from the silent *e* to the preceding vowel, and mark the vowel with a horizontal line above it to indicate that the vowel is long.

Vowel *r* and Silent *e* Word List							
-are			**-ere**		**-ire** **-yre**		
bare	stare	scare	here		dire	wire	inspire
care	ware	snare	mere		fire	spire	perspire
dare	share	beware			hire	retire	require
hare	blare	prepare			lyre	desire	admire
mare	flare	hardware			mire	entire	squire
pare	glare	warehouse			sire	spire	expire
rare	spare				tire		inquire

Vowel *r* and Silent *e* Word List (continued)				
-ore			**-ure**	
			u as /yoo/	*u* as /oo/
ore	pore	shore	pure	lure
core	sore	chore	cure	endure
fore	store	bore		allure
gore	tore	more		
wore	lore			

Phoneme-Grapheme Mapping
(A Method for Bridging Sound to Print)

Name: _____ Date: _____

c	a͞	r						
sh	a͞	r						
f	i͞	r						
C	o͞	r						
c	u͞	r						
h	e͞	r						
r	e	t	i͞	r				
i	g	n	o͞	r				

Note: This map is another example of a student's emergent under-standing of the silent -*e* syllable in both one- and two-syllable words.

3:4

Combined Syllable Types: Two-Syllable Words

TUTORIAL This lesson provides opportunities for students to review, practice, and strengthen their understanding of the closed, open, and silent -*e* syllables through phoneme-grapheme mapping of multisyllable words. The two-syllable words in this lesson provide review of previously taught concepts, including the syllable types, blends, digraphs, and two-syllable silent -*e* compound words.

> **TEACH**
>
> Quickly review the three syllable types—closed, open, and silent -*e*. Provide several single-syllable words and instruct students to sort them into syllable-type categories. Combine two of the words into a single word. Instruct students to read the word and tell what syllable types were combined to make the new word. Repeat the process with two different words. Explain to students that this lesson will review many of the sound/spelling concepts that they have learned.

MAPPING PROCEDURE

Because these are combination lessons, a variety of review mappings are reinforced. Refer to specific mapping instruction for the syllable type probed in each of the word lists that follow.

> **TEACH**
>
> In words of more than one syllable, the silent -*e* syllable is very prevalent in the final syllable position, as the following word lists demonstrate.

Combined Closed and Silent -e Syllables Word List

a	e	i	o	u
cascade	compete	admire	enclose	pollute
compare	complete	empire	backbone	confuse
dictate	extreme	describe	explode	dispute
escape	athlete	collide	compote	accuse
estate	stampede	combine	oppose	include
inflate	concrete	confide	explore	excuse
insane	convene	advise	backstroke	commune
invade	adhere	incline	suppose	compute
landscape	obscene	ignite	tadpole	consume
mistake		contrive	expose	costume
membrane		umpire	trombone	conclude
octane		hemline	ignore	obtuse
pancake		inside	dispose	intrude
stagnate		inquire	transpose	impure
translate		entire	fishpole	produce
welfare		retire	enthrone	exclude
regulate		exile	implore	
filtrate		advice	unclothe	
insulate		baptize		
contemplate		pastime		
illustrate		unwise		
deregulate		invite		
consummate		subscribe		
infiltrate		ignite		
confiscate		textile		
separate		sunshine		
duplicate		reptile		
educate		inscribe		
		dislike		
		acquire		
		expire		

"Combined Open and Silent -e Syllables" Word List

a	e	i	o	u
beside	locate	produce	behave	decide
beware	prepare	retake	debate	decline
deflate	seclude	predate	profile	provoke
secede	diphase	secure	reduce	tribune
dipole	reprise	triphase	became	oblige
recline	profuse	retrace	supreme	beguile
Chinese		provide	rebuke	recede

Combined Silent *e* and Closed Syllables Word List

| b | ā | s | m | e | n | t |

basement	pavement	boneless	careful	careless
casement	cuteness	dateless	hateful	dukedom
hopeful	hopeless	movement	lateness	likeness
nameless	placement	ripeness	sameness	timeless
spiteful	tubeless	tireless	useless	wasteful
wireless	lifeless	merely	soreness	fateful

Combined Silent *e* and Open Syllables Word List

| n | ī | c | l | y |

nicely	likely	direly	finely	lamely
lately	wisely	lonely	namely	timely
widely	rudely	stately	homely	sorely
lovely		purely	safely	rarely

Busy Silent ε and Past Tense -εd

TUTORIAL By now, your students should be aware of just how busy a silent *e* can be within a word. It often can have one or more of the following jobs:

- Silent *e* can make the preceding vowel long, as in the silent -*e* syllable pattern. This is demonstrated by drawing an arrow from the *e* to the preceding vowel, over which you draw a line.

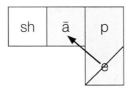

- Past tense -*ed* can be pronounced as one sound, /t/ or /d/. If a base word ends in silent *e* but has dropped the *e* to add the ending -*ed,* then show and cross out silent *e* and write the -*ed* in one box. Both the silent *e* and past-tense spelling are shown.

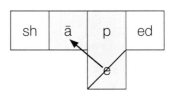

- Silent *e* can work with *c* to signal the soft *c* or /s/ sound. Students show this by placing the *e* in the same box as the *c* and looping the two letters together, as shown in the previous lessons [r | a (ce)]. When a base word ends in a final -*ce*, it creates the unvoiced /s/ sound. Therefore, when an -*ed* is added to the word, it takes on the unvoiced /t/ sound of -*ed* and is placed in one sound box. Always keep -*ed* together if the morpheme (-*ed*) is pronounced as one phoneme, /t/ or /d/. If silent *e* is dropped, it can be crossed out but left in the mapping system as shown below.

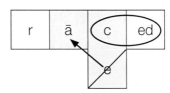 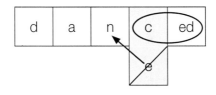

TEACH
The silent *e* in *danced* and *changed* does not make the preceding vowel long because there is an extra consonant (*n*) between the first vowel and the final *e*.

- Silent *e* can work with *g* to signal the soft *g* or /j/ sound. Students show this by placing the *e* in the same box as the *g* and looping the two letters together. When a base word ends in a final *-ge*, it represents the voiced /j/ sound. Therefore, when *-ed* is added to the word, it takes on the voiced single-phoneme /d/ sound of *-ed* and is placed in one box.

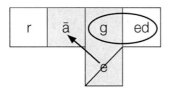 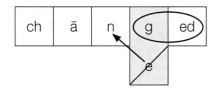

- Silent *e* protects the *v* from being the last letter in an English word. Students show this by putting an X through the *e*. An arrow to the preceding vowel is not necessary unless the preceding vowel is long. In this case, students draw one slash through the *e* and place a line over the preceding vowel.

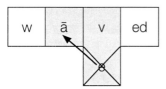 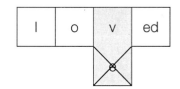

TEACH

Instruct students to read the silent *-e* syllable in *wave*. Discuss verbs and direct students to demonstrate the verb *wave*. Explain to students that there is a very important spelling, *-ed,* that is added to verbs to indicate past tense, meaning that the action happened in the past. Add *-ed* to *wave*. Read the new word: *waved*. Say, "We *waved* our hands when we saw the word *wave*."

"Silent *e* is a very busy letter. It makes the *a* in *wave* say its name. And when *-ed* is added, the extra *e* gets dropped. Silent *e* also keeps *wave* from ending in *v*, because words cannot end in a *v* in our language. Busy, busy *e*!"

Repeat this process with *changed.* Talk about the extra job that *e* has in *changed* when it softens the *g* to make the sound of /j/. Point out that *-ed* will represent either the phoneme /d/ or /t/ in words. Because *-ed* is a meaningful unit, the spelling letters *-ed* are never separated.

MAPPING PROCEDURE

Refer to the mapping procedures presented previously for other examples of the busy silent *e* and past tense *-ed*.

Silent and Past Tense *-ed* Word List				
Soft *c* and Busy Silent *e*			**Soft *g* and Busy Silent *e***	
d i c ed			e dg ed	
aced	pounced	induced	aged	damaged
faced	pranced	reduced	caged	discouraged
graced	iced	advanced	paged	rummaged
laced	juiced	balanced	raged	encouraged
paced	chanced	bounced	staged	scrimmaged
placed	danced	braced	waged	bandaged
raced	spliced	rejoiced	fudged	sabotaged
spaced	fenced	voiced	nudged	salvaged
traced	forced	spruced	budged	emerged
diced	glanced	minced	lodged	obliged
priced	lanced	enticed	edged	sieged
riced	spiced	pieced	dodged	gouged
sliced	noticed	policed	voyaged	challenged
			sponged	arranged

Single short vowel sound plus final *v* and silent *e*			Single long vowel sound plus final *v* and silent *e*			
l ĭ v ed			sh ā v ed			
live	love	give	paved	craved	strived	arrive
shove	shoved	glove	saved	shaved	behaved	survived
gloved	delved	valve	caved	shaven	revived	thrived
evolve	evolved	involved	waved	slaved	derived	roved
shelved	halved	loved				
lived	solved					

Silent and Past Tense *-ed* Word List (continued)	
Other long vowel sound plus final *v*	***r*-controlled vowels plus final** *v*

| h | ea | v | ed |

| c | ur | v | ed |

Other long vowel sound plus final *v*		*r*-controlled vowels plus final *v*	
heaved	moved	swerved	starved
peeved	improved	nerved	curved
sleeved	removed	conserve	carved
weaved	proved	conserved	served
retrieved			
For more help mapping long and other vowels, please see Unit 6.		For more help mapping *r*-controlled vowels, please see Unit 7.	

Phoneme-Grapheme Mapping
(A Method for Bridging Sound to Print)

Name: _____   Date: _____

W	i	sh	ed				
S	l	a	sh	ed			
d	a	sh	ed				
Sh	ou	ed					
r	en	t	e	d			
t	w	i	s	t	e	d	
t	i	ed					
s	p	l	a	sh	ed		
M	i	ss	e.	d			
b	oo	t	e	d			
a	g	ed					

Note: This map illustrates a student's emerging understanding of the three sounds of past tense *-ed* (note the error in *missed*).

The -ve Rule

TUTORIAL In English spellings, the letter *v* is never the final letter in a word. Words with short vowels also end in *-ve,* as in *have, give, live,* and *love.* The silent final *e* that follows the *v* in these words has no function other than to preserve the "sanctity" of the *v.* Therefore, words ending in *-ve* seldom follow the magic *e* rule.

Since the *e* in these words does not influence the preceding vowel sound, no loop back to the preceding vowel is necessary, as was previously demonstrated. However, an X is made across the *e* to show the letter is not heard, even though it is placed in a sound box.

"English words do not end in the letter *v.* Think of the *v* as needing an *e* to hold it up, or else it will fall over!" Show students the word *hive.* "In this word, the *e* holds up the *v* and is the magic *e* too; the vowel in the word says its name, /ī/." Show students the word *have.* Explain that the vowel sound is short, so the role of *e* is to keep the word from ending in *v.* When teaching the mapping procedure, make the distinction between the silent *-e* syllable with a long vowel sound and the syllable in which *e* props up and protects the *v.* Contrast their different mappings.

MAPPING PROCEDURE

If the *-ve* is part of a silent *-e* syllable whereby the *e* is used to make a long vowel sound, then the *e* should be placed in the same box as the *v.* The *e* is a silent letter and does not get its own box. The *e* should then be looped to the preceding vowel to show its relationship with that vowel. This is demonstrated by drawing an arrow from the *e* to the preceding vowel, over which you draw a line.

Silent *e* can also protect the *v* from being the last letter in the word. We show this by putting the *v* and *e* side by side in one box and drawing an X through the *e* (because the *e* is unheard. An arrow to the preceding vowel is not necessary because the vowel sound is not long.

See the mapping examples in the word lists that follow.

Vowel + -ve Word List			
Long Vowel		**Short Vowel**	**Other Vowel**
h ī v / e		h a v̶e̶	s er v̶e̶
hive	behave	have	carve
live	survive	live	starve
strive	wove	give	curve
arrive	thrive	love	serve
contrive	rave	valve	nerve
derive	save	evolve	leave
eve	cave	involve	heave
knave	wave	glue	improve
pave	dove	halve	prove
cove	rove	dove	weave
gave	dive	olive	forgive
stove	clove	salve	conserve
Steve	crave	solve	move
brave	drive	twelve	peeve
dive	engrave	shelve	remove
drove	grave	delve	retrieve
five	octave	shove	sleeve
grove	slave	dove	suave
shave			swerve

Suffix -ive Word List					
e	x	p e n s i v̶e̶			
native	detective	defective	inventive	effective	elusive
massive	relative	primitive	defensive	inattentive	expensive
cursive	festive	impressive	destructive	possessive	objective
motive	captive	expressive	intensive	offensive	conducive
festive	active	instinctive	sensitive	negative	

When Vowel y Replaces Vowel i

"When *y* comes in the middle of a base word, it generally takes the place of the vowel *i*. That means it can make either the short or long *i* sound, depending on the syllable type. We are going to study this type of word this week through three of the syllable types: silent -*e*, open, and closed. The majority of the words that fall into this category are derived from Greek." (The starred words in the word list are not from Greek.)

MAPPING PROCEDURE

Since the *y* is taking the place of a single short or long vowel sound, the *y* should be placed in one box.

y Replaces i Word List					
In Silent -e Syllables			**In Closed Syllables**		
When y is used instead of i in a silent -e or open syllable, it makes the long sound of i.			**When y is used instead of i in a closed syllable, it makes the short sound of i.**		

t	ȳ	p

g	y	m

s	y	s	t	e	m

style	type	enzyme	gym	bicycle	crypt
lyre	rhyme	restyle	crystal	cylinder	cynic
analyze	psyche	thyme	cyst	dialysis	sympathy
rye*	dye*	bye*	dysfunction	dyslexia	Egypt
pyre	hype	tyke*	abyss	gypsy	homonym
	lye*		hymn	hypnosis	onyx
			rhythm	syllable	symbol
			symphony	symptom	synonym
y at the end of an open syllable			syntax	synthetic	system
			typical	tryst	lynch
			Lynn	oxygen	physics

h	y	ph	e	n

dynamite	dynasty	tycoon*
encyclopedia	typhoon	hybrid
cyclops	hydrogen	hyper
hyphen	cyclone	python

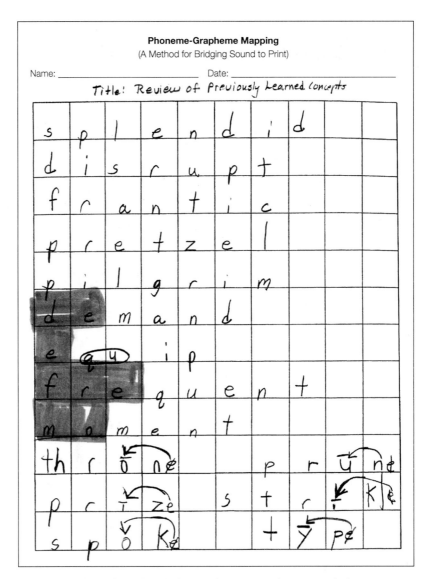

Phoneme-Grapheme Mapping
(A Method for Bridging Sound to Print)

Name: _____ Date: _____

Title: Review of Previously Learned Concepts

s	p	l	e	n	d	i	d		
d	i	s	r	u	p	t			
f	r	a	n	t	i	c			
p	r	e	t	z	e	l			
p	i	l	g	r	i	m			
d	e	m	a	n	d				
e	qu		i	p					
f	re	q	u	e	n	t			
m	o	m	e	n	t				
th	r	ō	nė			p	r	u	nė
p	r	ī	zė		s	t	r	i	kė
s	p	ō	kė			t	y	pė	

Note: A review of previously learned concepts is extremely important to solidify learning. This lesson revisits the three previously introduced and practiced syllable types to include closed, open, and silent -e syllables.

Unit 4

A Bridge to Morphology

Introduction to Morphology

Morphology is the study of morphemes, which are the smallest meaningful units of language. Morphemes can be one letter (-s) or more than one letter (-est). Morphemes can be one syllable, many syllables, or an entire word. Morphemes include compounds, prefixes, base words, roots, suffixes, and Greek combining forms, such as *poly, mono,* and *chrome.*

An affix is a term used to describe any prefix or suffix that is attached (affixed) to a base word or root. These morphemes have two forms: inflectional morphemes and derivational morphemes. An inflectional morpheme is a suffix that marks a word's tense, number, or degree without changing its part of speech. A derivational morpheme can be either a prefix or a suffix that when added to a base word or root helps to build a new word by changing the word's meaning, part of speech, or both. The three types of inflectional morphemes are described below.

Types of Inflectional Morphemes		
Inflectional morphemes added to the end of nouns to signify possession, gender, or number	Inflectional morphemes added to the end of verbs to signify tense, mood, or voice	Inflectional morphemes added to the end of adjectives to signify comparison
-'s as in Jeff's -s as in boys -es as in boxes	-ing as in smelling -ed as in smelled -en as in taken	-er as in smaller -est as in tallest

Prefixes are morphemes that appear before the base word or root and alter the meaning (and are, therefore, derivational). The most common English prefixes come from three sources: Anglo-Saxon (Old English), Latin, and Greek. Some words have more than one prefix, so it is important that students identify the base word or root when reading and spelling an unfamiliar word. By adding the meaning of each prefix to the base word or root, students can begin to unwrap the meaning of a word.

Of the twenty most frequently used prefixes in English, all but two are of Anglo-Saxon or Latin origin. The first prefixes taught to students should be those that occur most frequently with Anglo-Saxon base words: *a-, de-, dis-, fore-, in-, un-, mis-, pre,* and *re-.* Of nearly 3,000 prefixed words found in textbooks for students in grades 3–9, words beginning with *dis-, in-* (meaning not), *re-,* and *un-* occurred in more than 58 percent of the prefixed words (White, Sowell, and Yanagihara, 1989). Students first encounter the prefix *a-* as the schwa in words such as *asleep, away, alike,* and *around,* so discussing this prefix when introducing the schwa is appropriate. In fact, you should include instruction about the schwa before teaching this unit.

The English language contains more derivational suffixes than inflectional suffixes. However, four inflectional suffixes (-s, -es, -ed, and -ing) were found in about 65 percent of 2,000 commonly suffixed words (White, Sowell, and Yanagihara 1989). The derivational suffixes -ly, -er, (-or), -ion (-tion, -ation, -ition), as well as -able and -ible were found in another 17 percent of commonly suffixed words.

When you add a derivational suffix to a base word, you often change its part of speech. The following chart lists several common English suffixes that can determine the part of speech of a base word or root. English includes many additional suffixes, but this book's mapping procedures and word lists will feature those used commonly in primary and intermediate grades, as well as those that can be added to Anglo-Saxon base words without changing the spelling of either the base word or suffix.

Common Derivational Suffixes that Can Change Parts of Speech			
Derivational noun suffixes	Derivational adjective suffixes	Derivational verb suffixes	Derivational adverb suffixes
-er, or as in skier, actor	-ful as in fearful	-en as in tighten	-ly as in speedy
-ment as in basement	-less as in careless	-ate as in create	-ily as in speedily
-ship as in township	-some as in awesome		
-ness as in happiness	-y as in bossy		
-ion as in action	-able as in teachable		
-sion as in compulsion	-ible as in crucible		
-tion as in revolution	-ic as in public		
-ty as in cruelty	-ive as in responsive		
-al as in refusal	-ous as in curious		
-fold as in tenfold	-ish as in selfish		

Derivational rules can be unpredictable. The meaning and pronunciation of derivational morphemes can change depending on the morphemes they are combined with, but they are usually spelled consistently. A derivational suffix can also change the stress pattern on a syllable. For example, when the suffix -ous is added to the word courage, the stress switches from the first syllable to the second and actually makes the vowel sound in the second syllable of the base word easier to hear and spell.

Students can begin learning about derivational morphemes as early as second grade and should begin with common derivational prefixes and suffixes that do not require a phonological or orthographic change in the base word or root to which the affix is attached (un-, re-, dis-; -ment, -ness, -ful). Such words are generally of Anglo-Saxon origin and can stand alone as a word in English (pack, hand, peace); can be combined to make compounds (backpack, handbag, peacetime); and can be affixed by adding prefixes and suffixes (repack, handful, peacefulness). By late second grade and into third grade, students must learn some of the rules needed for suffix addition because the spelling of the base words are often affected. Most average students are generalizing their knowledge of prefixes, suffixes, and roots to decipher the meanings of hundreds of new words by fourth grade (Myerson 1978; Tyler and Nagy 1987; Wysocki and Jenkins 1987).

Morphology is a large area of study, and so this unit will focus on the introduction and mapping of the group of morphemes called affixes. Although an overview is provided for the most commonly used affixes, word lists will only be provided for those affixes used most frequently in the elementary grades.

Using the Affixo Chart

The Affixo Chart is a useful tool for strengthening the concept of affixes, helping students determine the divisions in words with affixes, and supporting the spelling options when applying affixes to roots and bases. It can be used, in addition to phoneme-grapheme mapping, to reinforce analysis of words with single and multiple affixes.

Directions: Provide the word to be analyzed. It may have one or multiple prefixes and/ or suffixes.

1. Direct students to identify the base word or root and to write it in the middle column.

2. Work outward from the root/base, identifying suffixes and prefixes that are a part of the original word.

3. Write the affixes in the prefix and suffix boxes to build the word.

4. Note spelling changes by marking them as they are marked during phoneme-grapheme mapping.

WHEN TO USE THE AFFIXO CHART

A blackline master of the Affixo Chart is provided in Appendix B. Use the Affixo Chart to:

- Introduce a new affix.

- Practice the spelling rules associated with adding affixes to roots and bases.

- Reinforce phoneme-grapheme mapping procedures.

- Review spelling concepts with affixes.

- Provide independent spelling practice.

- Provide extended practice with difficult concepts.

Affixo Chart

Prefix	Prefix	Prefix	Base Word Or Root	Suffix	Suffix	Suffix
			help	ful	ness	
			tire	less	ly	
			invent	ive	ness	
			equip	ment		
			thank	ful	ly	
			thank	less	ness	
			splendid	ly		
			frequent	ly		

I try to include words with affixes in word study lessons. The Affixo Chart gives students an opportunity to analyze the structure of their spelling words.

Plural s/ɛs

TUTORIAL Anglo-Saxon words use consistent spellings for plurals, but there are three different pronunciations:

- /s/ after base words that end in unvoiced consonants.
- /z/ after base words that end in voiced consonants.
- /es/ after base words that end in /ks/ as in *boxes*, /s/ as in *glasses*, /ch/ as in *churches*, /sh/ as in *dishes*, /j/ as in *ledges,* and /z/ as in *fizzes*. A phoneme is added (/e/ in the *es* ending).

When the plural suffix *s* is added to words ending in the unvoiced consonant /t/, the final consonant is often barely detectable or becomes disguised by the addition of the plural ending. For example, you can clearly hear the final /t/ in the word *nest*, but it becomes disguised, or coarticulated with the /s/, when you say its plural form (*nests*). Therefore, you often see young children write this plural as *nes* or *ness*. To avoid this error, it is important to teach students the base word concept early. If they say and spell the base word before adding the plural, this error is often avoided.

TEACH

Show students the word *hat.* Say, "I have one *hat*." Add an *s* to *hat.* Ask students to read the new word, *hats,* and use it in a sentence. Contrast the meaning of singular *hat* and plural *hats.* Remove the *s;* tell students that *hat* is the base word. "When it becomes plural, meaning more than one, we add the *s.*" Put the *s* back on *hat; s* is the suffix that changes the meaning of *hat.* Ask, "How does it change the meaning? It now means more than one *hat: hats.* What sound do you hear at the end of *hats*?" (/s/.)

Repeat this process with *crow,* only when the ending sound is isolated, it will be /z/.

Repeat the process with *lash.* Ask students to isolate the phonemes in *lashes* to help them hear the two phonemes in the suffix, *-es.* To make this word plural, add *-es.*

Even though students will learn about the disguised /t/ at the ends of some base words on Day One, teach the unique mapping procedure for base words ending in *t* on Day Two.

Note: It is important to ask students to say, isolate, and spell the base word when working with suffixes.

MAPPING PROCEDURE

The plurals should be mapped as follows:

- The single phonemes /s/ and /z/ should be represented by placing the *s* in a single box.

- The phonemes /e/ and /s/ should be represented by two separate boxes. They add two additional sounds, one of which is a vowel. This vowel sound adds an additional syllable to the base word.

- When the base word is a closed syllable that ends in *t,* this ending sound is often coarticulated with the plurals and becomes difficult for students to isolate. Instruct students to say and spell the base word before they add the plural. This helps students to not omit the final letter sound when the plural *-s* is added. During the mapping phase of these words, students should include the final consonant in its own box, even though it may be difficult to discriminate its sound once the plural *-s* is added. Instruct them to draw small, light, horizontal lines through the box to demonstrate "the letter's attempt to disguise its sound," as demonstrated in the following word list.

Plural -*s* Word List			
-*s* as /s/		**-*s* as /z/**	**-*es* as /e/ /s/**
n e s t s		h i ll s	a sh e s
drips	quotes	slaves	gushes
chops	boats	queens	boxes
slots	snaps	wheels	wishes
shots	jeeps	flames	waxes
bats	sinks	feels	dishes
hats	spanks	needs	fishes
mats	desks	blows	mashes
laps	tapes	crows	crashes
taps	plates	kills	flashes
lets	creeps	skins	splashes
pets	roasts	colds	foxes
fits	quits	lungs	axes
hits	skates	chains	mixes
lips	throats	shines	passes
tips	asks	finds	classes
dots	treats	things	dresses
lots	husks	sizes	misses
pots	slopes	noses	fusses
nuts	strokes	blades	glasses
flaps	jokes	games	buzzes
ships	scrapes	waves	fizzes
spots	spites	grades	ashes
ants	lasts	stoves	lashes
tents	gusts	brides	
nests	fists	glides	
hunts	rents	besides	
melts	drifts	skids	
drops		goals	

4:3

The Inflectional Suffixes -ing and -en

TUTORIAL The three inflectional suffixes that when added to the end of verbs signify tense, mood, or voice are *-ing*, *-en*, and the past tense *-ed*. This lesson addresses the inflectional suffixes *-ing* and *-en*; Lesson 4.4 addresses the past tense suffix *-ed*.

A verb has three principal parts: the present, the past, and the past participle. All six verb tenses are formed from these principal parts. The past and past participle of regular verbs are formed by adding *-ed* to the present form. However, irregular words such as drive, eat, bite, break, speak, steal, take, weave, and write become past participles with the addition of the suffix *-en*.

TEACH

"Today we will learn about two more endings we can add to words without changing their parts of speech. The inflectional morphemes *-ing* and *-en* are used to give verbs their sense of time (tense), mood, or voice. You will need to use a helping verb like am, is, are, has, or had in front of these two morphemes."

MAPPING PROCEDURES

Because *-ng* is a digraph that makes one sound, it should be placed in one sound box. The preceding short *i* should be placed in a box of its own.

The suffix *-en* has two phonemes and so should be placed in two separate boxes, as shown in the following word list. Students often confuse this suffix with the letter name for the alphabet symbol *n* and may try to place both the *e* and *n* in one box or omit the *e* entirely when they spell this ending, as in *brokn*.

Inflectional Suffixes *-ing* and *-en* Word List		
Inflectional Suffix *-ing*		**Inflectional Suffix *-en***
i | ng		e | n
acting	drilling	broken
ailing	eating	driven
alarming	batting	chosen
amazing	fighting	fallen
arching	hunting	frozen
banking	keeping	given
being	killing	mistaken
belonging	knowing	spoken
bidding	lasting	stolen
bowling	leading	taken
boxing	leaning	bitten
breaking	loading	eaten
burning	meeting	forgotten
calling	picking	gotten
camping	singing	gidden
charming	sneaking	written
clearing	speeding	awaken

4:4

The Inflectional Suffix -ed

TUTORIAL In the beginning stages of decoding and encoding, first graders often spell the suffix -ed as they hear it. Since there are three possible sounds for -ed, it is not unusual to see these novice spelling attempts:

- *Wisht* for *wished*
- *Pland* for *planned*
- *Plantid* for *planted*

Students must learn that although they hear three different sounds for this inflectional suffix, it truly has just one spelling, and that is -ed. They must also understand that the addition of this suffix changes the meaning of the word to past tense. Meaning and spelling should be married at this point in their instruction.

There are three sounds for this suffix:

- -ed makes the unvoiced sound of /t/ (a single phoneme) when the base word ends in an unvoiced consonant sound, such as /k/, /f/, /h/, /p/, /s/, /x/ /sh/, /ch/, /ph/, and /th/ (as in <u>thin</u>).

wished	sniffed	bumped	passed	boxed	crunched

- -ed makes the voiced sound of /d/ (a single phoneme) when the base word ends in a vowel or a voiced consonant sound, such as /b/, /d/, /g/, /j /, /l/, /m/, /n/, /r/, /v/, /z/, /ng/ (as in *banged*), /th/ (as in *ba<u>the</u>*), or in the voiced /zh/ (as in *gara<u>ge</u>*).

climbed	banged	caged	rolled	calmed	caned
starred	loved	buzzed	bathed	measured	

- -ed makes the sounds of two phonemes, /e/ and /d/. It is sometimes pronounced /i/ and /d/ when the base word ends in either the unvoiced /t/ or the voiced /d/. Because it contains a vowel as one of its phonemes, -ed adds an additional syllable to the base word.

planted	indented	printed	handed	reminded	bonded

Give students small pieces of paper. Show the word *fold*. Ask students to *fold* their paper into the smallest square they can. Then show the words *aim* and *toss*. Ask them to *aim* their folded paper toward the wastebasket and *toss* it in. Have fun with this, and when the chaos has subsided, add *-ed* to *fold* and say, "We *folded* the paper." Add *-ed* to *aim* and say, "We *aimed* it at the wastebasket." Add *-ed* to toss and say, "We *tossed* it and most of us *missed*!" List the words *folded, aimed, tossed,* and *missed* on the board. Lead students to isolate the base words and identify the common ending *-ed,* which means "we did this in the past" or "we are through doing this." Direct students to isolate the ending sound(s) represented by *-ed* in *missed, /t/; tossed, /t/; aimed, /d/;* and *folded, /e/ /d/.* "We add *-ed* to verbs to show that the action happened in the past, and the *-ed* can make three different sounds!"

MAPPING PROCEDURES

When the suffix *-ed* comes after a base word that ends in an unvoiced consonant sound, it makes the single phoneme /t/. Therefore, both the *e* and the *d* should be placed in one box to represent the single sound of /t/ made in these words.

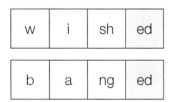

w	i	sh	ed

b	a	ng	ed

When the suffix *-ed* comes after a base word that ends in a voiced consonant sound, it makes the single phoneme /d/. Therefore, both the *e* and the *d* should be placed together in one box to represent the single sound of /d/ made in these words.

b	u	zz	ed

When the suffix *-ed* comes after a base word that ends in either *d* or *t,* we hear the two phonemes /e/ and /d/. Therefore, the letters *e* and *d* should be placed in two separate boxes to indicate these two individual sounds.

p	l	a	n	t	e	d

Note: Place the two *d*'s in one box for *nodded* because we do not hear two *d*'s. The additional *d* ensures that the preceding vowel remains short by retaining the first syllable as a closed syllable.

MAPPING MULTIPLE CONCEPTS WITH -ED

Review and become familiar with the following phoneme-grapheme mapping concepts. Be prepared to explain the concepts and mapping procedures to students when mapping the three sounds of *-ed*.

Raked and hoped. The *e* has two purposes in *raked* and *hoped*.

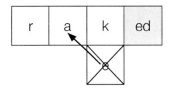 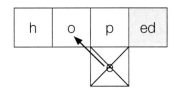

- The original *e* is dropped, but the *e* in *-ed* keeps the silent *e* principle at work.
- The *e* also works with *-ed* to represent the past tense. Because it makes the single sound of /d/, *-ed* is placed in one box.

Iced. The *e* has three jobs in *iced*.

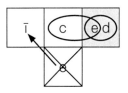 The *e* is looped twice to show two of the three relationships.

- The original *e* is dropped, but the *e* in *-ed* keeps the silent *e* principle at work.
- The *e* also works with *-ed* to represent the past tense. Because it makes the single sound of /d/, *-ed* is placed in one box.
- The *e* works with the *c* to create the soft sound of /s/.

Danced. The *e* has two jobs in *danced*.

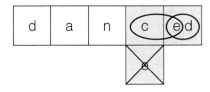 The *e* is looped twice to show both relationships.

- The *e* acts with the *c* to make the soft sound of /s/.

- The *e* also works with *d* to make the -*ed* suffix. Because it makes the single phoneme /t/, both letters are written in one box.

TEACH

Some students see the final *e* at the end of the base word *dance* and erroneously assume it is a silent -*e* syllable, thereby causing the preceding vowel to be long. Point out that there are two consonant sounds (*n* = /n/ and *c* = /s/) between the vowel *a* and the silent *e* in *dance*, so the silent *e* rule does not apply. The *e* after the *c* in *danced* is only there to soften the *c*, so it can say /s/ instead of /k/.

Caged. The *e* has three jobs in *caged*.

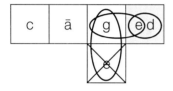

- The original *e* is dropped, but the *e* in -*ed* helps to keep the silent *e* principle at work.

- The *e* acts with the *g* to make the soft sound of /j/.

- The *e* also works with the *d* to make the -*ed* suffix. Because it makes the single phoneme /d/, both letters are written in one box.

The Three Sounds of *-ed* Word List		
-ed = /t/ One Sound/One Box	*-ed = /d/* One Sound/One Box	*-ed = /e/ /d/ or /i/ /d/* Two Sounds/Two Boxes
`a` `s` `k` `ed`	`sh` `ow` `ed`	`e` `n` `d` `e` `d`

-ed = /t/		-ed = /d/		Two Sounds	
jumped	axed	showed	informed	loaded	coated
winked	helped	cleaned	lived	folded	dated
bumped	forced	filled	skilled	handed	drafted
rushed	forked	yelled	smelled	planted	frosted
fished	flunked	seemed	spelled	trusted	needed
asked	missed	snowed	used	acted	parted
dashed	passed	sailed	armed	heated	printed
lumped	hoped	smiled	ganged	needed	rusted
blinked	hushed	trained	heeled	lasted	sanded
dressed	slumped	buzzed	lettered	dented	seated
splashed	iced	aimed	edged	ended	slanted
crushed	kicked	trailed	revealed	rented	tented
fussed	packed	stained	tied	hinted	tested
stamped	yanked	screamed	longed	dusted	drifted
mixed	voiced	blazed	served	lifted	granted
bossed	risked	posed	aged	melted	wilted
crossed	panted	chimed	drilled	painted	bunted
messed	limped	crowed	tilled	blasted	booted
taxed	puffed	flowed	filmed	twisted	added
loafed	blinked	squealed	grilled	bonded	belted
fixed		mowed	happened		

Inflectional Comparative Suffixes -er and -est

TUTORIAL There are three forms of adjectives:

- Positive adjectives describe a noun or pronoun without comparing it to anyone or anything else.
  Example: My bedroom is *neat*.

- Comparative adjectives compare two people, places, things, or ideas and are formed by adding the inflectional suffix *-er* to the base word.
  Example: My classroom is *neater* than my sister's bedroom.

- Superlative adjectives compare three or more people, places, things, or ideas by adding the inflectional suffix *-est* to the base word.
  Example: My bedroom is the *neatest* room in the whole house.

It is beneficial to have students think of the word *best* in relationship to superlative adjectives. For example, the neatest child might be thought of as the child who is the best at being neat. Because the short *e* is easier to hear in the word best, this analogy can help children to correctly spell the suffix *-est* rather than *-ist*, which is a common error.

Positive adjectives form a very large group of words that can be mapped according to their respective syllable types and are therefore are covered in other units throughout this book. This lesson addresses the meaning and mapping of the two inflectional adjectives *-er* and *-est*.

TEACH

"There are three types of adjectives in the English language. Most of us use the first type of adjective the most. It is called a positive adjective because it does not compare a person or thing to anyone or anything else.

Example: My classroom is *cold.*

The second type of adjective is called a comparative adjective. We use this adjective when we are comparing two people, places, things, or ideas. This type of adjective usually ends in the suffix *-er.*

Example: My classroom is *colder* than Jayne's classroom.

The third type of adjective is called a superlative adjective. We use this adjective when we are comparing three or more people, places, things, or ideas to each other. This type of adjective usually ends in *-est.*

Example: My classroom is the *coldest* in the entire school.

MAPPING PROCEDURE

Follow the examples in the word lists that follow.

Adjectives of Comparison Word List		
Positive Form	**Comparative Form** Suffix *-er*	**Superlative Form** Suffix *-est*
	er	e s t
black	blacker	blackest
blue	bluer	bluest
brave	braver	bravest
bright	brighter	brightest
calm	calmer	calmest
clean	cleaner	cleanest
cool	cooler	coolest
crisp	crisper	crispest
damp	damper	dampest
dark	darker	darkest
far	farther	farthest
fast	faster	fastest
firm	firmer	firmest
fit	fitter	fittest
great	greater	greatest
green	greener	greenest
hard	harder	hardest
high	higher	highest
late	later	latest
light	lighter	lightest
long	longer	longest
low	lower	lowest
mild	milder	mildest
near	nearer	nearest
old	older	oldest
quick	quicker	quickest
sharp	sharper	sharpest
short	shorter	shortest
slow	slower	slowest
dim	dimmer	dimmest
wet	wetter	wettest
hot	hotter	hottest
mad	madder	maddest
red	redder	reddest
sad	sadder	saddest

Derivational Prefixes

TEACH

"We have just finished learning about some morphemes or affixes that can be added to words that do not change their parts of speech. Next, we learn about another group of affixes called derivational prefixes. These prefixes can be added to Anglo-Saxon base words and Greek and Latin roots.

A prefix is a small unit of meaning, or a morpheme, that is placed in front of a base word or root and can change the meaning of the base word. Prefixes are a lot like prepositions; *sub* means under, *ad* means to or toward, *ex* means out of, and so forth. Some words have more than one prefix, so it is important to locate the base word or root when reading an unfamiliar word. We can add the meaning of each prefix to the base word or root to unwrap the meaning of the entire word. We are going to learn a few prefixes each day that will help us read and write a lot of words."

Select two to three prefixes from the following word lists to introduce each day. As you write each prefix on the overhead, explain its meaning. Ask students to generate words they know that contain the target prefix and list them on the overhead or board. Once the four lists are compiled, ask students to select three words from each of the four prefix lists to write on an Affixo Chart (see Appendix B). For example:

Prefix	Prefix	Base or Root	Suffix	Suffix
dis	re	spect		
	un	do		
	in	exact		

The following day, ask students to explain the meanings of the words they placed on the Affixo Chart by using the meaning of the prefix to help them construct their responses. Model the responses on the overhead or board. The following explanations are based on the introduction of the prefixes *pre-* and *fore-*.

- A *pretest* is a *test* you take *before* the real test.

- The *foreground* of a picture is the part of the picture that is *in front of* most of the objects or items in a picture.

MAPPING PROCEDURE

Use the examples above each of the following word lists to help you.

Common Prefixes *un-*, *re-*, *in-*, and *dis-* Word List				
Prefix *un-*		**Prefix *re-***	**Prefix *in-***	**Prefix *dis-***
u n		r e	i n	d i s
not or opposite of	to undo or reverse	back or again	not	not, absence of, apart
unhappy	unarm	recount	inept	dislike
unjust	unbend	reinvest	inadequate	distrust
unsafe	unbind	reuse	inadvisable	disable
unlike	unchain	rejoin	inattentive	disarm
unfair	unclothe	recall	incapable	disband
unfit	unfold	remark	incomplete	disbar
unrest	unglue	remove	incurable	disclose
unwise	unhitch	reorder	indecent	discount
unknown	unlace	repay	indecisive	discuss
unable	unlash	replace	independence	disfigure
uneasy	unload	reprint	independent	disgrace
unlawful	unlock	resign	indestructible	dishonest
unskilled	unpack	restore	indifferent	dishonor
unthinkable	unseat	retell	indignant	disinterest
unsound	unstuck	rethink	indirectly	dislodge
untruthful	unwrap	retrace	ineffective	disorder
unmindful	unzip	return	inexact	displace
unaware	untie	rewrite	infant	disposal
unfounded		rework	infinity	dispose
unusual		record	infirmary	dispute
unpaid		Refer	injustice	disrupt
unwilling		reflect	inobservant	dissolve
unclean		reflex	inorganic	distance
		reform	insane	distant
		refuse	insensible	distract
		regain	insensitive	distraction
		regress	insignificant	
		reject	insufficient	
		relate	invalid	
		relax		
		release		
		respect		
		respectful		

Common Prefixes *mis-*, *pre*, *a-*, *de-*, and *fore-* Word List				
Prefix *Mis-*	**Prefix *Pre-***	**Prefix *a-***	**Prefix *de-***	**Prefix *fore-***
m i s	p r e	a	d e	f o r e
A prefix meaning bad or badly wrong or wrongly	A prefix meaning before or earlier	A prefix meaning on or in; to	A prefix meaning down or away from	A prefix meaning before
misfire	predate	across	debate	forearm
mishap	prefer	adrift	debrief	foreword
misuse	preheat	afire	decay	forecast
mismatch	precook	ahead	decline	forecaster
misname	premix	alike	decode	foreclose
misplace	prename	alive	decompose	forefather
misprint	prepay	alone	deduct	forego
misread	preplan	along	defeat	foregone
misspell	prepackage	aloud	defer	foreground
mistake	presell	amuse	deflect	forehand
mistreat	presold	apart	defog	forehead
miscall	pretest	arise	deform	foreman
misbehave	prewrite	around	delight	moremost
misbelieve	prewrap	aside	deplane	forereach
mischief	pretype	asleep	deport	forerunner
miscount	prearrange	await	deportation	foresee
misdirect	precede	awake	debark	foreshadow
misgivings	preclude	away	decamp	foresight
mishandle	predetermine	awoke	decease	forestall
mishear	predict	abide	declaim	foretell
mislead	prediction	abound	deduce	forewarn
misspent	prefer	above	deduction	foreclosure
mistaken	preflight	afoot	defect	
mistrial	prehistoric	among	defection	
	prejudge	anoint	deferral	
	premeditate		defile	
	prepare			
	presenter			
	preserve			

4:7

Derivational Suffixes

TEACH

"Derivational suffixes are affixes that often change the parts of speech of the base words or roots to which they are added. For example, the adjective *happy* becomes the noun *happiness* with the derivational suffix *-ness*. English has more derivational suffixes than inflectional suffixes (although the four inflectional suffixes *-s*, *-es*, *-ed*, and *-ing* are used most frequently). More than half of the words you will read and spell in your content area textbooks and materials will likely contain a derivational morpheme. The majority of derivational suffixes are used to create nouns and adjectives."

Select two or three suffixes at a time to introduce to students. As you write each suffix on the overhead or board, explain its meaning. Ask students to generate some words they know that contain the target suffix, and list them on the overhead or board. Once the lists are compiled, ask students to select three words from each of the suffix lists to write on an Affixo Chart (see Appendix B).

Remember that prefixes and suffixes can be strung together before and after a base word or root. This can be deceiving, as in the case of the *-ation* form of the suffix *-ion*. The suffix *-ation* is actually a combination of the derivational suffixes *-ate* and *-ion*. However, the silent *e* in *-ate* is dropped because the suffix that is being added (*-ion*) begins with a vowel. This occurrence can be clearly shown on the Affixo Chart, where you will have students write the original spelling of the base word, root, or affix and note any letters that are dropped or added, as in the following example.

Prefix	Prefix	Base or Root	Suffix	Suffix
		sharp	ly	
		teach	er	
		doct	or	
		act	ion	
		imagine	ate	ion
		ignite	ion	

MAPPING PROCEDURE

See examples of the most frequently used suffixes at the head of each of the following word lists.

Common Derivational Suffixes -ful, -ness, -less, -ment, and -ly Word List				
-ful	**-ness**	**-less**	**-ment**	**-ly**
f u l	n e ss	l e ss	m e n t	l y
Adjective suffix meaning full of or full	Noun suffix meaning state of	Adjective suffix meaning without	Noun Suffix meaning act of, state of, or result of an action	Adverb Suffix meaning like or manner of
fearful	bigness	ageless	basement	proudly
harmful	badness	blameless	amendment	smoothly
hurtful	fitness	breathless	amusement	loudly
careful	flatness	careless	apartment	madly
playful	gladness	childless	arrangement	sadly
trustful	greatness	cloudless	assessment	badly
spoonful	lightness	endless	assignment	gladly
restful	loudness	faceless	assortment	nightly
painful	madness	faithless	department	blindly
helpful	neatness	faultless	disagreement	kindly
handful	politeness	groundless	document	sweetly
thankful	promptness	hatless	element	freshly
mouthful	quaintness	helpless	enjoyment	highly
hateful	roundness	homeless	entertainment	neatly
powerful	sadness	hopeless	fragment	coldly
wishful	shortness	joyless	equipment	lightly
armful	shyness	lifeless	environment	brightly
fistful	sleeplessness	loveless	enlargement	nearly
faithful	slowness	nameless	pavement	clearly
cheerful	smartness	noiseless	shipment	hardly
lawful	softness	painless	statement	formerly
graceful	strictness	pointless	treatment	deadly
dreadful	sweetness	priceless	tournament	costly
forgetful	swiftness	restless	experiment	dearly
hopeful	tightness	shameless	engagement	lately
joyful	vastness	shiftless	installment	monthly
shameful	wellness	sleepless	judgment	sickly
truthful	wetness	sleeveless	management	softly
tasteful	witness	soundless	payment	yearly
thoughtful	happiness	timeless	punishment	weekly
tearful	prettiness	tireless	retirement	rarely
delightful		voiceless	amazement	mainly
doubtful		voteless	advancement	instantly
forceful		wingless	announcement	honestly
respectful		wordless	contentment	fatherly

Write your words in syllables below. Put only one syllable in a box.

be	hind			
stu	dent			
re	spect			
si	lent			
re	fund			
dis	re	spect	ful	
do	nate			
de	fine			
u	nite			
re	tire			
re	quire			
si	lent	ly		
non	re	fund	able	
re	tire	ment		
re	quire	ment		

Note: In this particular lesson on common affixes, the student is able to see the relationship of the affix to syllable division rules. Anglo-Saxon base words such as *tire*, *fund*, and *hind* separate easily from their affixes. However, words with Latin roots and *unite* often have their meaning-based units (morphemes) separated when dividing by syllable type.

Common Derivational Suffixes -y, -er, -or, -ic, -en Word List				
-y	**-er**	**-or**	**-ic**	**-en**
y	er	or	i c	e n
Adjective suffix meaning inclined to	Noun or pronoun suffix meaning one who, that which	Noun suffix meaning one who; that which	Adjective suffix meaning of, pertaining to, or characterized by	Verb suffix meaning made of or to make
beefy	baker	actor	academic	blacken
bumpy	banker	advisor	automatic	cheapen
cheery	blinker	ancestor	civic	dampen
chewy	boiler	collector	classic	darken
chilly	catcher	contractor	egotistic	deepen
crafty	milker	creator	elastic	enlighten
cranky	coaster	dictator	enthusiastic	flatten
creaky	cooler	director	geometric	freshen
creepy	dancer	divisor	gigantic	harden
crispy	cracker	editor	historic	lengthen
dirty	driver	educator	logistic	lighten
drafty	gardener	elevator	magic	loosen
dusty	holder	erector	materialistic	ripen
feathery	keeper	escalator	microscopic	soften
flaky	laughter	generator	music	strengthen
frosty	locker	governor	mystic	thicken
glittery	player	impostor	narcotic	tighten
grumpy	robber	incubator	naturalistic	toughen
healthy	shopper	instructor	optimistic	waken
hilly	sparkler	inventor	Pacific	weaken
lazy	surfer	juror	patriotic	widen
needy	**Verb suffix -er**	legislator	poetic	**Adjective suffix -en**
rubbery	lower	liberator	public	barren
sandy	scatter	moderator	romantic	broken
scrappy	scamper	narrator	rustic	drunken
snowy	slobber	navigator	scientific	frozen
starchy	splatter	professor	symbolic	mistaken
stormy	swelter	projector		olden
sunny	chatter	protector		spoken
tasty	barber	radiator		golden
thorny	center	spectator		oaken
thrifty	flicker	supervisor		silken
lucky		survivor		
wordy		tractor		
waxy		translator		

More Complex Suffixes Easily Affixed to Base Words

"We have already learned several suffixes that can be added to base words and roots that will change their part of speech. There are a few more suffixes worth learning that can be easily added to base words without usually requiring a spelling change. We will be learning six more of these in this lesson."

MAPPING PROCEDURE

Follow the examples at the head of each word list that follows.

Suffixes *-ship*, *-some*, and *-hood* Word List		
-ship	**-some**	**-hood**
sh | i | p	s | o | me	h | oo | d
A noun suffix meaning office, state, dignity, skill, quality, or profession	An adjective suffix meaning characterized by a specified quality, condition, or action	A noun suffix meaning condition, state, or quality
authorship	awesome	boyhood
captainship	fearsome	brotherhood
censorship	handsome	childhood
championship	lonesome	fatherhood
chairmanship	threesome	girlhood
citizenship	tiresome	knighthood
companionship	troublesome	likelihood
courtship	twosome	livelihood
dictatorship	wholesome	manhood
fellowship	bothersome	motherhood
friendship	cumbersome	neighborhood
guardianship	adventuresome	priesthood
hardship	meddlesome	sainthood
kinship		sisterhood
leadership		womanhood
membership		
ownership		
partnership		
relationship		
scholarship		
seamanship		
sponsorship		
township		
workmanship		

Suffixes *-ish*, *-most*, and *-fold* Word List		
-ish	*-most*	*-fold*
i | sh	m | o | s | t	f | o | l | d
An adjective suffix meaning origin, nature, or resembling	An adjective suffix meaning most or nearest to	A noun suffix meaning related to a specified number or quantity
bookish	bottommost	twofold
boyish	endmost	multifold
clownish	furthermost	manifold
dampish	inmost	fiftyfold
darkish	innermost	tenfold
devilish	lowermost	hundredfold
dullish	middlemost	multifold
foolish	northernmost	thousandfold
fortyish	outermost	
freakish	southernmost	
girlish	topmost	
longish	undermost	
reddish	upmost	
selfish	uppermost	
sheepish		
skittish		
sluggish		
smallish		
softish		
Spanish		
stylish		
Swedish		
sweetish		
thickish		
thinnish		
youngish		
British		
babyish		

Derivational Suffixes -able and -ible

TEACH

"The suffix *-able* is usually added to Anglo-Saxon base words (*reasonable, eatable, printable*) whereas *-ible* is usually added to Latin roots (*impossible, legible, edible*). Remember that a base word can stand by itself if the suffix is taken away, but a root needs a prefix or a suffix to become an independent word."

Suffixes *-able* and *-ible* Word Lists	
Suffix *-able* a | b | le	**Suffix *-ible*** i | b | le
An adjective suffix that means able, can do. It is usually used with Anglo-Saxon base words.	An adjective suffix that means able, can do. It is mostly used with Latin roots.

allowable	likable	accessible
bearable	arguable	collapsible
buyable	believable	compatible
comfortable	charitable	comprehensible
drinkable	deceivable	convertible
eatable	definable	corruptible
employable	desirable	credible
enjoyable	disputable	destructible
explainable	excitable	edible
exportable	flammable	eligible
fixable	forgivable	expressible
passable	hospitable	extendible
payable	improvable	flexible
portable	lovable	forcible
readable	notable	illegible
reasonable	observable	intelligible
remarkable	receivable	legible
repairable	recognizable	possible
repayable	regrettable	reducible
returnable	retrievable	reprehensible
sailable	solvable	resistible
sinkable	storable	responsible
smellable	swimmable	reversible
suitable	tastable	sensible
taxable	valuable	terrible
teachable	weavable	
workable	respectable	

A Suffix of Rebellion, Tension, and Deception: Coping With -ion, -sion, and -tion

TUTORIAL The suffixes *-ion*, *-sion*, and *-tion* can often be problematic for students. Do not introduce these concepts unless students have been introduced to the schwa vowel sound. These three suffixes each contain the schwa vowel sound, and the spelling of the initial phoneme varies among the three suffixes. To further complicate matters, the suffix *-ion* is often misrepresented as being the suffix *-tion* or *-sion*. This occurs when *-ion* is preceded by a base word, root, or suffix that has an *s* or *t* as the final letter after a silent *e* is dropped. However, as the first example below illustrates, the root of *tension* would be *ten* if the suffix were *-sion* and not *-ion*.

Prefix	Prefix	Base or Root	Suffix	Suffix
		tens(e)	ion	
	super	vis(e)	ion	
		creat(e)	ion	
		decor	at(e)	ion

Additionally, there is not always a one-to-one correspondence between the sounds students hear and the letters they write in these suffixes. Depending on the word to which the suffixes are added, the first phoneme can be one of two or three different phonemes. For this reason, the suffixes are arranged according to their sound-spelling correspondences and not their morphological endings. Each of the sounds and spellings for the suffixes *-ion*, *-sion*, and *-tion* are identified in the word lists in this lesson.

TEACH

Read a few of the words from each of the word lists. Ask students to tell you the suffix they hear in each word. Repeat the suffix and show students how it is spelled. Explain that these are rebellious suffixes and that their job is to calm the tension and tame the deception through mapping the sounds and spellings.

MAPPING PROCEDURE

Study the examples to become familiar with the shading and notation of the schwa in these suffixes. When isolating the sounds in the suffixes *-ion*, *-sion*, or *-tion*, you will often hear three sounds. In a few words, such as *cushion*, *fashion*, and *legion*, the *-ion* suffix makes just two sounds, because the *i* and *o* combine to make the schwa vowel.

-*ion* Word List		
-*ion* as /yən/	**-*ion* as /ēən/**	**-*ion* as /ən/ o**
i ə n	i ə n	io n
o n i ə n	s c o r p i ə n	l e g io n
battalion companion onion	accordion	cushion
billion cotillion reunion	criterion	fashion
bullion dominion stallion	oblivion	religion
bunion hellion scallion	scorpion	legion
union medallion trillion	champion	
million opinion	clarion	

-*sion* Word List	
-*sion* as /shən/	**-*sion* as /zhən/**
si ə n	si ə n
t e n si ə n	v i si ə n
/sh/ /ə/ /n/	/zh/ /ə/ /n/
admission impression	vision incision
aggression intermission	aspersion precision
mansion mission	conversion evasion
commission recession	diversion dispersion
tension dimension	emersion evasion
comprehension discussion	excursion invasion
pension extension	immersion occasion
compulsion expansion	inversion supervision
concession expression	submersion television
concussion expulsion	version cohesion
confession	collision

-tion **Word List**	
-tion as /shən/	**-tion as /chən/**

/sh/ /ə/ /n/		/ch/ /ə/ /n/
citation	association	question
collation	calculation	congestion
activation	aviation	ingestion
admiration	computation	combustion
adoration	concentration	suggestion
administration	congratulations	
animation	condensation	
alteration	coordination	
application	creation	
appreciation	dedication	
articulation	destination	
education	decoration	
exclamation	donation	
generation		

Phoneme-Grapheme Mapping
(A Method for Bridging Sound to Print)

Name: _____   Date: _____

b	ĭ	ll	i	o	n				
c	ŭ	sh	i	o	n				
f	ă	sh	i	o	n				
s	c	or	p	i	o	n			
t	ĕ	n	si	o	n				
v	ĭ	si	o	n					
ā	v	i	ā	ti	o	n			
c	r	ē	ā	ti	o	n			
qu	e	s	ti	o	n				

Note: This map shows a student's growing understanding of the complex phoneme-grapheme relations of three troublesome suffixes. It is very important that students return to concrete sound blocks to manipulate when they encounter difficulty with a given concept. Some students will try to visually remember a mapping sequence rather than check themselves using blocks. Sound blocks give you a window on the student's phonemic segmentation skills.

Some Frequently Used Derivational Suffixes Found in More Complex Text

"The following suffixes are frequently found in more upper-level texts and are important to learn because you will be seeing them in your content area studies."

MAPPING PROCEDURE

Follow the examples below.

Suffix *-ous*	Suffix *-ty*, *-ity*	Suffix *-al*, *-ial*	Suffix *-ive*
ou | s	t | y i | t | y	a | l i | a | l	i | ve
Adjective suffix meaning full of or having	**Noun suffixes meaning state or quality of**	**Adjective suffixes meaning relating to or characterized by**	**Adjective suffix meaning causing or making**
adventurous	anxiety	betrayal universal	active
anonymous	cruelty	cardinal several	attentive
cavernous	entirety	correctional plural	congestive
dangerous	frailty	criminal dental	consecutive
desirous	liberty	confessional final	constructive
enormous	ninety	seasonal devotional	cooperative
extraneous	novelty	diagonal eternal	creative
fabulous	acidity	disposal funeral	cursive
famous	capacity	educational liberal	decisive
generous	captivity	emotional literal	defensive
hazardous	electricity	federal moral	descriptive
humorous	facility	external optional	destructive
igneous	finality	original rational	effective
jealous	humidity	formal recital	elective
joyous	legality	functional regional	eruptive
miraculous	locality	general reversal	expensive
monstrous	mentality	gradual ritual	explosive
mountainous	nationality	horizontal remedial	massive
nervous	oddity	personal principal	native
poisonous	personality	internal skeletal	negative
populous	publicity	journal spinal	passive
scandalous	quality	manual terminal	perceptive
simultaneous	quantity	medical thermal	positive
slanderous	reality	mental mortal	primitive
spontaneous	severity	universal visual	receptive
tremendous	simplicity	professional nasal	relative
vigorous	stupidity	national colonial	sensitive
	totality	normal denial	punitive

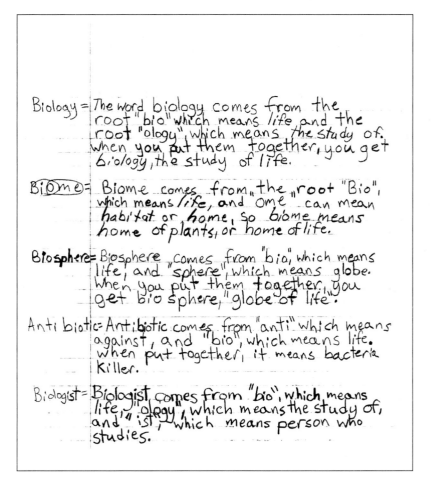

Biology = The word biology comes from the root "bio" which means life and the root "ology", which means the study of. When you put them together, you get biology, the study of life.

Biome = Biome comes from the root "Bio", which means life, and "ome" can mean habitat or home, so biome means home of plants, or home of life.

Biosphere = Biosphere comes from "bio", which means life, and "sphere", which means globe. When you put them together, you get biosphere, "globe of life".

Antibiotic = Antibiotic comes from "anti" which means against, and "bio", which means life. When put together, it means bacteria killer.

Biologist = Biologist comes from "bio", which means life, "ology", which means the study of, and "ist", which means person who studies.

Note: During a unit about plant study, this student demonstrates an understanding of morphology, using a knowledge of roots and affixes to construct meaning-based definitions.

— Unit 5 —

The Consonant -le Syllable

Introduction to the Consonant -*le* Syllable

A consonant -*le* syllable is always found at the end of a base word, as in *ta-<u>ble</u>* and *bab-<u>ble</u>*, and, as the name implies, is spelled with a consonant and -*le* combination. This syllable contains a schwa vowel sound, so it can appear that you are only pronouncing the preceding consonant phoneme plus the /l/. However, it is more correctly represented as shown below with the words *able* (/a/ /b/ /l/) and *candle* (/c/ /a/ /n/ /d/ /l/).

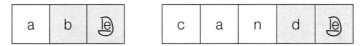

Remember that consonant *n* can sound like /ng/ when it is heard before a hard /g/, as in angle:

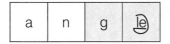

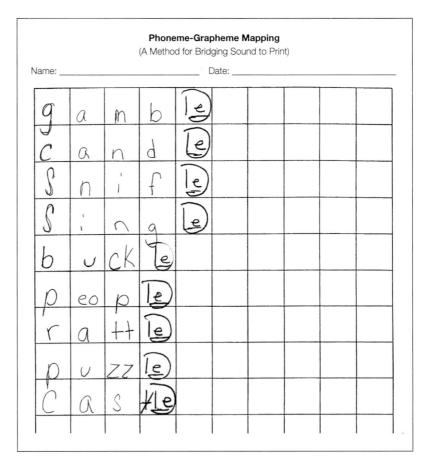

Note: The student's error on the map above allows for a teachable moment. Have the student shade the consonant -*le* syllables, as shown in the word *sniffle*, and the student should see that an open (not a closed) syllable is made in the first syllable.

Mapping the Consonant -le Syllable

Choose several words from the word list that follows. Tell students they are going to learn the consonant -*le* syllable. Consonant -*le* syllables are only found at the ends of words and are spelled with a consonant followed by *le*. Read a few of the words to the students, asking them to listen for the consonant -*le* syllable at the ends of the words. Instruct students to say the consonant -*le* syllable: *table–ble; riddle–dle, waffle–fle.* Direct students to identify the schwa. Explain the perceived schwa sound. When students hear the schwa sound, there is no vowel, but they still show the schwa in the mapping procedure. Show students the words and direct them to identify the letters in the consonant -*le* syllable.

MAPPING PROCEDURE

Study the examples to become familiar with the shading and notation of the schwa. When isolating the sounds in the consonant -*le* syllable, we generally hear two sounds, the consonant and the /l/. The consonant in the consonant -*le* pattern is usually discernible, but the schwa is coarticulated with the /l/, making it sound like the consonant /l/ sound is the only sound being spoken. However, we know that every syllable in our language needs to have a vowel sound, so we treat the -*le* in the consonant -*le* syllable as one grapheme and draw a schwa symbol around the entire grapheme *le* to mark the existence of a vowel sound.

Note that some teachers choose to map the consonant -*le* syllable as three sounds, treating the schwa as a discreet vowel sound rather than one that is coarticulated. In such cases, wrap the schwa symbol around the *le* graphemes, as shown below:

When mapping multisyllabic words, do not have students skip boxes between syllables. Rather, instruct students to color each syllable a different color. Words do not always break evenly between sound boxes due to silent letters, vowel teams, consonant oddities, and so on, as earlier examples readily show.

Consonant -*le* Word List					
a b ⟨le⟩		i d ⟨le⟩		t r i f ⟨le⟩	
-ble		**-dle**		**-fle**	
bubble	bumble	bundle	riddle	baffle	sniffle
ramble	mumble	candle	dwindle	rifle	trifle
gamble	rumble	handle	saddle	trifle	waffle
table	feeble	puddle	ladle	raffle	muffle
able	agreeable	middle	huddle	ruffle	
stable	cable	cradle	muddle	stifle	
thimble	tumble	idle	fiddle		
humble	grumble	paddle			
tremble	stubble	cuddle			
-gle		**-kle***		**-ple**	
ea g ⟨le⟩		⟨p i (ck) le⟩		m a p ⟨le⟩	
bugle	dangle	buckle	tinkle	people	rumple
gargle	wrangle	ankle	crinkle	apple	crumple
giggle	smuggle	fickle	twinkle	dimple	topple
jiggle	snuggle	pickle	fickle	ripple	rumple
jungle	haggle	tickle	spackle	simple	trample
single	eagle	crackle	sparkle	sample	dapple
tingle	beagle	sprinkle		maple	staple
mingle	shingle				
bangle	wiggle				
tangle					

*-*ck* makes one sound: /k/. Due to coarticulation, the /k/ is heard in both syllables. Therefore, students must loop the *ck* with each syllable to show its joint ownership, as shown in the word *pickle*. Otherwise, students might think the first syllable is an open syllable and pronounced /pi/.

TEACH The -*stle* words still have two phonemes. The *t* is silent, placed in the box with the *s* and crossed out to acknowledge its silence.

Consonant -*le* Word List (continued)

-*tle*		-*zle*	-*stle*	
c a t ⓛⓔ		f i z ⓛⓔ	c a s̶t̶ ⓛⓔ	
battle	shuttle	puzzle	castle	bristle
rattle	whittle	dazzle	rustle	nestle
cattle	throttle	razzle	bustle	jostle
bottle	whittle	fizzle	hustle	gristle
little	mettle	drizzle	whistle	trestle
settle		sizzle	wrestle	pestle
nettle		frazzle	thistle	

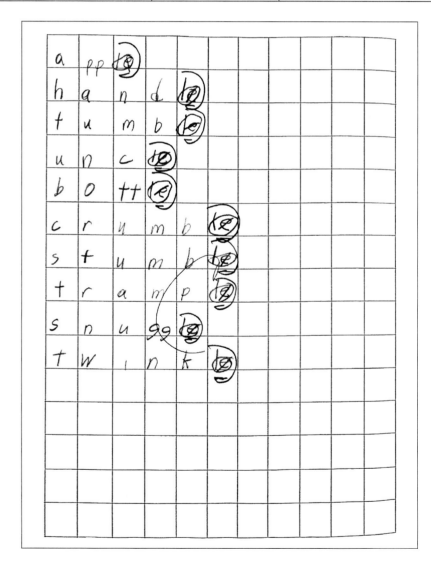

The Syllable Writing Grid is an excellent tool for helping students read and spell words containing the consonant -*le* syllable. Teach students to recheck their lists to ensure they have added a consonant before the -*le* in the same column. Then ask students to identify what type of syllable they have created in the first syllable. This method helps students catch errors such as *craddle* for *cradle* and *botle* for *bottle* because they readily see whether they have created an open or closed first syllable.

Syllable Writing Grid

Name: _____ Date: _____

Write your words in syllables in the boxes below. Then use this grid to help you sort your syllables onto the Syllable Sorting Grid.

Write the first syllable of the word here.	Write the second syllable of the word here.	Write the third syllable of the word here.
a p	p/e	
han	d/e	
tum	ble	
un	c/e	
bot	tle	
crum	b/e	
stum	ble	
tram	ple	
snug	g/e	
twin	k/e	
a	b/e	
sta	p/e	
to	b/e	
sta	ble	
sin	gle	
tan	gle	
tic	k/e	
ex	am	ple
rec	tan	gle
cra	dle	

Blackline masters of the Syllable Writing Grid and the Syllable Sorting Grid are provided in Appendix B.

Phoneme-Grapheme Mapping
(A Method for Bridging Sound to Print)

Name: _____ Date: _____

a	pp	(le)							
h	a	n	d	(le)					
t	u	m	b	(le)					
u	n	c	(le)						
b	o	tt	(le)						
c	r	u	m	b	(le)				
s	t	u	m	b	(le)				
t	r	a	m	p	(le)				
s	n	u	gg	(le)					
t	w	i	n	k	(le)				
a	b	(le)							
s	t	a	b	(le)					
t	a	b	(le)						

This student correctly maps twin consonants in one sound box and appropriately places the grapheme *-le* in one box to represent the co-articulated schwa and consonant /l/. The grapheme is then wrapped with a schwa to mark the existence of a vowel sound.

The Vowel Team Syllable

Introduction to the Vowel Team Syllable

A vowel team syllable has a group of two, three, or four letters that team up to create a unique vowel sound. In the case of a vowel team, the members of the multiletter grapheme work together to produce one vowel sound. The vowel sound can be long, short, or a diphthong. The letters comprising the vowel team do not always need to be vowel letters, as the name might seem to imply. In fact, some vowel teams can contain more consonant letters than vowel letters, as the following examples illustrate:

igh as in *night* | n | igh | t |

ough as in *though* | th | ough |

Some phonics programs introduce vowel teams as only those patterns that make a long vowel sound, such as *ai, ay, oa, ee,* and so on. Some teachers may even have their students recite the age-old chant, "The first vowel does the talking while the second vowel does the walking (or is silent)." However, this rule works less than 30 percent of the time, as Table 8 demonstrates.

Table 8 Vowel Teams			
Vowel Teams That Follow Talking/Walking Pattern	**Vowel Teams That Do Not Follow Talking/Walking Pattern**		
First vowel says its name. The second vowel is silent.	**First vowel does not say its name.**	**Multiletter Vowel Teams**	**Diphthongs**
ai as in *rain* ay as in *day* ee as in *feet* ea as in *meat* oa as in *boat* oe as in *toe* ie as in *tie* ei as in *ceiling* ue as in *cue* ou as in *shoulder* oe as in *toy* ey as in *key*	ei as in *heist* ey as *they* ow as in *snow* ew as in *pew* eu as in *feud* ou as in *soup* oo as in *food* oo as in *foot* ou as in *cougar* ou as in *tough* au as in *sauce* aw as in *saw* ea as in *bread* ea as in *steak* eu as in *deuce* ue as in *avenue* ui as in *suit*	eigh as in *eight* eigh as in *height* igh as in *night* ough as in *though* ough as in *bought* ough as in *bough* augh as in *caught* eau as in *beau* (French) **Oddball** ow as in *snow**	oi as in *oil* oy as in *boy* ow as in *cow*

*second letter is not a vowel

Teaching Long-Vowel Spellings

When students begin to learn about long vowel spellings, they call on their phonological awareness to help them locate the positions of vowel sounds in words. Is the sound in the initial, medial, or final position? Does the phoneme occur at the end of a syllable or the end of a base word? These auditory skills are extremely important (for example, when trying to decide which of the eight spellings for /ā/ should be used in a specific word) because long vowel spelling patterns are more predictable in specific positions in a word. With the aid of phonemic awareness and instruction in phonics generalizations, students can begin to master the particularly large body of spellings that represent long vowels.

Long Vowel Spelling Choices

Table 9 is a valuable tool for supporting instruction and helping students to remember the positional phonemes and associated spelling choices. Can we expect students to memorize the spellings and positions of the 38 phoneme-grapheme correspondences for the five long vowels? *Phoneme-Grapheme Mapping* does not teach long vowel sounds by this memorization method. By having a visual reference while learning one vowel grouping at a time, the entire process of selecting the correct grapheme becomes more doable as well as cumulative.

The chart is divided into two component parts: frequently used long vowel choices and less frequently used long vowel choices. Provide a copy of the Long Vowel Spelling Choices Chart (see Appendix B) for each student. Explain the headings and general vocabulary to acquaint them with it. Provide the following example to illustrate how to use it:

> "If I want to spell *rain* and I am not sure how to spell the vowel sound I hear in the middle, /ā/, I can look at this chart, find long *a* on the left, and go across to the two columns headed "middle of a base word or syllable." I see that I have two choices that are frequently used: silent *e* rule (*a-e*) or *ai*. Which one is it? Right! The long vowel sound in *rain* is spelled *ai*."

Discuss frequently used versus less frequently used spellings with the students. Instruct them to color the vowel names in the first column and the third and fourth columns (labeled "Middle of Word") yellow. This focuses their attention quickly to the key points of the matrix.

Next, instruct students to fold the chart along the dotted line that separates the frequent spellings from the less frequent spellings and fold back the less frequent section so it is not visible. The lessons will focus on the most frequently used spellings first.

Table 9 Long Vowel Spelling Choices							
Frequently Used Spellings				**Less Frequently Used Spellings**			
Spellings of . . . at . . .	At the **END** of a syllable (open syllable)	In the **MIDDLE** of a base word or syllable		At the **END** of a base word	These spellings are not used as often			
Long *a*	**a** ta ble	**a-e*** name	**ai (n, l)** rain, rail	**ay** day	**eigh** eight	**ei** vein	**ey** they	**ea** break
Long *e*	**e** be gin	**ee** feet	**ea** seat	**y** funny	**e-e*** eve	**ie** chief	**[c] ei** ceiling	**ey** key
Long *i*	**i** si lent	**i-e** time	**igh** night	**y** my	**ie** pie	**y-e** type	—	—
Long *o*	**o** o pen	**o-e*** robe	**oa** boat	**ow** snow	**ou** shoulder	**oe** toe	—	—
Long *u* /y/ /oo/ (two phonemes)	**u [yu]** mu sic	**u-e*** cute	—	—	**ue** cue	**ew** pew	**eu** feud	—
Long *u* /oo/ (one phoneme)	**u** ru by	**u-e** rule	**ou/oo** soup food	—	**ue** clue	**ew** grew	—	—

Used by permission of Wilson Anderson.

*These patterns are silent *e* syllables. The dash means a consonant sound needs to come between the vowel and the final, silent *e*.

Long Vowel Bingo

Long vowel bingo helps students become familiar with Table 9, Long Vowel Spelling Choices. The game requires students to listen for a specific long vowel sound and to determine the position of that sound in the word. This exercise helps students find their way around the chart so they can later access it independently during reading and written language activities.

1. Provide each student with a copy of the Long Vowel Spelling Choices chart (see Appendix B). This will be their bingo board.

2. Begin with the most frequently used long vowel *a* spellings on the chart. Instruct students to cover the other vowel rows with a large index card so they can only see the vowel *a* row.

3. Dictate several one-syllable, long vowel *a* words to the students. (A list of these words is found in the long vowel *a* spelling Lesson 6:1.) Ask students

to segment the words into individual phonemes so they can best decide where in the word they hear the long vowel *a* sound. Is it at the end of a syllable? In the middle of a base word? At the end of a base word?

4. Have the students place a bingo chip over the column heading that best describes where they heard the long *a* sound. Once they have put their chip on the correct positional heading, turn their attention to the spelling choices below their chip. If they hear the long *a* at the end of an open syllable, for example, they place their chip on the first column heading and see the choice below: single *a*. If they hear the long *a* in the middle of a word, they have to decide which of the two spellings (*a-e* or *ai*) is correct. (One helpful clue is that if long *a* is followed by /n/ or /l/, it is frequently—but not exclusively—spelled *ai*.

5. Continue the game by dictating eight-to-ten randomly selected, one-syllable, long vowel *a* words until you are sure the students are segmenting the phonemes correctly (i.e., selecting the appropriate spelling/grapheme choice).

6. When the students have demonstrated an understanding of the *a* spelling, move to the long *e* vowel. (This should occur in two separate lessons.) Repeat steps 1–5 for only the long vowel *e* choices. Once the students understand clearly how to listen for the long *e* sound and select the appropriate positional spellings, instruct them to discriminate between both long vowel *a* and long vowel *e* words simultaneously.

7. Continue this procedure daily until all five vowel-rows have been reviewed. Long vowel *u* has two possible pronunciations, so plan on spending more than one day on this difficult concept.

8. Once the students are fairly familiar with the frequent spellings, they can unfold the Long Vowel Spelling Choices Chart. Discuss the less frequent spellings that are not so easily accessed by position. These spellings need to be learned through a combination of sound and visual memory as well as by understanding some word family connections. For example, *eight* can be taught alongside the words *eighty, eighteen, weigh, weight,* and so on. Table 9 provides word lists for each long vowel to assist with teaching the less frequent spellings through word families.

The bingo game helps students become familiar with using the chart so that they can do so independently. However, this introduction will not ensure complete, accurate application unless it is followed up with daily reinforcement and the chart is made available to students on a daily basis. Securing it in their word study notebook is a good idea.

Continue working with long vowels by focusing on one long vowel spelling word group per week as part of the students' weekly word list and study. The remainder of Unit 6 includes word lists and mapping techniques for instructing students in the spelling of words containing long vowels.

Mapping Procedure: More Difficult Vowel Teams

Vowel teams are best learned through word sorting activities and multiple opportunities in which to practice the various patterns. Phoneme-grapheme mapping is an excellent activity to help students see the variant members of each team and how their sounds translate to print. Vowel teams are mapped by placing all the letters of the team in one sound box:

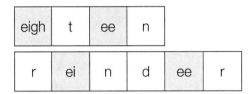

Tough. The **gh** in *tough* represents the sound /f/; the *ou* vowel team represents the short *u* sound.

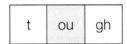

Weigh and **height.** The *eigh* vowel team in *weigh* and *height* represents two completely different sounds. You hear the long *a* in *eight* and the long *i* in *height*. However, in both words, the single sound is represented by four letters, which are all placed in a single box.

 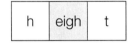

Caught. The four-letter vowel team *(augh)* is placed in just one box, because all four letters are used to represent the short *o* sound in *caught*.

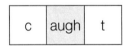

Beau and **beauty.** Although the pattern *eau* is taken from the French, there are many frequently used words in English (such as *bureau, chateau, plateau, beauty, beautiful, tableau*) that use this pattern. Although the *eau* is pronounced differently in the following examples, the three-letter team stands for one distinct sound in each word, so it is placed in one box.

 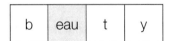

Long Vowel a Spellings

Prior to mapping the long vowel sounds, read the introduction to Unit 6. Prepare students for this lesson by following the instructional processes outlined in the unit introduction.

TEACH

> Discuss the meaning of *team*. Ask students what people on a sports or work team have in common. Help them to understand that teammates work together toward a common goal and teams can have varying numbers and members.
>
> Teach the vowel team syllable. In the case of a vowel team, the team members work together to produce one vowel sound. The letters that comprise the vowel team do not always need to be vowel letters (*a, e, i, o, u*), as the name might seem to imply. In fact, some vowel teams can contain more consonant letters than vowel letters! Show students a variety of words that have multiple letters for a one-vowel sound. Instruct students to look at the Long Vowel Spelling Choices Chart (see Table 9 and Appendix B). Direct them to find the vowel teams on the chart.

MAPPING PROCEDURE

The mapping procedure for vowel teams applies the phoneme-grapheme mapping rule of one sound in one box. The graphemes for long vowels have more than one letter; therefore, boxes contain multiple letters for one sound. Following are examples of the more straightforward mappings. The more complex mapping procedures follow.

VOWEL TEAMS: LONG VOWEL A

As students begin to transition from phonetic to morphemic spelling, they must begin to distinguish between homophones, which abound in long-vowel spelling patterns. Words such as *hay* and *hey* sound the same but are spelled differently and have different meanings. Therefore, students should learn them in meaningful phrases in conjunction with their spelling patterns. Students should also be taught a few of these words at a time rather than an entire unit. In the word list that follows, homophones are marked with an **H**.

Long Vowel *a* Word List			
At the End of a Syllable (open syllable)	**In the Middle of a Base Word**	**At the End of a Base Word**	**Spellings That Are Not Used Very Often**
a ta ble	*a-e* name — *ai* (n, l) rain, rail	*ay* day	*eigh* as in *eight* *ei* as in *vein* *ey* as in *they* *ea* as in *break*
able	safe	jail	spray	**eigh**
apron	gave	rain	lay	eight — eighty
David	hate	aim	stay	eighteen — freight
table	flame	brain	day	neighbor — neigh
vacant	frame	paint	gray	weigh — weight
patron	grade	nail	May	sleigh
agent	same	stain	pay	**ei**
navy	plate	train	play	beige — heir
cable	skate	chain	hay (**H**)	reindeer — rein
caper	shave	trail	clay	skein — reign
fable	trade	snail	tray	vein — veil
maple	scrape	drain	stray	chow mein
staple	came	grain	sway	**ey**
stable	chase	faith	way (**H**)	they — hey (**H**)
baby	slave	quail	bay	grey — obey
haven	age	quaint	ray	whey — prey (**H**)
crazy	behave	claim	say	disobey — convey
lady	haste	mailman	driveway	purvey — survey
taper	jade	maintain	sideways	frey — trey
naval	invade	retail	daylight	**ea**
label	inflate	rainy	crayon	great — steak
labor	membrane	airlift	delay	break
paper	blade	tail (**H**)	subway	
vacation	grave	sail (**H**)	highway	
relation	rate		relay	
fixation			display	

MAPPING MORE COMPLEX LONG VOWEL A WORDS

Reindeer. There are two vowel teams in this word (*ei* and *ee*), which must both be placed as a team in their own boxes:

r	ei	n	d	ee	r

Reign. It takes a three-letter grapheme to create the /ā/ sound in this word.

r	eig	n

Beige. The *g* is not part of the vowel team in this word. It needs to be paired with the *e* to make the soft *g* sound.

b	ei	~~ge~~

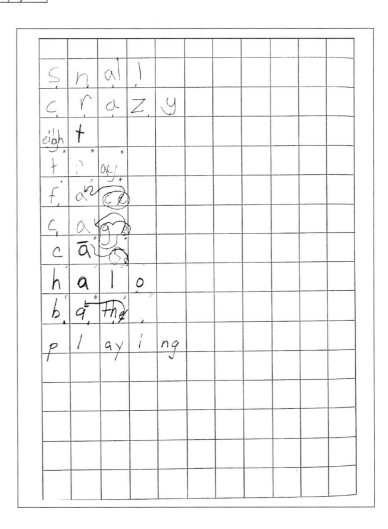

6:2

Long Vowel ε Spellings

TEACH

Introduce the lesson by explaining to students that they will learn long *e* spellings.

MAPPING PROCEDURE

Long vowel teams and long-vowel CVC*e* spellings are mapped as illustrated in the word list that follows.

Long Vowel e Word List				
At the End of a Syllable (open syllable)	**In the Middle of a Base Word**		**At the End of a Base Word**	**Spellings That Are Not Used Very Often**
e be gin	*ee* feet	*ea* seat	*y* funny	*e-e* as in *eve* *ie* as in *chief* *ei* as in *ceiling* *ey* as in *key*

At the End of a Syllable	In the Middle of a Base Word		At the End of a Base Word	Spellings That Are Not Used Very Often	
				e-e	
begin	keep	mean	rainy	eve	Pete
began	deep	clean	snowy	these	theme
became	feed	cream	dirty	delete	athlete
become	free	team	soapy	stampede	mere
recent	green	heat	jumpy	**ie**	
repel	need	leaf	sandy	brief	relief
ego	sheep	meal	rusty	priest	niece
zero	speed	read	frosty	thief	pier
veto	bleed	dream	dusty	fierce	hygiene
recess	weed	steam	grumpy	pierce	movie
recite	screen	treat	grouchy	shield	shriek
rely	sheet	seat	handy	siege	wield
remain	queen	cheat	bumpy	rookie	prairie
repeal	wheel	leash	creepy	brownie	bogie
rerim	sleep	scream	needy	**ei**	
retell	sleet	lean	curly		
retail	jeep	deal	brainy	caffeine	codeine
preheat	fleet	wheat	windy	conceit	conceive
precook	between	peanut	sporty	seize	protein
pretend	keen	teapot	speedy	receive	seize
degree	weep	steamship	thirsty	receipt	weird
refuse	spree	heap	mighty		
secret	meek	east	oily	**ey**	
tepee	greet	stream	handy	hockey	donkey
reseed	greed	beast	misty	chimney	turkey
fever	indeed	reveal	ready	trolley	medley
Hebrew	canteen	beneath	twenty	money	monkey
seclude	cheek	eaves	thirty	pulley	valley
cedar	flee	peacock	ugly	volley	whiskey
secure	refugee	teacher	plenty	Jeffrey	Mickey
secede	tree	easy	nursery	journey	kidney

Phoneme-Grapheme Mapping
(A Method for Bridging Sound to Print)

Name: _____ Date: _____

r	e	c	e	n	t				
z	e	r	o						
s	c	r	ee	n					
g	r	ee	n						
h	ea	t							
d	r	ea	m						
r	ai	n	y						
m	ea	n							

MAPPING PROCEDURE: MORE COMPLEX LONG VOWEL E WORDS

Receipt. There are two long-vowel spellings in the word *receipt.*

- An open syllable is the first syllable and so is shaded.

- The less frequent spelling of /e/ as *ei* is found in the second syllable.

Additionally, the *e* in the *ei* pattern is responsible for the soft sound of *c,* so it needs to be looped across the two boxes. Also, the silent letter *p* must be crossed out because it is not heard.

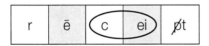

Fierce. The final *e* in *fierce* does not create a silent *e* syllable. Its only job is to work with the *c* to make the soft /s/ sound. That is why *c* and *e* are placed in the same box.

Deceive. The purpose of the final *e* in *deceive* is to keep it from ending in a final *v*. An X is put through the final *e* to show that it does not make a sound.

Long Vowel i Spellings

TEACH

Before beginning this lesson, it is recommended that a review lesson on the spellings of long *a* and *e* be performed. Choose a combination of words from both the long *a* and the long *e* lists. Segment sounds and map the spellings. After the review, move into Lesson 6:3 on long vowel *i* spellings. Introduce the lesson by explaining to students that they will learn the long *i* spellings. Continue with the lesson steps.

MAPPING PROCEDURE

The letters representing the sound of long *e* should be mapped as presented in the word list that follows.

Long Vowel *i* Word List				
At the End of a Syllable (open syllable)	**In the Middle of a Base Word**		**At the End of a Base Word**	**Spellings That Are Not Used Very Often**
i si lent ī v y	*i-e* time k ī t e	*igh* night l igh t	*y* my m y	*ie* as in *pie* *y-e* as in *type* p ie t ȳ p e
tiny	kite	light	why	***ie***
hi-fi	while	tight	my	lie tie
tidy	quite	bright	myself	pie pried
icy	side	high	try	die died
silo	size	fight	cry	tried vie
ivy	hide	might	dry	tie tied
pilot	five	night	fly	applied complied
virus	fine	flight	fry	***y-e***
minus	time	fright	sky	cycle cyclone
rival	life	sight	spy	cypress dyad
final	mile	slight	shy	dynamite enzyme
riot	smile	sigh	sty	gyrate hybrid
diet	dime	thigh	sly	hype hyper
bias	hive	delight	pry	hyphen lyre
bible	pipe	tightrope	ply	myopia style
biceps	shine	midnight	spry	psyche stylus
biology	ride	highway	by	psychology zygot
biography	bride	flashlight	guy	pylon Pyrex
bionic	crime	blight	thy	python rhyme
cipher	prize	plight	wry	thyme thyroid
diabetic	beside	limelight	ally	typhoid typhoon
diameter	revive	right	apply	typhus tyrant
diagnose	incline	wheelwright	comply	tyre xylem
dial	driveway	Dwight	deny	xylophone
Diana	sunshine	insight	reply	
fiber	spite	knight	supply	
hibernate	swipe	nigh	dignify	
license	swine	upright	glorify	
lima	chime	playwright	specify	
lilac	prime		decry	
lion	twine		imply	
migrate	thrive			

Phoneme-Grapheme Mapping
(A Method for Bridging Sound to Print)

Name: _____ Date: _____

f	r	igh	t						
s	igh	t							
t	igh	t	e	n					
l	igh	t	e	n					
t	y	pe							
ī	v	y							
k	ī	te							
ī	c y								
d	ī	e	t						
s	p	r	y						

MAPPING PROCEDURE: MORE COMPLEX LONG VOWEL I WORDS

Diet. Because *diet* is a two-syllable word, it is divided between the *i* and *e*. Some students might perceive the *i* and *e* as a vowel team and incorrectly put them in one box. It is important to teach students that there are times when the two vowels are split to make two syllables, as in the words *diet, poet,* and *create*.

d	ī	ĕ	t

Cipher and cycle. The *c* needs to be looped with the vowel that follows it because the *i* and *y* are responsible for making the soft /s/ sound. A *c* in a box by itself without a loop would mean it makes the hard /k/ sound, as it does when it stands with any other consonants or the remaining three vowels (*a, o,* or *u*).

Xylophone. In a limited number of words, *x* says /z/, and *xylophone* is one of them. Because there is a one-to-one correspondence between the sound of /z/ and the letter *x*, it is placed in one box. The two open syllables in *xylophone* should be shaded differently so that they are distinguishable.

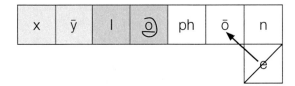

Long Vowel o Spellings

6:4

Introduce the lesson by explaining to students that they will learn the long *o* spellings.

MAPPING PROCEDURE

Long vowel teams should be placed in boxes according to the examples in the following word list.

Long Vowel *o* Word List			
At the End of a Syllable (open syllable)	**In the Middle of a Base Word**		**At the End of a Base Word**	**Spellings That Are Not Used Very Often**

At the End of a Syllable (open syllable)	In the Middle of a Base Word		At the End of a Base Word	Spellings That Are Not Used Very Often
o o pen ē g o	*o-e* robe h o p e	*oa* boat oa t	*ow* snow l ow	*ou* as in *shoulder* *oe* as in *toe* s ou l t oe
open	hope	load	show	boulder
polo	home	coat	throw	cantaloupe
hobo	pole	boat	grow	poultry
holy	bone	goat	low	shoulder
photo	those	loaf	snow	soul
poet	stove	soap	blow	**oe**
robot	hose	float	mow	toe doe
omit	stole	toast	bowl	foe goes
motel	rose	roast	crow	Joe hoe
totem	robe	coast	flow	Moe oboe
total	note	boast	blown	roe tiptoe
hotel	vote	goal	growth	woe Crusoe
donate	rope	foam	snowflake	mistletoe
bonus	drove	oats	window	Monroe Poe
mocha	froze	gloat	below	Tahoe
Mohawk	slope	moat	elbow	
produce	code	moan	stow	
locate	doze	poach	glow	
polar	mope	coach	widow	
solar	chose	roach	fellow	
clover	clothe	coal	follow	
local	quote	coax	tomorrow	
cocoa	prone	croak	hallow	
vocal	strode	hoax	Halloween	
police	cope	roam	minnow	
mohair	cone	soak	meadow	
In final syllables	choke	whoa	pillow	
hello	code	oaf	rainbow	
ego	joke	aboard	shadow	
Jell-O	poke	afloat		
ditto	spoke	charcoal		

Phoneme-Grapheme Mapping
(A Method for Bridging Sound to Print)

Name: Jonathan S,　　　　　　　Date: _____

Sh	ow							
Sh	ow	ed						
W	i	n	d	ow				
g	r	ow	n					
S	h	ow	p	l	ow			
t	oe	n	ai	l				
h	oe							
d	oe							
Sh	ōͮ	l	d	er				
b	ōͮ	l	d	er				
b	oa	t						
o	p	e	n					
r o	b	o	t					

MAPPING PROCEDURE: MORE COMPLEX LONG-VOWEL O WORDS

Poet. Since *poet* is a two-syllable word, it is divided between the *o* and *e*. However, some students might perceive the two vowels side by side as a vowel team and put both letters in one box. It is important to teach them that there are times when the two vowels are split to make two syllables, as in the words *diet, poet,* and *create*.

p	ō	ĕ	t

Cocoa. In this word, *oa* does come at the end of the base word—although *cocoa* was originally spelled *cacao,* from the plant.

c	ō	c	oa

Clothe. Clothe has a silent *e* syllable because the digraph **th** represents just one consonant sound. That is all that is needed to meet the one vowel–one consonant sound–final *e* pattern of a silent *e* syllable.

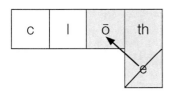

Coached. The seven letters in *coached* create just four sounds, thanks to the vowel team, digraph, and unvoiced /t/ for the *ed,* which represents a single phoneme.

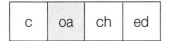

Shoulder. Many times, students mispronounce this word as /sh/ /oo/ /d/ /er/ because they are familiar with the one-syllable word *should.* Knowing that long *o* is a possibility for *ou* may reduce the frequency of this error.

Halloween. The grapheme *ow* is generally found at the end of base words. The base word of *Halloween* is *hallow* (meaning *holy*). Literally, *Halloween* means All Hallow's Eve or the night before a holy day. (November 1 is All Saints Day in the Catholic religion.)

H	a	ll	ow	ee	n

Long u When It Sounds Like the Two Phonemes /y/ + /o͞o/

INTRODUCTION: LONG VOWEL U SPELLINGS

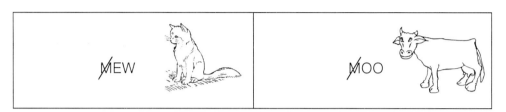

MEW

MOO

Long *u* is the most complex of all the long vowel sounds because there are two ways to pronounce it. Many phonics programs describe long vowels as "those sounds that say a letter's name." However…

- The letter name for *u* is actually comprised of two phonemes, /y/ + /o͞o/, as in the word *mew.*

- To complicate things further, long *u* can also sound like the single phoneme /o͞o/, as in the word *moo.*

Some students have difficulty hearing the difference between these two sounds for the same vowel. It is useful to have students delete the phoneme or phonemes before the long vowel *u* and use the onset pattern to help them hear whether or not the familiar word *you* (/yoo/) is heard. If it is heard, then that word contains the extra /y/ phoneme.

Try this: "Say *few.* Now, say *few* without /f/." Answer: /y/ /o͞o/.

Since the long *u* in few contains two phonemes, it is mapped across two boxes, as shown below. Regardless of how the long *u* that bears the two phonemes /y/ + /o͞o/ is spelled, its grapheme(s) are spread across two boxes.

f	ew

Now try this: "Say *chew.* Now, say *chew* without /ch/." Answer: /oo/.

Because the long *u* in *chew* contains just one phoneme, its grapheme representation is placed in just one box as shown.

ch	ew

Activity: Long Vowel u Sorting Grid. Give students a sorting grid like the one pictured below (see Appendix B). Using pictures or dictated words, randomly ask students to ascertain which long *u* they hear in each word (phoneme /o͞o/, or phonemes /y/ and /o͞o/). Then have students glue the pictures or write the word under the correct heading. Once again, the picture cues serve as a reminder for the two choices. Many students have difficulty hearing sounds in the medial position of words. For this reason, it is helpful to heave them delete the phoneme(s) before the long *u* sound, as described.

M̶EW		M̶OO	
u = /y/ /o͞o/		**u = /o͞o/**	
bugle	cube	ruby	you
Other *long y* words to dictate in random order:			
human	cute	duty	tulip
cute	use	super	prune
future	huge	rumor	plume
pupil	mule	tube	hoop

TEACH

Use the introduction material to teach the /y/ /o͞o/ sound of long *u*. Show students the picture of the cat. Instruct them to say *mew* and listen to the vowel sounds in the word. Ask them to say *mew* without the /m/. Assist students to isolate /y/ /o͞o/. Make sure they realize that when they hear the long sound of /y/ /o͞o/ in this lesson, there are two phonemes. Continue with the lesson steps.

MAPPING PROCEDURE

Follow the examples in the word list that follows.

Long Vowel *u* = /y/ /o͞o/ Word List			
MEW			
At the End of a Syllable (open syllable)	**In the Middle of a Base Word**	**At the End of a Base Word**	**Spellings That Are Not Used Very Often**
u mu sic /myo͞o/ /sik/ [p][ū][n][y]	*u-e* cute /kyo͞ot/ [ū][s]↘[e]	*e-w* pew /pyo͞o/ [p][ew]	*ue* cue /kyo͞o/ *eu* feud /fyo͞od/ [c][ue] [f][eu][d]
human Cuba cupid pupil bugle truly puny humid music mucus mutiny cubic puma humor cupola fuel future fury furious humane	cube cute use fuse mule huge consume accuse refuse acute fume Yule July muse mute volume	few pewter ewe pew hew hewn nephew mew phew! skew skewer spew whew!	**ue** argue cue continue hue revue venue rescue value **eu** feud eulogy feudal Eugene euphoria Europe Euclid euthanasia euphemism

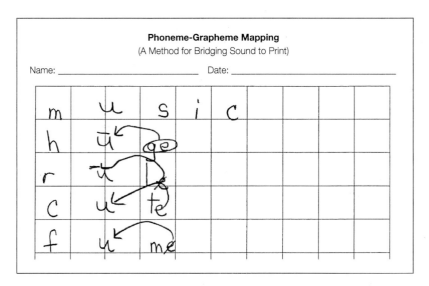

MAPPING PROCEDURE: MORE COMPLEX LONG VOWEL U [/Y/ + /ōō/] WORDS

Music, mule,* and *huge. The long *u* in the first three words is spelled with a single *u*. However, since that pronunciation contains the two phonemes /y/ and /ōō/, the single consonant *u* is spread across two boxes.

Notice how the *e* in *huge* serves two purposes:

- The silent *e* makes the preceding vowel long.

- The *e* works with the *g* to make its soft sound /j/. Therefore, the two letters are looped to show this relationship.

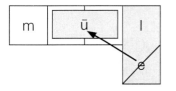 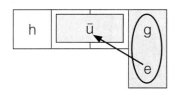

Argue, nephew,* and *eulogy. These three words contain the less frequent spellings of long *u*, pronounced /y/ + /ōō/. That is why the two-letter grapheme pairs of *ue, ew,* and *eu* are spread across two sound boxes.

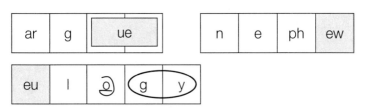

The second syllable in *eulogy* is an open syllable because it ends in a vowel. However, it is pronounced as a schwa, so we call it a **schwa open syllable**. Shade it and wrap the schwa symbol around it. Notice how the *g* and *y* are looped across two boxes because the *y* following the *g* is what helps the *g* say the soft /j/.

Long u When It Sounds Like the Single Phoneme /o͞o/

TEACH

Use the introduction material to teach the /o͞o/ sound of long *u*. Show students the picture of the cow. Instruct them to say *moo* and listen to the vowel sound in the word. Ask them to say *moo* without the /m/. Assist students to isolate /o͞o/. Make sure they realize that when they hear the long sound of /o͞o/ in this lesson, it will represent one phoneme. Compare and contrast the two sounds of long *u*. Continue with the lesson steps.

MAPPING PROCEDURE

The examples in the word list that follows will help you teach students to map this complex vowel.

Long Vowel *u* = /oō/ Word List					

MOO

At the End of a Syllable (open syllable)	In the Middle of a Base Word			At the End of a Base Word	Spellings That Are Not Used Very Often
u rū by /roō be/	*u-e* rūle /roōl/	*ou* soup /soōp/	*oo* food /foōd/	*ew* hew /noō/	*ue* as in *clue* /kloō/ *ew* as in *dew* /doō/
r | u | b | y	r | ū | l e	s | ou | p	f | oo | d	d | ew	c | l | ue
ruby	rule	coupon	balloon	new	blue	clue
student	crude	group	afternoon	knew	due	flue
duty	tube	recoup	bloom	blew	glue	fondue
truly	dude	rouge	blooper	brew	true	pursue
tulip	rude	route	caboose	chew	residue	issue
rubric	duke	toupee	cartoon	crew	retinue	revenue
ruin	plume	you	choose	dew	statue	subdue
frugal	dune	youth	cocoon	drew	Sue	true
super	June	youthful	coop	jewel	Tuesday	untrue
jubilant	prune	wound	doodle	lewd		
jubilee	tune	boutique	doom	Lewis		
judo	flute	crouton	goof	mildew		
Jupiter	brute	ghoul	goon	screw		
juniper	assume	goulash	goose	sewer		
jury	Bruce	Louis	fool	stew		
lunar	dupe	louver	harpoon	shrew		
nucleus	fluke	roulette	hoop	shrewd		
numeral	nude	toucan	hoot	grew		
nutrient	prude	souvenir	loop	flew		
rubella	brute		mood	threw		
rumor	truce		moon	yew		
superb	include		noodle			
supervise	exclude		moose			
	spruce		ooze			
	ruler		roof			
			scoop			
			shoot			
			snoop			
			soon			
			room			
			school			
			spook			
			spool			
			tooth			
			tool			
			troop			
			spoon			
			typhoon			

Judging from the length of columns in the word list, which spelling for long *u* occurs more frequently in the middle of a word? *u-e*? *ou*? *oo*?

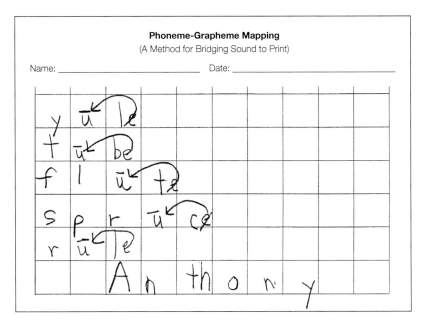

MAPPING PROCEDURE: MORE COMPLEX U /ōō/ WORDS

Superb, assume, **and** ***acoustic.*** These three words contain a schwa vowel. *Assume* is divided between the two *s*'s, which makes the first syllable a closed-schwa syllable. *Acoustic* is divided after the first *a*, which makes the first syllable an open-schwa syllable. (The schwa is explained more completely in Lesson 1:3.)

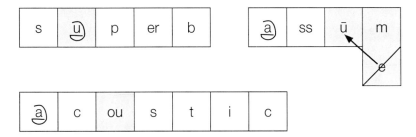

Caboose. The first syllable in *caboose* is also an open-schwa syllable. The final *e* in *caboose* serves no purpose other than to keep the word from looking like a plural.

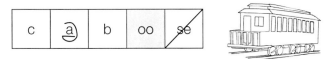

Knew. Remember to cross out the silent *k* in *knew*.

X̶n	ew

Tuesday. There are two vowel teams in *Tuesday*.

T	ue	s	d	ay

The Three Sounds of Vowel Team ea

TUTORIAL The vowel team *ea* has three sounds: /ē/, /ā/, and /ĕ/. It is important for students to learn all three because two of them, /ē/ and /ĕ/, are used frequently.

"The vowel team *ea* has three different sounds: /ē/, /ā/, and /ĕ/." Ask students which sound they have already learned. (Long *e* as in /ē/.) Teach students the following clever chant to help them remember the three sounds of *ea*:

"Eat a great breakfast."

MAPPING PROCEDURE

The *ea* in each of the three spellings should be placed in one box because the two letters represent one phoneme in each pronunciation.

ea Word List		
ea Says /ē/ as in eat	**ea Says /ā/ as in steak**	**ea Says /ĕ/ as in bread**
ea t	s t ea k	b r ea d

eat	decease	clear	reveal	steak	bread	breakfast
beacon	decrease	cleat	sea	great	head	breast
bead	defeat	conceal	seam	break	breath	meadow
beagle	dream	cream	seal	yea	dead	meant
beak	each	weak	season	Yeats	deaf	measure
beach	eager	treat	seat		death	peasant
beam	eagle	deal	scream		dread	pheasant
bean	ear	dean	sheaf		feather	pleasant
beard	ease	dear	sheath		ahead	read
beast	east	weave	team		lead	ready
beaver	Easter	year	sneak		heading	spread
beneath	easy	gleam	leak		health	steady
bleach	eaves	grease	spear		heather	sweat
bleacher	fear	heal	speak		heaven	sweater
bleak	feast	heap	squeal		heavy	thread
breathe	feat	hear	steal		weather	leaven
cease	feature	heat	steam		instead	tread
cheap	flea	heave	streak		jealous	treasure
cheat	freak	peach	stream		leapt	wealth
clean	gear	yeast	tea		leather	weapon
			teach			

MAPPING PROCEDURE: MORE COMPLEX EA WORDS

Squeamish. Remember to place the *q* and *u* close to each other and loop them, as they are constant partners.

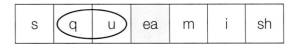

Pheasant. The digraph **ph** (/f/) is placed in one box because it is a digraph and makes one sound. The second vowel sound is a closed-syllable schwa and is marked accordingly.

ph	ea	s	a̲	n	t

Treacherous. *Treacherous* has eleven letters but just seven sounds: four phonemes that contain more than one letter. As vocabulary levels increase in the upper grades, multisyllabic words show less and less of a one-to-one correspondence between sounds (phonemes) and the letters (graphemes) that represent them. Note the schwa vowel-team syllable at the end of this very complex word.

t	r	ea	ch	er	ou̲	s

Phoneme-Grapheme Mapping
(A Method for Bridging Sound to Print)

Name: _____ Date: _____

S	n	ai	l				m	ēa̲	n	
C	r	a	z	y			b	ēa̲	s	t
eigh	t							t	ēa̲	
t	r	ay					t	ēa̲	ch	
f	ay	Ç								
c	a	ay					b	r	eā	k
	n	igh	t				s	t	eā	k
	u	sȩ								
J	u	l	y				h	ĕa̲	v	y
S	m	oo	th				d	ĕa̲	th	
m	u	s	i	c			m	ĕa̲	n	t
c	u	tȩ								
r	u	i	n							
	t	u bȩ								

Vowel Diphthongs

INTRODUCTION: VOWEL DIPHTHONGS

A diphthong has two parts that glide together through a noticeable change in mouth position. As you start the sound, the front of your mouth moves, and then the back, or vice versa, depending on the diphthong being made. There are two clear diphthongs in English: /ou/ and /oi/. Each is spelled by a pair of vowel teams.

/oi/ = *oi, oy*   /ou/ = *ou, ow*

as in *oil* and *boy*   as in *out* and *owl*

Try this simple exercise to help students experience the gliding firsthand. Students use a mirror to view the mouth position change.

First, try to isolate the first diphthong:

"Say *oil* without the /l/." (/oi/.)

"Where did your mouth begin this sound?" (Front of mouth.)

"Where did your mouth glide to as you finished the sound?" (Back of mouth.)

Then, isolate the second diphthong:

"Say *out* without the /t/." (/ou/.)

"Where did your mouth begin this sound?" (Back of mouth.)

"Where did your mouth end this sound?" (Front of mouth.)

Since /oi/ and /ou/ are single vowel phonemes, they are mapped in one box as shown below.

 and

 and

Give students hand mirrors. Tell them that they will be learning two new vowel sounds called **diphthongs.** "The mouth position changes when we say a diphthong, and the mirrors will help you see how the mouth changes."

The first new sound is/oi/ as in *oil*. Instruct students to say /oi/ slowly and to watch in their mirrors how their mouths start with the lips pursed out front followed by a sliding movement that takes their mouths open and back. Have them say *oil* without the /l/ and watch again.

The second diphthong is /ou/ as in *out*. Instruct students to say /ou/ slowly and to watch in their mirrors how their mouths start open and back followed by a sliding movement that brings their lips pursed and forward. Have them say *out* without the /t/ and watch again. Continue with the lesson steps.

MAPPING PROCEDURE

See examples in the word list that follows.

Vowel Diphthongs Word List			

/oi/ as in boy		/ou/ as in owl	

oi | l	t | oy	ou | t	c | ow

TEACH With just a few exceptions, the *oi* spelling is used in the initial and medial positions of words.	**TEACH** With just a few exceptions, the *oy* spelling is used in the final position of words.	**TEACH** The most frequent medial spelling of these diphthongs is *ou*.	**TEACH** Have students take note of how many *ow* words are followed by an *l, n,* or *er.*

oi		*oy*	*ou*			*ow*	
oil	disjoint	boy	about	noun	voucher	bow	pow
boil	typhoid	cowboy	out	amount	bounty	cow	powder
broil	loiter	buoy	ouch	ounce	compound	brow	power
coil	doily	coy	our	bounce	county	brown	rowdy
coin	sequoia	decoy	bound	pouch	council	browse	scowl
spoil	steroid	destroy	cloud	pound	sound	chow	shower
joint	sirloin	employ	couch	pout	spouse	chowder	sow
join	trapezoid	enjoy	count	pronoun	grouch	clown	towel
loin	turmoil	Floyd	proud	crouch	spout	coward	tower
point		foyer	round	devout	sprout	cower	town
poise		soy	roust	discount	stout	cowl	trowel
poison		toy	doubt	scour	mound	crowd	vow
quoit		Troy	flour	scout	lounge	crown	vowel
recoil		envoy	foul	shout	trouser	allow	wow
rejoice		corduroy	found	slouch	trout	growl	yowl
soil		**Exceptions**	sour	council	snout	how	
toil		vo*y*age	pout	ground	mount	Howard	
toilet		lo*y*al	hound		mouse	howl	
voice		ro*y*al	loud		mouth	jowl	
void		bo*y*cott				meow	
adjoin		bo*y*senberry				now	
celluloid		clairvo*y*ance				owl	
disappoint		flambo*y*ant				prowl	
embroider		gargo*y*le				plow	

MAPPING PROCEDURE: A FEW DIFFICULT CONCEPTS

Voyage. This word has a silent *e* that does not influence the preceding vowel, so the *e* should be slashed because we don't hear it. However, it needs to be looped with the *g* to show its role in softening the *g* to create the sound /j/. The vowel in the second syllable is a schwa.

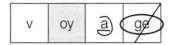

Spouse. This word also has a silent *e* that does not influence the preceding vowel. The final *e* in *spouse* is there to ensure the reader does not think the *s* is acting as a plural *s*.

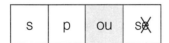

Clairvoyance. The 12 letters in this word combine to make 9 sounds. The final *e* does not influence the preceding vowel. However, it needs to be looped with the *c* to show its role in softening the *c* to create the sound /s/.

c	l	ai	r	v	oy	a	n	ce

Diphthong Sentences With
Prepositional Phrases

1. The boy heard noise off in the distance

2. Behind the crowd, by the tree was a dog.

3. I heard a howl down the street between the trees.

4. My sister was rowdy as a clown at the concert.

5. It was very oily underneath my Father's car from motor fluid

6. I placed my decoy around the corner, below the birdhouse.

7. I like to rejoice after winning a baseball game.

8. I like to annoy my mother after she comes home from shopping

Note: As part of a spelling assignment on diphthongs and prepositions, students were asked to use eight of their spelling words in complete sentences that contained *at least* one prepositional phrase. This student was able to use multiple prepositions in six of his eight sentences.

The Sound of /aw/ Spelled au and aw

TUTORIAL Useful generalizations exist to help the speller determine whether to use *au* or *aw* to spell the rounded back vowel sound /aw/. Which in some dialects is pronounced like short o /ŏ/.

- Use *au* at the beginning or in the middle of a word unless the sound of /aw/ is followed by a single *n* or *l*. In that case, use *aw*.

  Examples:

because	drawn	saucer
shawl	lawn	crawl

  Some notable exceptions:

hawk	awful	awkward	restaurant	Paul
squawk	awning	Hawthorne		

- Use *aw* when you hear /aw/ at the end of a base word.

  Examples:

draw	jaw	saw	lawyer

TEACH

Instruct students to hold hand mirrors and watch their mouths as they say *octopus.* Direct them to hold the /o/ sound and note how their mouth looks. Then instruct them to say *awning,* once again holding the vowel sound, this time /aw/. Direct them to compare the vowel sound in *octopus* to the vowel sound in *awning.* Their mouths round up with /aw/. Explain that they will learn two spellings for this sound.

The position of each spelling is explained in the word list headings.

MAPPING PROCEDURE

See the examples provided in the *au* and *aw* Word List.

au and aw Word List			
au for /aw/		**aw for /aw/**	
TEACH Use *au* when you hear /aw/ at the beginning or in the middle of a word.	**TEACH** Use *au* when you hear /aw/ and it is followed by an *n* or *l* anywhere in the word.	**TEACH** Use *aw* when you hear /aw/ at the end of a base word.	**TEACH** Use *aw* when you hear /aw/ and it is followed by a final *n* or *l* in the base word.

<table>
<tr><td colspan="2">| au | t | o |</td><td colspan="2">| h | au | l |</td><td colspan="2">| s | aw |</td><td colspan="2">| y | aw | n |</td></tr>
<tr><td>auto</td><td>clause</td><td>haunt</td><td>maul</td><td>aw</td><td>paw</td><td>fawn</td><td>awl</td></tr>
<tr><td>August</td><td>audit</td><td>jaunt</td><td>cauldron</td><td>claw</td><td>saw</td><td>pawn</td><td>bawl</td></tr>
<tr><td>caution</td><td>Austin</td><td>laundry</td><td>hydraulic</td><td>craw</td><td>law</td><td>brawn</td><td>brawl</td></tr>
<tr><td>autumn</td><td>autism</td><td>laundress</td><td>caulk</td><td>flaw</td><td>lawyer</td><td>dawn</td><td>crawl</td></tr>
<tr><td>faucet</td><td>autograph</td><td>gauntlet</td><td>haul</td><td>guffaw</td><td>draw</td><td>drawn</td><td>drawl</td></tr>
<tr><td>fraud</td><td>automobile</td><td>gaunt</td><td>fault</td><td>jaw</td><td>gnaw</td><td>lawn</td><td>scrawl</td></tr>
<tr><td>sauce</td><td>laud</td><td>launch</td><td>Paul</td><td>naw</td><td>haw</td><td>pawn</td><td>shawl</td></tr>
<tr><td>saucer</td><td>auxiliary</td><td>jaundice</td><td>assault</td><td>raw</td><td></td><td>scrawny</td><td>sprawl</td></tr>
<tr><td>author</td><td>bauxite</td><td>paunch</td><td>somersault</td><td>caw</td><td></td><td>yawn</td><td>trawler</td></tr>
<tr><td>cause</td><td>automatic</td><td>staunch</td><td>tarpaulin</td><td>coleslaw</td><td></td><td>spawn</td><td>yawl</td></tr>
<tr><td>because</td><td>autopsy</td><td>sauna</td><td>cauliflower</td><td></td><td></td><td>trawl</td><td></td></tr>
<tr><td>exhaust</td><td>nautical</td><td>saunter</td><td>vault</td><td></td><td></td><td>tawny</td><td></td></tr>
<tr><td>pause</td><td>applause</td><td>taunt</td><td></td><td></td><td></td><td></td><td></td></tr>
<tr><td>pauper</td><td>astronaut</td><td></td><td></td><td></td><td></td><td></td><td></td></tr>
<tr><td>gauze</td><td>auction</td><td></td><td></td><td></td><td></td><td></td><td></td></tr>
<tr><td>sausage</td><td>audio</td><td></td><td></td><td></td><td></td><td></td><td></td></tr>
<tr><td>saucy</td><td>audition</td><td></td><td></td><td></td><td></td><td></td><td></td></tr>
<tr><td>trauma</td><td>Australia</td><td></td><td></td><td></td><td></td><td></td><td></td></tr>
<tr><td>applaud</td><td>autocrat</td><td></td><td></td><td></td><td></td><td></td><td></td></tr>
</table>

MAPPING PROCEDURE: A FEW DIFFICULT CONCEPTS

Saucer and **faucet.** Loop the *c* with the vowel that follows it to show how they pair up to soften the *c* while also producing the vowel sound in that syllable.

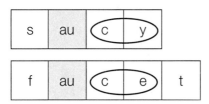

s	au	c	y

f	au	c	e	t

Exhaust. Two phonemes, /k/ and /s/, represent the grapheme *x*. Therefore, it is mapped across two boxes. Also, since the *h* is silent, it does not go in a box of its own. It is placed with the *au* and then crossed out to show its silence.

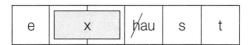

e	x	ẖau	s	t

Lawyer. Since *law* is the base word of *lawyer,* the *aw* spelling is found in the middle of this word. However, it is used at the end of the base word, so the spelling choice remains *aw.*

l	aw	y	er

Cauliflower and **author.** *Cauliflower* is an eleven-letter word that is reduced to eight phonemes due to the number of sounds represented by more than one letter. The same is true of the word *author,* in which six letters represent three phonemes. The lack of one-to-one correspondence between sound and letter is truly evident in these two words.

au	th	or

c	au	l	i	f	l	ow	er

The Two Sounds of oo

TUTORIAL The letters *oo* can represent two distinctively different sounds. To help students remember these two sounds, use pictures that provide cue words representing both sounds. Here are two for you to choose from.

- A picture of a ghost reading a book can conjure the — phrase *boo book.*

- A picture of a *footstool* can also help students remember the two sounds of *oo*.

Since the sound of /o͞o/ as in *boo* and *stool* is more frequently used than the sound of /o͝o/ in *book* or *foot*, students should be encouraged to use that sound first to try to pronounce a word. If that doesn't work, they should try the remaining sound.

> **TEACH**
>
> Choose one or both of the picture cues to introduce the two sounds of *oo*. Instruct students to say the cue words, *boo–book* and *foot–stool.* Isolate the two sounds. Instruct students to say the two sounds while watching their mouths in a hand mirror. Tell students that the spellings for each of these two sounds may be *oo*.

MAPPING PROCEDURE

The mapping of the *oo* sounds is mostly straightforward. See the examples in the word list and the more complex mappings in the following section.

oo as in *foot* and *stool* Word List						
/o͞o/ as in *boo*					/o͝o/ as in *book*	
b | oo					b | oo | k	
boo	stoop	pool	swoop	drool	book	booklet
noon	hoop	proof	tool	mood	brook	cook
boot	hoot	roof	noon	balloon	cookie	crook
booth	igloo	room	tooth	food	foot	good
smooth	kazoo	roost	troop	bamboo	hood	hoof
cool	loop	root	shampoo	moon	hook	hooky
coon	loom	school	raccoon	fool	hooray	manhood
coop	loose	scoop	zoo	voodoo	look	nook
doom	loot	scoot	zoom	snoop	shook	stood
droop	moo	shoot	noon	gloom	took	wood
goof	oops	soon	caboose	goon	rook	toots
ooze	cocoon	goose	pooch	spook	woof	wool
groom	poodle	spool	spoon	stool		
Exceptions						
door poor floor						
brooch blood flood						

MAPPING PROCEDURE: MORE COMPLEX OO WORDS

Typhoon and schooner. Since **ph** is a digraph and makes one sound, it is placed in one box. The **ch** in *schooner* stands for the single phoneme /k/, so it is placed in one box.

t	ȳ	ph	oo	n

s	ch	oo	n	er

Goose, loose, and ooze. When a one-syllable word ends in the sound of /s/, as in *goose* and *loose*, a silent *e* generally follows it. However, it is not there to make the preceding vowel long as in the silent -*e* syllable pattern. This *e* is there to ensure that the reader does not assume the *s* is a plural marker and read the word as more than one *loo* or more than one *goo*. This can also be true when a one-syllable word ends in the sound of /z/, as in *ooze,* since plural *s* can sound like /z/ when the final consonant sound in the base word is a voiced sound (e.g., *plug–plugs; rim–rims*).

g	oo	sҿ

l	oo	sҿ

oo	zҿ

Boogie. The sound of /ē/ is represented in this word by the vowel team *ie* and makes just one sound. Therefore, both letters are placed in one sound box. Students do not loop the *g* with the *i* in *boogie* because the *i* does not soften the preceding *g* in this word. Remember, *e*, *i,* and *y* often (not always) soften.

| b | oo | g͡ie | | |

Phoneme-Grapheme Mapping
(A Method for Bridging Sound to Print)

Name: _____ Date: _____

b	oo	t								
t	y	ph	oo	N						
t	y	c	oo	N						
r	oo	s	t	er						
M	oo	se								
b	oo	k								
Sh	oo	k								
S	t	oo	d							
b	r	oo	k							

Unit 7

r-Controlled (or vowel-r) Syllables

Introduction to *r*-Controlled Syllables

The ***r*-controlled syllables**, sometimes called vowel-r syllables, are syllables in which the vowel is controlled by the *r*. Common spellings for the vowel in this syllable are *ar, or, ir, er,* and *ur*. If a spelling has a vowel team (e.g., *dear*) or a silent e pattern (e.g., *care*), it is not an *r*-controlled syllable. The *r*-controlled syllables occur often and are challenging for students to learn because the /r/ sound is difficult to locate in words, and the words' spellings are many and varied. Students require ongoing and frequent review to master the *r*-controlled spellings.

When a vowel letter is followed by the letter *r*, the vowel sound is different from either the long or short vowel sound. It is important to teach students that the *r* always comes after the vowel and helps to give the vowel its unique sound.

The five main vowels (*a, e, i, o,* and *u*) combine with *r* to make three distinct sounds most of the time, as in Table 10.

Table 10 Vowel + *r* Sounds		
ar* /ar/** **as in *art	***or* /or/** **as in *orbit***	***er, ir, ur* /er/** **as in *her, sir,* and *fur***
car	for	germ girl turn
chart	born	thermal birth burn
bark	thorn	shorter . thirst church
tarp	fort	smaller first churn

The *er* spelling is the most common one for /er/. It is frequently found at the end of a word or syllable as in *father* and *perhaps*.

Students often place the *r* in front of the vowel because /r/ is the first sound they hear. This mistakenly creates a consonant blend and forms the following incorrect spellings by the novice speller:

frist for *first*   *gril* for *girl*   *brithday* for *birthday*

However, once students clearly understand *r*-controlled vowel spellings and blends, they are less apt to continue making these errors.

Sound variations of *r*-controlled vowels:

- *ar* in an unaccented syllable says /er/, as in *dollar, collar, forward*

- *ar* as a suffix says /er/, as in *polar, angular, circular*

- *ar* can also say /or/ after a *w*, as in *war, ward*

- *or* after a *w* says /er/, as in *work, worm, word*

- *or* in an unaccented syllable at the end of a word says /er/, as in *doctor, professor, donor*

r-Controlled Syllables: ar

Prepare a letter card with a muscular illustrated *r* to introduce *r*-controlled syllables.

"Today we will learn the *r*-controlled syllable. The *r*-controlled syllable has a bossy letter. This boss is very picky and always wants to come after the vowel letter and then control what the vowel says. This bossy letter is the *r*." Show the picture of the bossy *r*.

"Say *art* and the sounds in *art,* /ar/ /t/. Do you hear the bossy *r*?" Show the bossy *r* picture. "Will it come first? No, because it always wants to come after a vowel letter." Show students the word *art,* ask them to identify the vowel letter, *a,* and underline the vowel combination *ar.*

"Say *dollar* and the sounds in *dollar,* /d/ /o/ /l/ /r/. Do you hear the bossy *r*? Will it come first? No, because it always wants to come after the vowel letter." Show students the word *dollar,* ask them to identify the vowel letter, *a,* and underline the vowel combination *ar.*

Explain that they will start with the bossy *r* spelling *ar,* and they will learn others in later lessons. Continue with the lesson steps to teach the *r*-controlled spelling *ar* and its phoneme relationships.

MAPPING PROCEDURE

The sound /är/ is the most frequently occurring sound for the spelling ar. Words applying this phoneme-grapheme relationship are listed first in the word list that follows.

r-Controlled Syllables: ar Word List		
är as /ar/		
ar t	är ch	m ar b le
art	dart	marlin
arc	depart	Mars
arch	discard	marble
Arctic	charge	marvel
archer	far	marsh
ark	farce	mart
argue	farm	marten
arm	garb	martyr
armor	garden	nark
army	gargle	par
arson	garland	part
artery	garlic	park
Arthur	garment	parlay
article	garnet	parlor
artist	garnish	parse
bar	garter	parsnip
barb	gnarl	parson
barber	go-kart	part
bard	guard	partake
barge	guardian	tar
bark	harbor	radar
barn	hard	regard
barter	hardly	sharp
car	hark	sarcasm
carbon	harm	scar
carcass	harness	scarf
card	harp	scarlet
cargo	harsh	seminar
carp	harvest	shard
carpet	jaguar	shark
cart	jar	smart
carton	jargon	snarl
cartoon	knar	spar
carve	larceny	spark
chard	lard	tardy
yard	largo	starch
charm	lark	stark
chart	marble	charge
cigar	tzar	yarn
tarp	margin	starve
dark	mark	
darn	market	
large	yard	
tart		

Phoneme-Grapheme Mapping
(A Method for Bridging Sound to Print)

Name: _____ Date: _____

ar	t	i	s	t						
s	m	ar	t	e	s	t				
g	p	ar	k	ed						
ch	ar	g ed								

ar Word List (continued)		
ar as /er/ **at the End of a Word**	**ar as /ár/**	**arr as /ár/** **in an Accented Syllable**
l i ar	ár i d	arr ow
angular stellar	Aaron	arrow
cellular triangular	Arab	arrogant
circular vulgar	Arabic	barracks
familiar altar	arable	barracuda
granular beggar	aragon	barrel
lunar burglar	parent	barren
molecular calendar	arid	barrier
muscular caterpillar	tariff	carriage
particular cedar	parish	carry
peculiar cellar	parity	carrot
perpendicular collar	parody	carrier
polar cougar	pharaoh	garret
popular dollar	proletariat	Harris
rectangular grammar	Sarah	marriage
regular hangar	tariff	marry
secular sugar	Mary	narrow
similar molar		parrot
singular mortar		tarry
solar nectar		wheelbarrow
spectacular vinegar		
pillar		
scholar		
liar		
Exceptions are, afar, bar, bazaar, car, cigar, far, jaguar, jar, mar, and star	*Note:* Words such as *care, blare, dare, fare, hare, glare, pare, rare, stare,* and *ware* are treated as silent -e syllables in this book.	

MAPPING PROCEDURE: MORE COMPLEX AR WORDS

***Archaic* and *archer*.** The digraph **ch** has two different sounds in these two words. It makes the sound of /k/ in *archaic,* and it makes the sound of /ch/ in *archer*. Because single phonemes are produced, the letters are placed in one sound box.

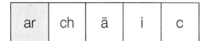 

ar	ch	ā	i	c

ar	ch	er

Farce. Note that *c* and *e* are placed in the same box because the *e* is needed to soften the *c* so that the reader will not pronounce the word as /fark/.

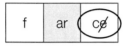

f	ar	c̸e̸

Scholar. The *ar* in *scholar* sounds like /er/. It is used as a suffix ending added to the root *school*.

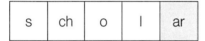

s	ch	o	l	ar

r-Controlled Syllables: or

This lesson teaches that the letters *or* make the sound of /or/ when they occur in the initial or medial position of a word. They can also make the sound of /er/ when they occur in an unaccented syllable at the end of a word. (In addition, *or* makes the sound /er/ when it follows the letter *w,* as in *word.* This concept is covered in the Lesson 7:3 on *r*-controlled vowels and consonant *w*.)

TEACH

"Today we will learn another *r*-controlled spelling and its sounds. Say *corn* and the sounds in *corn*, /k/ /or/ /n/. Do you hear the bossy *r*? Will it come first? No, because it always wants to come after a vowel letter." Show students the word *corn* and ask them to identify the vowel letter, *o,* and underline the vowel combination, *or.*

"Say the word *actor,* and the sounds in *actor,* /a/ /k/ /t/ /r/. Do you hear the bossy *r*? Will it come first? No, because it always wants to come after a vowel letter." Show the students the word *actor* and ask them to identify the vowel letter, *o.* Underline the vowel combination, *or.* Continue with the lesson steps.

MAPPING PROCEDURE

Students map *or* in a single box, as in the following mapping examples of *morning* and *author*.

m	or	n	i	ng

au	th	or

r-Controlled Syllables: *or* Word List

or as /or/ in the Initial or Medial Position			*or* as /er/ in the Unaccented Final Position	
			Means "a person who does . . ."	Other nouns
a c **or** n			au th **or**	ar m **or**
acorn	force	morning	actor	anchor
born	forceps	morsel	ancestor	arbor
border	ford	mortal	censor	armor
lord	foreign	mortar	auditor	ardor
chord	forest	mortgage	author	calculator
chorus	forge	mortify	captor	clamor
cord	fork	mortuary	collector	color
cork	forlorn	nor	commentator	corridor
corn	form	norm	competitor	elevator
corner	fort	normal	conductor	equator
cornet	forth	north	contractor	error
corpse	forty	or	director	factor
corral	forum	oral	doctor	favor
deport	forward	orange	donor	fervor
distort	gory	orbit	editor	flavor
divorce	horde	orchard	educator	generator
dorm	hormone	orchestra	emperor	harbor
dormant	horn	orchid	governor	honor
dormer	hornet	ordain	instructor	horror
pork	horrible	order	janitor	humor
endorse	horrid	ordinary	juror	labor
escort	horrify	Oregon	legislator	major
enforce	horror	organ	mayor	minor
export	horse	orient	mentor	mirror
extort	Jordan	ordeal	operator	monitor
Florence	morbid	ornate	proctor	motor
Florida	morgue	port	professor	odor
for	morn	scorch	sailor	parlor
forage	storm		sculptor	prior
score	thorn		senator	projector
scorn	torment		spectator	razor
shorn	torso		sponsor	rigor
short	tort		tailor	rotor
snort	vortex		tenor	rumor
sordid	York		traitor	savor
sort			tutor	splendor
stork			victor	terror
			visitor	tractor
			neighbor	tremor
				tumor
				vapor
				visor

The words that follow also contain the sound /or/. Group them with the silent -*e* syllable words because the sound and the pattern follow the silent *e* principle of making the preceding vowel long.

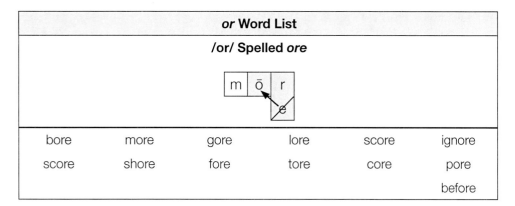

or Word List					
/or/ Spelled *ore*					
bore	more	gore	lore	score	ignore
score	shore	fore	tore	core	pore
					before

OR PHONEME-GRAPHEME MAPPING

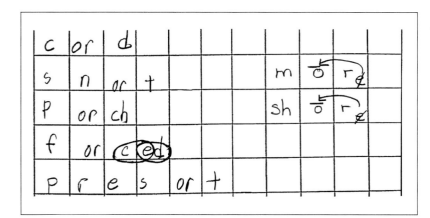

r-Controlled Syllables: er

TUTORIAL The sound of /er/ has three spellings: *er, ir,* and *ur.* Unquestionably, *er* is the most often used of the three. It is not only used within a word that is followed by a consonant, but it is also a popular suffix ending. When *er* is attached to a base word, it can produce a noun, pronoun, verb, or adjective. Examples of these transformations are included in the word list.

TEACH

Teach students that the next *r*-controlled syllable is *er.* It is the most popular spelling of all the *r*-controlled vowels. It is used within words followed by a consonant. And it is used as a suffix, added to a base word. Provide examples of words with *er,* isolate the /er/, and then show students the spelling: *fern, farmer, cavern, closer.*

MAPPING PROCEDURE

See examples that follow.

r-Controlled Syllables: *er* Word List				
er as /er/ (within a word when followed by a consonant) `f	er	n`	**er as /er/** (as a suffix to create a noun or a pronoun) `ar	ch	er`	**er as /er/** (as a suffix ending to create a verb) `or	d	er`	**er as /er/** (as a suffix ending to create an adjective)	
			Comparative Form of an Adjective `d	ar	k	er`	**Other Adjectives** `i	nn	er`
adverb expert	anger farmer	alter	better	bitter
adverse fern	answer fender	anger	blacker	clever
alert fertile	archer gardener	answer	bluer	either
artery germ	baker glimmer	banter	braver	inner
assert German	banker grocer	barter	brighter	other
avert govern	banner grounder	blister	calmer	tender
bakery herb	batter hamburger	blunder	cleaner	upper
Berlin herd	binder helper	bother	closer	amber
berserk hermit	bleacher hunter	chatter	cooler	elder
berth insert	blender informer	cluster	crisper	former
cavern interest	diner jester	cover	damper	improper
celery intern	blocker jumper	enter	darker	proper
cistern invert	blister keeper	filter	dimmer	sober
checkers jerk	boarder lather	flicker	elder	somber
clerk kernel	border letter	fluster	farther	subcaliber
concern lantern	bother lobster	foster	faster	slender
serve merge	boxer manger	gather	fatter	sinister
concert modern	brother marker	glimmer	firmer	tender
conserve nerd	bumper member	hammer	fitter	yonder
converge nerve	burner number	hinder	greater	
converse opera	burger order	linger	greener	
convert pattern	buzzer partner	litter	harder	
covert percent	caller porter	lower	higher	
culvert perch	camper power	murder	later	
derby perfect	cancer reporter	mutter	lesser	
dessert perfume	catcher river	offer	lighter	
discern perhaps	chapter scorcher	order	longer	
disperse perk	clover singer	pamper	milder	
diverge permit	clutter splinter	ponder	moister	
divert perplex	counter teacher	prefer	nearer	
erg serf	cracker teenager	refer	older	
person tern	danger thinker	remember	quicker	
excerpt verb	dimmer thunder	scamper	redder	
serpent	winter trainer	scatter	sadder	
serve	wonder whisper	utter	stronger	
		wager	thinner	
		Adverbs	weaker	
		ever never		
		hither later		
		rather sooner		

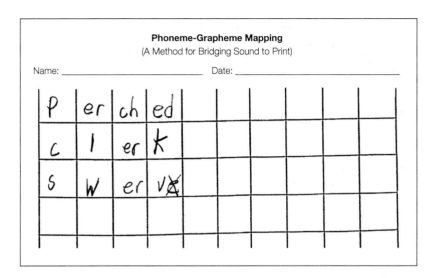

MAPPING PROCEDURE: MORE COMPLEX ER WORDS

Answer. The silent *w* is placed with the *s* and then crossed out because it is not heard.

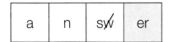

Smarter. Note the presence of two *r*-controlled vowels. They reduce a seven-letter word to five boxes.

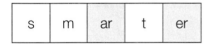

Either. The vowel team *ei*, digraph **th,** and an *r*-controlled vowel reduce this six-letter word to three boxes. When students lack an understanding of this mismatch of letters and sounds, they might spell the word *either* as *ethr*.

r-Controlled Syllables: ir

TUTORIAL The grapheme *ir* generally represents /er/ when it occurs in any position in a word. However, it can also stand for /ear/ in a much smaller sampling of vocabulary. The grapheme *ir* represents /ear/:

- When another *r* follows *ir* as in *irrigate*.
- When a vowel other than *e* immediately follows the *ir,* as in *iridescence*.

TEACH

Teach students that the next *r*-controlled spelling is *ir*. "The bossy *r* likes to follow the vowel and controls the vowel sound, saying /er/." Provide examples of words with *ir,* isolate the sound /er/, and then show students the spelling: *bird, circle, shirt.*

"Sometimes the *ir* spelling makes the sound /ear/. Say *irrigate*. Isolate the /ear/ sound." Show students the word. Repeat with *miracle.*

MAPPING PROCEDURE

See examples in the word list that follows.

r-Controlled Syllables: *ir* Word List				
ir as /er/			**ir as /ear/**	
			ir-r	**ir plus any vowel other than e**
	b | ir | ch		m | irr | or	m | ir | a | c | le
birch	quirk	sirloin	cirrus	Hiroshima
bird	squirm	skirt	irremovable	Iroquois
birth	squirt	smirk	irreplaceable	lira
chirp	shirk	stir	irresistible	miracle
circle	shirt	swirl	irresolvable	iridescent
circuit	sir	twirl	irresponsible	pirouette
circus	third	girder	irritant	
confirm	thirst	girl	irritate	
dirt	virgin	girth	mirror	
elixir	Virgo	infirm	irrational	
fir	virtual	irk	irregular	
firm	virtue	mirth	irreparable	
first	whir	gird		
flirt	whirl	stirrup		

MAPPING PROCEDURE: MORE COMPLEX EXAMPLES OF IR

Circus. Because the first *c* is soft due to the *i* that follows it, loop the *c i* to show this relationship. The second *c*, which produces the hard sound of /k/, is not looped because it is the more often produced sound of *c*.

c	ir	c	u	s

Sirloin. The seven letters become reduced to five sounds because of the *r*-controlled vowel sound /ir/ and the diphthong /oi/.

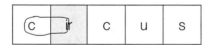

s	ir	l	oi	n

Elixir. Remember to map *x* across two boxes because it consists of the two phonemes /k/ and /s/.

ē	l	i	x	ir

SPELLING TESTS

Have students take their spelling tests in syllables. Grade them according to the syllables they spell correctly rather than the number of words correct, as in the spelling test example.

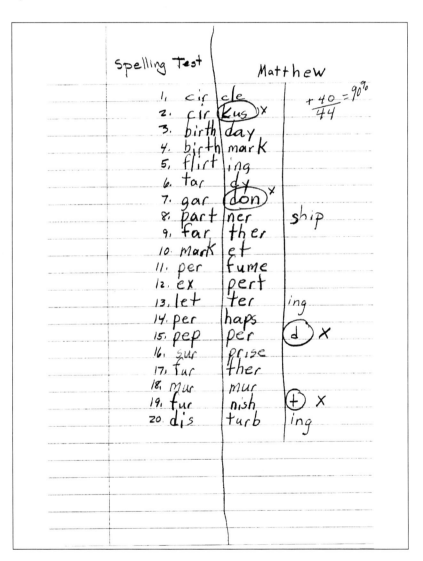

This student's score, based on the number of syllables correct, is 90%. His score based on the number of words correct would have been 85%. From this test, you can see a review of the sounds of the suffix *-ed* is warranted.

r-Controlled Syllables: ur

TUTORIAL The sound /er/ can be represented as *ur* or *urr*.

TEACH

Teach students that the next *r*-controlled spelling is *ur*. Provide examples of words with *ur*, isolate the sound /er/, and then show students the spelling: *fur, burn, surf.* Sometimes the spelling of this *r*-controlled vowel is *urr*. Use the words *hurrah* and *purr* as examples.

MAPPING PROCEDURE

See examples in the word list that follows.

r-Controlled Syllables: *ur* Word List					
ur as /er/				*urr* as /er/ (or /u/ /r/)	
ur ch i n				p urr or p u rr	
absurd	curve	purse	curb	purr	purr
Arthur	disburse	slur	curd	burr	scurry
blur	disturb	slurp	curl	burro	hurrah
blurb	fur	spur	curse	burrow	surrey
burly	furl	spurn	cursive	currant	turret
burden	furtive	spurt	curt	current	furry
burg	gurgle	sturdy	Curtis	curry	
burlap	Hamburg	sulfur	curtsy	currier	
burl	hurdle	surf	perturb	flurry	
burlington	hurl	surge	purge	furrier	
Burma	hurt	surmise	purple	furrow	
burn	hurtful	surplus	purpose	furry	
burnt	incur	surprise	nurse	hurry	
burp	excursion	survive	turn		
burst	lurch	turban	turnip		
Burton	lurk	yurt	urban		
church	murder	turf	urge		
churn	murk		urn		

MAPPING PROCEDURE: MORE COMPLEX EXAMPLES OF UR

***Furtive* and *survive*.** The final *e* in these words has two uses. In *furtive*, the *e* is crossed out because its *only* job is to protect the *v*. No word in English ends in a final *v*; Therefore, words ending in the final sound of /v/ always have an *e* immediately following the *v*. In *survive*, the final *e* has two jobs. It creates a silent *-e* syllable so the preceding vowel is long, and it protects the *v* from being the final letter in the word.

Perturb. This word contains two *r*-controlled vowels: *er* and *ur*.

p	er	t	ur	b

Gurgle. The *ur* produces the sound of /er/ in this word. Remember to place the *le* in one box and wrap the box with a giant schwa. The two graphemes jointly represent the schwa sound /u/ plus /l/ in the final consonant *-le* syllable.

g	ur	g	le

***urr* Words.** Many *urr* words have an alternate pronunciation with a clearly heard /u/ separate from /r/, as illustrated below.

b	urr	o

b	u	rr	o

or

f	urr	ow

f	u	rr	ow

Phoneme-Grapheme Mapping
(A Method for Bridging Sound to Print)

Name: _____ Date: _____

c	ir	c	u	s				
b	ir	th	m	ar	k			
t	ar	d	y					
p	ar	t	n	e	r			
m	a	r	k	e	t			
e	x	p	er	t				
p	er	h	a	p	s			
s	ur	p	r	i	se			
m	ur	m	ur					
d	i	s	t	ur	b			
f	or	t	r	e	ss			

This student sample reviews all *r*-controlled syllables.

COMBINING SPELLING WITH LANGUAGE USAGE LESSONS

This fourth grade student created these sentences after a mini-lesson on punctuating adjectives in a series. The spelling focus was *r*-controlled vowels.

Combining Spelling with Language Usage Lessons

1. The lonely, ill, bird is bored.
2. The artist is very crazy, and clever.
3. The evil, fat turtle bit a person.
4. The rich, rotten girl is very spoiled.
5. The rotten, cazy, clerk is very mean.
6. The big, ugly, scar is from a bee.
7. The big, strong, bull charged at the man.
8. The long, small, cord was unplugged.

Note: Rather than having students simply use five of their spelling words in sentences, it is more beneficial to combine grammar/mini-lessons with spelling instruction. By targeting specific sentence-building strategies, students can practice these skills on a regular basis.

r-Controlled Vowels and Consonant w

TEACH

"Say *war.*" Ask students to say the sounds in *war,* /w/ /or/. Show them the word and direct them to the spelling of /or/. Underline the spelling *-ar.*

"Say *word.*" Ask students to say the sounds in *word,* /w/ /r/ /d/. Show them *word* and direct them to the spelling of /r/. Underline the spelling *-or.*

What do students notice about the letter just before the *r*-controlled spelling? It is a *w* in both words.

"When *ar* follows a *w,* it makes the sound of /or/. When *or* follows a *w,* it makes the sound of /er/."

MAPPING PROCEDURE

See the following examples and the examples in the word list.

r-Controlled Vowels and w Word List	
war as /wor/	**wor as /wer/**
w	ar		w	or	d

war	warranty	word	worth
ward	warren	wording	worthless
warm	warrior	work	worthwhile
warn	Warsaw	workbook	worthy
warmth	Warwick	workshop	workable
warp	thwart	world	worry
wart	warble	worldly	worse
dwarf	warbler	worldwide	worsen
swarm	warden	worm	worship
swarthy	warfare	wormhole	worst
	warrant		wort

Exceptions	**Exceptions**
toward /tord/	sword /sord/
Edward /ed-werd/	worn /worn/
	worsted /woos-tid/

w	ar	m	th

w	orr	y

th	w	ar	t

w	or	th	y

— Unit 8 —

A Few Good Rules

Unit 8 contains more in-depth exploration and practice of a few of the "good ol'" rules that govern the way spelling changes when suffixes are added. These lessons can be inserted and taught throughout the program, whenever you recognize that students would benefit from explicit rule instruction. Or, you can teach them as a separate unit. Before learning the concepts in these lessons, students need to be familiar with root and base words, suffixes, vowels, consonants, and syllable division of written words.

The Doubling Rule With Single-Syllable Base Words

TUTORIAL There are four important prerequisite skills students need before you introduce the doubling rule. They must be able to:

1. Define and identify a base word.

2. Define and identify a suffix.

3. Identify whether a suffix begins with a vowel or a consonant (as in Table 11).

4. Understand what a syllable is and the difference between one- and two-syllable words.

Table 11 Common Suffixes											
Common Suffixes Beginning With a Vowel							Common Suffixes Beginning With a Consonant				
-able	-an	-en	-er	-ible	-ish	-or	-ful	-less	-ness	-sion	-tion
-age	-ant	-ence	-ery	-ic	-ist	-ous	-fy	-ly	-s	-some	
-al	-ed	-ent	-est	-ing	-ive	-y	-hood	-ment	-ship	-ster	

WHAT IS THE DOUBLING RULE (THE 1–1–1 RULE)?

If a *one-syllable base word* ends in *one consonant* with *one vowel before it,* double the final consonant of the base word before adding a suffix that begins with a vowel. Do not double the final consonant if the suffix begins with a consonant.

This long explanation can be very confusing for students. To simplify this rule, use the discrete questions on the Doubling Rule Chart (see Appendix B).

• If the answer is yes to *all* the questions on the chart, double the final consonant of the base word before adding a suffix.

• If the answer is no to *any* of the questions, do not double the consonant; just add the suffix to the base word. Never double the final letters *w, x,* or *y.* **Exceptions:** *damage* and *manage*.

The Doubling Rule With Single-Syllable Base Words

Doubling Rule Chart for Single Syllable Base Words

Base word	Suffix or ending	Does the base word have one syllable?	Does the base word end in a short vowel sound?	Does the base word end in one consonant sound?	Does the suffix begin with a vowel?	Double the final consonant if answer to all questions is yes.	Do not double the final consonant if answer to any question is no.
Example: stop	-ing	yes	yes	yes	yes	stopping	
Example: play	-ed	yes	no	no	yes		played
mad	est	yes	yes	yes	yes	maddest	
swim	er	yes	yes	yes	yes	swimmer	
hop	ing	yes	yes	yes	yes	hopping	
snob	ish	yes	yes	yes	yes	snobbish	
grim	ly	yes	yes	yes	no		grimly
gope	ing	yes	no	X	X		gaping

MAPPING PROCEDURE

Students write the double letters in one box because the letters make just one sound. For spelling purposes, the consonant is doubled. It is helpful to have students shade the base word and the suffix different colors, as in the following examples.

m	a	dd	e	n

m	a	dd	er

m	a	d	n	e	ss

Doubling Rule: Single-Syllable Base Word List					
The Final Consonant Is Doubled			**The Final Consonant Is Not Doubled**		
b | i | gg | e | s | t			f | i | t | n | e | ss		
big	bigger	biggest	bigness	madness	madly
maddest	biggish	madder	flatness	flips	trimly
flipper	madden	flatly	redness	redless	trapful
flippable	flipped	flipping	entrapment	strapless	shipment
snub	flippant	flippish	ships	traps	chipless
trimmed	snubbed	snubbish	whipless	spinless	fatness
trim	trimming	trimmer	manless	spotlessness	kinship
red	trimmest	trimmable	rams	tags	manhood
reddish	redder	redden	jobless	jobs	tagless
trapper	trapped	trapping	fitness	snobbish	bagless
shipping	trappable	shipped	crabless	shagless	skinless
chipped	shipper	shippable	shopless	gladly	gladness
chipper	chipping	ramming	thinly	*thinness*	swims
taggable	rammed	slugger	badly	hipless	topless
whipped	nabless	snubbable	grimly	sadly	sadness
grimmest	whipping	fattest	seamanship	spinster	gridless
sadder	tagged	bagging	crashed	equipment	chewy
baggy	sadden	snobbish	staying	smallest	healthy
bagger	bagged	shaggy	stayed	outfoxed	misty
shagged	snobby	skinnest	displacement	handsome	moldy
skinned	shagging	quitter	smallest	madness	snowy
skinny	skinner	drumming	friendship	grassy	sticky
drum	blotter	mopping	gruesome	staying	thrifty
drummer	drummed	shopper	bending	establishment	madly
shop	mopped	stopped	standing	bumpy	bossy
shopped	shopping	thinned	tallest	hops	handsome
stopping	stoppable	clipper	boxed*	homeless	fistful
rot	thinning	clippable	fixed*	novelist	outfoxed
clipped	rotten	hopper	boxful*	thicken	bulky
hopped	clipping	skipping	foxy*	enjoyment	cheery
bitter	hopping		mixing*		
	bitten		axed*		
swimming	swimmer	funny			

*Although these base words end in one short vowel followed by a single consonant, the letter *x* makes two consonant sounds /k/ and /s/, so the doubling rule does not apply.

Accent or Stress

TUTORIAL Syllables of content words (as opposed to function words, such as articles *a* and *the*) are stressed for one of several reasons:

- Sometimes stress reflects the part of speech, as in the stress alternation of these words:

  CONvict (noun) versus *conVICT* (verb)

  CONtent (noun) versus conTENT (adjective)

  PRESent (noun) versus preSENT (adjective and verb)

- Compound words in English have a distinctive stress pattern. Consider *house-boat, blackbird, lighthouse, crackpot,* and *backwater.* In each of these, the first syllable is stressed. These words contrast in some instances with the same words in noncompound form, such as *the tall, black bird* or *the newly painted, light house.* (*Himself* and *myself* depart from this pattern.) A linguistically sensitive learner will use the phonological cue of stress to understand compounds.

- Multisyllabic words with affixes, especially those of Latin origin, usually have the accent or stress on the root morpheme:

  com PAR a ble

Teachers may neglect to teach stress because many students have difficulty understanding the concept at a young age. However, by upper elementary school, students need to understand accent (stress) so that they can apply it to more sophisticated spelling rules, such as doubling the final consonant in multisyllabic words, which is explained in the next lesson.

8:3

The Doubling Rule for Words of Two or More Syllables

TUTORIAL There are some important prerequisite skills students need before they can learn the more complicated doubling rule for two or more syllables. They must be able to:

- Define and identify a base word.
- Define and identify a suffix (see Table 11 in Lesson 8:1).
- Define accent or stress and ascertain the stressed syllable in a word.
- Understand that accents (stresses) usually do not fall on prefixes.

WHAT IS THE DOUBLING RULE FOR TWO OR MORE SYLLABLES?

If a word has two or more syllables, double the final consonant of the base word when adding a suffix that begins with a vowel if the following conditions apply:

- The accent, or stress, is on the last syllable.
- The final syllable ends in one consonant with only one vowel before it.
- The suffix that will be added begins with a vowel.

To help students apply this rule, use the discrete questions on the Doubling Rule Chart for Multisyllabic Words (see Appendix B).

- If the answer is yes to *all* the questions on the chart, double the final consonant of the base word before adding a suffix.
- If the answer is no to *any* of the questions, do not double the consonant; just add the suffix to the base word.

MAPPING PROCEDURE

When doubling occurs, place the duplicate consonant in the same box as the final consonant (because you do not hear an extra sound).

Doubling Rule: Multisyllable Word List

Double the final consonant in words of two or more syllables that end in VC and have the stress on the final syllable of the base word	Do not double words of two or more syllables that end in VC and do not have the stress on the final syllable of the base word
a d m i tt e d	n u m b er ed
stressed final syllable	**unstressed final syllable**

admittance	forgetting	transferred	piloted	exhibited	alphabetize
committing	excelled	controlling	galloped	discredited	localize
forgotten	excellent	deferred	numbering	intuition	penalize
permitted	referred	equipped	problematic	profitable	equality
occurrence	acquittal	transmitting	animalism	spirited	normalize
propeller	committee		egoism	inhabited	locality
inferred	unforgettable		emotionalism	ravenous	nationality
befitting	expelled		humanism	thunderous	hospitality
			inheritance	limited	visitor
			depositing		

Words Containing the Stem *-fit*	Words Ending in *-mit*
TEACH Double the final consonant in the following words when you add a suffix beginning with a vowel.	**TEACH** If the last syllable is *mit,* that syllable almost always gets the accent, so the *t* is doubled. (The *t* is doubled before adding an ending that begins with a vowel.
b e f i tt i ng	a d m i tt a n ce
stressed syllable	**stressed syllable**

Base word plus doubled consonant plus suffix	Base word plus doubled consonant plus suffix*		
befit	befitted	admit	admittance*	admitted*
misfit	misfitting	commit	committed*	committing*
refit	refitted	demit	demitted*	demitting*
unfit	unfitting	remit	remitted*	remittance*
		transmit	transmitted*	transmittance*
		omit	omitting*	omittance*
		permit	permitting*	permitted*

TEACH Never double the final consonant in the following words, because the accent is not on the last syllable.

p r o f i t a b le

profit	benefit	profitable	benefited

*Dictionaries often provide both spellings.

Doubling Rule: Multisyllable Word List (continued)		
Words Containing the Stem *-fer*		
TEACH For these words, with two *f*'s, never double the final consonant because the accent is on the first syllable.	**TEACH** For other words containing the stem *-fer,* double the final consonant if you are adding the following suffixes: -ed -al -ing	**TEACH** For the stem *-fer,* add the following suffixes *without* doubling the final consonant: -ent -ence -ency The stem *-fer* never takes the following suffixes: -ant -ance -ancy
	c o n f er ed c o n f er e n ce	
offer differ suffer	preferred preferring conferred conferring deferred deferring referred referring referral transferring transferred transferral	preference deference conference reference transference circumference*

Note: As the following example clearly demonstrates, any syllable type can contain a schwa sound. Such is the case in the two *r*-controlled syllables (*cir* and *fer*) shown in the word mapped below.

c ir c u m f er e n ce

Week of 2/7/2005   Student: **Keenan**

The Doubling Rule

To double the final consonant in **base words that have one syllable**…remember:			To double the final consonant in **base words that have more than one syllable** …remember:		
• The base word has just one syllable. • The base word ends in one vowel followed by one consonant. • You are adding a suffix that begins with a vowel.			• The base word has more than one syllable • The final syllable of the base word ends in one vowel followed by one consonant. • The accent must be on the final syllable. • You are adding a suffix that begins with a vowel		
1. dragged	6. untaxed	11. striped	16. admittance	21. transferring	26. visiting
2. putting	7. massive	12. restaged	17. equipping	22. conferring	27. traveling
3. stirred	8. splotchy	13. gaping	18. omitting	23. referring	28. honorable
4. druggist	9. locker	14. spiteful	19. regrettable	24. excellent	29. anchored
5. choppy	10. unmasked	15. hateful	20. beginning	25. rebelling	30. difference

__ Mon. Write words 1-15 in sound boxes. Color the base word yellow in each word. Study 10 min.

12 min.

___ Tuesday: Complete the attached rule chart. It will help you apply the second part of the doubling rule that relates to *multi-syllabic words*. Study 10 min.

Word and suffix	Does the Suffix begin with a vowel?	Does the base word have more than one syllable?	Does the base word end in one vowel and one consonant?	Is the accent on the final syllable?	Write the new word here.
1. admit + ing	yes	yes	yes	yes	admitting
2. patrol + ed	yes	yes	yes	no	patroled
3. disappoint + ed	yes	yes	no	yes	disappointed
4. rebel + ion	yes	yes	yes	yes	rebellion
5. deposit + ory	yes	yes	yes	yes	depository
6. patrol + man	no	yes	yes	no	patrolman
7. deliver + able	yes	yes	yes	no	deliverable
8. signal + ed	yes	yes	yes	no	signaled

___ Wed. Do Activity Sheet 21 (pg. 55). Study 10 min.

___ Thurs. Do Activity Sheet 22 (pg. 65) Study 10 min.

___ Fri. Test

Note: This lesson on the Doubling Rule helps students apply the second part of the rule as it relates to multisyllabic words. Students find the rule chart extremely helpful when first learning the rule because it clearly states what questions they need to ask themselves as they apply this very complex spelling rule.

8:4

The Silent e Rule

TUTORIAL There are three important prerequisite skills students need before you introduce the silent *e* rule. Students must be able to:

- Define and identify a base word.
- Define and identify a suffix (see Table 11, Lesson 8:1).
- Identify whether a suffix begins with a vowel or a consonant.

Review the exceptions to the rule before teaching the rule to students. Exceptions are listed in Table 12.

Common suffixes beginning with a vowel						Common suffixes beginning with a consonant			
-ed	-y	-er	-y	-or	-ic	-ful	-ment	-ness	-less
-en	-ing	-est	-ible	-ist	-ery	-sion	-some	-ship	-fy
-ous	-ant	-ent	-able	-ish		-s	-ster	-ly	-tion
-an	-al	-ive	-age	-ence		-hood			

WHAT IS THE SILENT E RULE?

When a base word ends in a silent *e*:

- Drop the *e* before adding a suffix that begins with a vowel.

  hope + ing = hoping   *like + able = likable*

- Keep the *e* before adding a suffix that begins with a consonant.

  hope + less = hopeless   *like + ness = likeness*

- There are four types of exceptions to this rule. Use the Phoneme-Grapheme Mapping Paper (Silent *e* Rule) (see Appendix B) to help students apply the rule.

Table 12 Exceptions to Silent *e* rule			
Some words keep the silent *e* before a suffix beginning with a vowel. When adding the suffixes *-ous* and *-able* to words with a *c* or *g* prior to the silent *e*, keep the silent *e* at the end of the base word to keep the *c* or *g* soft.	Some words drop the silent *e* before adding a suffix that begins with a consonant.	Some words keep the silent *e* to preserve their identity.	Three words change their spelling entirely when the suffix *-ing* is added to the base word.
courageous	truly	canoeing	dying (die)
outrageous	truth	shoeing	
advantageous	ninth	hoeing	
manageable	argument	toeing	tying (tie)
enforceable	wholly	mileage	
marriageable	judgment	dyeing	
traceable	acknowledgment	singeing	lying (lie)
peaceable	duly	tingeing	
serviceable		cueing	
noticeable			
pronounceable			

MAPPING PROCEDURE

Lesson 3:5 showed how to map busy silent -*e* (when the *e* has shared jobs). However, some words have suffixes that do not begin with an *e* that shares jobs. If a silent *e* in the base word is dropped, place the dropped *e* in the "drop box." Then cross out the *e* because it does not exist in the true spelling of the word. See the examples in word list that follows.

Silent e Rule Word List	
Drop the silent e before adding a suffix that begins with a vowel.	**Keep the silent e before adding a suffix that begins with a consonant.**

baking	wider	tuning	homeless	hopeless	requirement
raving	joker	poker	oneness	spineless	retirement
broken	moving	riding	sameness	timeless	statement
frozen	shaving	notable	lonesome	useless	settlement
staring	shaking	salable	purely	bravely	gruesome
smiling	sharing	smoking	rarely	crudely	troublesome
skater	caring	stony	careful	lately	wholesome
roving	salable	smoky	placement	rarely	closeness
icy	continuous	bridal	enticement	safely	forgiveness
cutest	biting	wading	hateful	strangely	tameness
safest	hoping	usable	tireless	tensely	rudeness
hiring	riding	shining	hopeless	careful	bareness
storage	awful	striped	hopeful	graceful	lifeless
stored	wiping	whining	shameless	disgraceful	priceless
scared	fuming	shamed	lonely	forceful	boredom
taming	tuner	defensive	amazement	grateful	popedom
slimy	cured	driving	achievement	spiteful	dukedom
adventurous	sliding	moping	amusement	useful	conciseness
spicy	bakery	winery	basement	excitement	edgewise
sizable	pleasant	flutist	replacement	engagement	likewise
drivable	debatable	judging	careless	enlargement	
purist	bravest	extremist	changeless	improvement	

Phoneme-Grapheme Mapping Rule Paper
(For use with the silent e rule)

Name: _____ Date: _____

b	ā	k	i	ng					
☐	☐	☒e	☐	☐	☐	☐	☐	☐	☐
sh	ā	k	i	ng					
☐	☐	☒e	☐	☐	☐	☐	☐	☐	☐
s	l	i	m	y					
☐	☐	☐	☒e	☐	☐	☐	☐	☐	☐
j	ō	k	er						
☐	☐	☒e	☐	☐	☐	☐	☐	☐	☐
s	t	r	i	p	ed				
☐	☐	☐	☐	☒e	☐	☐	☐	☐	☐
l	ō	ne	l	y					
☐	☐	☐	☐	y	☐	☐	☐	☐	☐

Note: When first teaching the silent e rule, it is helpful to use the mapping paper above. It provides students with a visual for the actual dropping of the e. Later, using the Affixio Chart to practice the silent e rule is a good strategy because students have to demonstrate their understanding of the rule's effect on the base word or root when adding suffixes.

8:5

The y Rule

TUTORIAL There are three important prerequisite skills students need before you introduce the *y* rule. Students need to be able to:

- Define and identify a base word.

- Define and identify a suffix (see Table 11, Lesson 8:1).

- Identify whether a vowel or a consonant comes before the final *y* in the base word.

WHAT IS THE Y RULE?

The important part of this rule is whether a vowel or a consonant comes before the final *y* of the base word. You do not have to think about whether the suffix begins with a vowel. Focus mainly on the end of the base word.

- If the letter before the final *y* is a vowel, keep the *y* and add any suffix:

  pl<u>ay</u>–pl<u>ay</u>ed   *ann<u>oy</u>–ann<u>oy</u>ance, ann<u>oy</u>ing*

- If the letter before a final *y* is a consonant, change the *y* to an *i* before you add any suffix, except any suffix beginning with an *i*.

  sp<u>y</u>–sp<u>i</u>ed   *sp<u>y</u>–sp<u>y</u>ing*

Review the exceptions to the y rule before teaching the rule to students. The exceptions are listed in Table 13.

Table 13 Exceptions to *y* Rule			
Vowel before the *y* exceptions		**Consonant before the *y* exceptions**	
slay + ed	slain	spry + ness	spryness
lay + ed	laid	shy + ness	shyness
mislay + ed	mislaid	sly + ness	slyness
day + ly	daily	dry + ness	dryness
gay + ly	gaily	shy + ly	shyly
pay + ed	paid	dry + ly	dryly
		sly + ly	slyly
		spry + ly	spryly

MAPPING PROCEDURE

Use the Phoneme-Grapheme Mapping Paper (Y Rule) in Appendix B to help students map words that use the *y* rule. Students place the *y* that has been changed to an *i* or dropped in the drop box. Then they cross it out because it does not exist in the true spelling of the word. Students write *i* in the boxes (as shown below) so that they end up with the true spelling of the word.

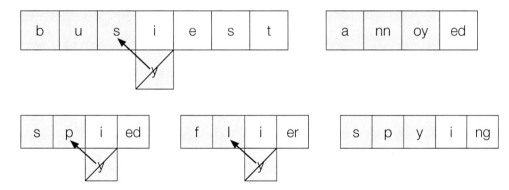

y Rule Word List					
The *y* is changed before adding a suffix			**The *y* remains when adding a suffix**		
gaily	glorious	complied	staying	replaying	strayed
paid	spied	implied	annoyance	annoying	copying
busiest	tinier	dried	annoyed	enjoying	spying
cried	tiniest	fried	enjoyment	paying	supplying
tiniest	copied	candied	enjoyed	employing	studying
flier	copier	countries	payment	destroying	hurrying
studious	busier	factories	decoys	deploying	relying
business	busiest	families	cowboys	obeying	bullying
supplied	merriest	babies	annoying	parleying	flying
luckiest	greedier	gullies	destroyer	surveying	caddying
hurried	carried	memories	destroyed	disobeying	lobbying
loneliness	carrier	plentiful	destroying	conveying	pitying
reliable	tried	historical	employable	graying	worrying
beautiful	twentieth	ponies	employment	preying	trying
mislaid	thirtieth	pennies	employer	praying	crying
laziest	sixtieth	discoveries	employed	volleying	frying
daily	fortieth	deputies	deployment	dismaying	prying
happiness	fiftieth	daisies		displaying	

Phoneme-Grapheme Mapping Rule Paper
(For use with Change the *y* to *i* Rule)

Name: _____ Date: _____

h	a	p	p	i	e	s	t		
☐	☐	☐	☐	☐ y	☐	☐	☐	☐	☐

t	i	n	i	er					
☐	☐	☐	☒ y	☐	☐	☐	☐	☐	☐

l	a	z	i	er					
☐	☐	☐ y	☐	☐	☐	☐	☐	☐	☐

B	a	b	i	es					
☐	☐	☐ y	☐	☐	☐	☐	☐	☐	☐

t	r	i	ed						
☐	☐ y	☐	☐	☐	☐	☐	☐	☐	☐

c	r	y	i	ng					
☐	☐	☐	☐	☐	☐	☐	☐	☐	☐

Spelling Connections

Designing a Spelling Program

Phonics and Spelling Through Phoneme-Grapheme Mapping provides a process, materials, and word lists for you to design your own spelling program. Many teachers realize that explicit and systematic processes improve students' reading and spelling skills. However, many teachers do not have the tools with which to implement a spelling program.

To create an individualized spelling program, complete the Spelling Program Evaluation (Appendix C) to become familiar with the components of a well-designed spelling program and to analyze what is currently in place. Then strengthen the program by incorporating components of *Phoneme-Grapheme Mapping*.

Following are guidelines for planning and implementing a spelling program that uses *Phoneme-Grapheme Mapping* as a springboard and primary source of word lists, tools, and methods of instruction. Simple directions to assist with the process, example student spelling lists, and sample take-home spelling sheets are included.

How to Create Spelling Lists for Your Classroom

Grouping words for spelling is an efficient way to provide focused units of instruction for students. One way to reinforce the structured language concepts taught in your reading/spelling program is to use a spelling list that can be modified according to each student's needs and abilities.

By teaching a single concept to the entire class, but providing spelling lists that span the learning abilities within it, you can provide the exposures students need to master these important concepts.

To create a class spelling list that meets the needs of your students, follow these simple steps:

1. Give a spelling inventory to determine the concepts/spelling patterns that require instruction.

2. Pick one syllable pattern around which to organize your list. (e.g., closed syllables, open syllables).

3. Depending on the range of needs among your students, select the number of words to have on your weekly list. (This can vary between 15 and 25 words, depending on the grade level you teach and/or the range of abilities in your classroom.)

4. Arrange your words in order of difficulty. For example, words 1–5 are easier than words 20–25. Be sure the words in each cluster of five maintain a consistent pattern.

5. Whenever possible, use words that you know students will be reading in their literature books or content areas of study. For example, if your third graders are learning a space science unit, include *ship* and *planet* on your closed-syllable list. In this way, you reinforce vocabulary across settings and provide multiple opportunities for practice.

6. *Remember to start with sound.* Always include an auditory component when you ask students to spell predictable words. Phoneme-grapheme mapping should be one of the first activities each week, as this helps students think about the relationship between the sounds in a word and the letters that represent the sounds.

7. Include weekly sentence-dictation exercises that use target words and any capitalization/punctuation rules you have taught and would like to reinforce. Providing a dictation practice sentence on the spelling list is also helpful.

8. As there are a small number of words that simply have to be memorized, including two-to-five of them on a list as challenge words is also appropriate.

Have you ever seen a throne?
Did Destiny ever win a prize?
Is the baseball team on strike?
When was the last time you
ate a prune?
How do you see a turtle?
Where is the pretzel?
Who spoke to the people?
Do you see a bottle?

Note: These sentence dictation exercises were given to students after the completed instruction in all six syllable types and a lesson on writing questions.

Using Common Words to Plan Weekly Spelling Lists

When planning your weekly spelling lists or looking for specific pattern words for word study lessons, be sure to start with frequently used words. By doing so, you are giving students the opportunity to practice patterns and words so often used in class work. The word lists on the next page classify 151 of the words most often found in elementary students' reading and writing by syllable type.

The Most Common Words in Students' Reading and Writing, by Syllable Type

Closed Syllables - Words Containing a Short Vowel Sound

a		e		i		o		u	
had	glad	when	then	in	into	got	box	but	up
back	black	went	them	it	if	on	not	run	fun
at	cat	get	let	is	his	off		us	bus
am	can	red	send	will	him			just	much
has	man	yes	with	did	which				
an	after	them	twenty	this	think				
ran	and	well		little	big				
than									

Open Syllable		Silent -e Syllable		Vowel Team Syllable			r-Controlled Syllable	
I	a	ride	twice	you	your	now	or	for
me	he	like	came	look	book	how	girl	first
my	by	time	here	good	school	brown	over	order
he	we	made	make	out	about	cow	car	her
she	be	write	home	our	house	down	part	after
so	no	know	use	day	play	oil	far	word
go	going	these	before	way	see	boy	number	work
		more		may	each	toy	letter	
				dear	green	say		
				received	seen	saw	**Consonant -le Syllable**	
				because			people	little

Irregular words that don't follow the syllable spelling patterns

-ve Rule

all	have	done	was	do	there	other	any
ball	give	some	what	who	their	mother	many
call	love	come	would	two	very	water	
old	twelve	one	could	the	are		
cold		once	friend		were		
told			said				

Homework Spelling List: Short Vowel *a*

Spelling list for the week of _____   Student: _____

Closed syllables with short *a*

Parent note: Over the past few weeks, we have been working on short vowels and initial blends. This week we have begun instruction in final blends. This week's spelling list adds final blend words to List 3. The other words serve as review for some students. In class, we will be learning to read and spell many more words with these patterns. Your child is responsible for the number of words noted at the bottom of this list. However, he or she can always learn more words, as we will be practicing all these patterns over the course of the week.

Initial and final consonants	Initial blends	Initial and final blends
1. mad	6. plan	11. plant
2. pat	7. trap	12. grasp
3. an	8. flat	13. draft
4. nap	9. slap	14. stamp
5. tap	10. grab	15. stand

Bonus: flatten, cabin, napkin

_____, please study words #_____* this week.
   (Student's name)

*Indicate the number of words in this blank, *as* in 1–5, 1–10, or 5–15.

Spelling Homework

The first homework spelling list sample is an introductory list for short *a*. Note the various levels of difficulty on the list. Each student in the class is assigned a different number of words, depending on whether the individual needs to review consonants, blends, digraphs, or all these concepts. Yet the teacher can instruct or review short *a*, closed syllables with the entire class.

Homework Spelling List: Short Vowel *u*

Spelling list for the week of _____ Student: _____

Closed syllables with short *u*

You are only responsible for learning words #_____ this week and the dictation sentence. If you want to learn the words on the other lists, you will earn extra credit.

Words with digraphs	-ff -ll -ss rule	Three-letter blends	Three-letter digraph blends	Two-syllable words
1. crunch	6. stuff	11. strum	16. shrub	21. muffins
2. chum	7. muss	12. strung	17. shrug	22. stuntman
3. crush	8. muff	13. struck	18. shrunk	23. crunchy
4. brunch	9. Buff	14. stunts	19. thrush	24. stuffing
5. thud	10. fussy	15. scrub	20. thrust	25. chumless

Dictation sentence: We ate muffins and crunchy stuffing for brunch.

You have a spelling assignment for each day of the week. In addition, you need to practice your words with a parent for 10 minutes each night. Then your parent needs to initial the study time in the blank before each day of the week.

_____ *Monday:* Map your first 15 spelling words in boxes with your teacher. Study 10 minutes.

_____ *Tuesday:* Complete the attached word sort paper. Study 10 minutes.

_____ *Wednesday:* Write 15 of your spelling words in the word strip boxes. Cut them apart. Sort them into alphabetical (ABC) order. Then glue them onto a separate piece of paper in alphabetical order. Study 10 minutes.

_____ *Thursday:* Use seven of your spelling words in sentences that ask a question. Be sure to use one of the question words below and end your sentence with a question mark. Study for 10 minutes. Take a pretest with your parent. Test tomorrow!

Who   What   Where   When   Why   How

_____ *Friday:* Test.

Note: This spelling list spans several concepts, as indicated in the column headers. It allows for individual needs through careful assignment of words.

Homework Spelling List: Long Vowel *i*

Spelling list for the week of _____ Student: _____

You are responsible for learning words #_____ this week and the dictation sentence. If you want to learn the words on the other lists, you will earn extra credit.

Parent note: We are in our second week of studying long vowel spellings. The students have been given a complete chart of all the long vowel spellings for their reference during reading and writing time. Learning how to use the chart effectively is very important, because a specific spelling is determined by the long sound's position in the word.

At the end of a syllable	In the middle of a base word	In the middle of a base word	At the end of a base word	Spellings not used very much
1. silently	6. nice	11. lighting	16. why	21. piecrust
2. silo	7. slide	12. tight	17. myself	22. untie
3. tiny	8. knife	13. high	18. slyly	23. type
4. pilot	9. twice	14. fright	19. trying	24. hyper
5. bicycle	10. rice	15. frighten	20. crying	25. cycle

Dictation sentence: The tiny child was silent and began to cry when he was frightened by the bright light.

_____ *Monday:* Map your words in boxes. Study 10 minutes.

_____ *Tuesday:* Complete the long-vowel sort paper. Study 10 minutes.

_____ *Wednesday:* Complete the Affixo Chart. Study 10 minutes.

_____ *Thursday:* Use six of your words in complete sentences that include a prepositional phrase, which you should underline. Use the attached list of prepositions to help you. Study 10 minutes.

_____ *Friday:* Test.

Long Vowel Sort

Long *i* at the end of a syllable (open syllable)	Long *i* in the middle of a base word	Long *i* in the middle of a base word	Long *i* at the end of a base word	Long *i* spellings that are not used very much
i	*i - e*	*igh*	*y*	*ie* as in p*ie*
as in <u>si</u>-lent	as in b<u>ike</u>	as in n<u>igh</u>t	as in fl<u>y</u>	*y - e* as in t<u>ype</u>

Note: This spelling list, which introduces the six spellings of long *i*, can be individualized by assigning a set number of words for students depending on their skill level.

Word Sorts and Affixo Charts

I frequently use word sorts (like the one in the following student sample) as a means of helping students internalize a concept. Students begin by writing their spelling words on index cards on Monday and using them throughout the week in word sorts. Once students have sorted the word cards according to their long vowel spelling patterns, I have them fill in a word sort chart. It is beneficial for students to repeatedly see the long vowel headings because to help them categorize the spelling choices in their long-term memory.

Long "I" Vowel Sort

Long "I: at the end of a syllable (Open syllable) **I** as in *si lent*	Long "I" in the middle of a baseword. **I - E** As in *bike*	Long "I" in the middle of a baseword. **IGH** As in *night*	Long "I" at the end of a base word. **Y** As in *fly*	Long "I" spellings that are not used very much. IE as in *pie* **Y-E** as in *type*
silently	nice	light	why	pie crust
silo	slide	tighten	myself	tieclip
tiny	knife	high	slyly	type
pilot	twice	fright	trying	hyper
bicycle	rice	frighten	crying	cycle

I try to include words with affixes in my word study lessons. The sample Affixo Chart that follows gives students an opportunity to analyze the structure of their spelling words. Note how the student writes a large • between *my* and *self* to illustrate that the word has two base words (it is a compound word).

PREFIX	PREFIX	BASE WORD OR ROOT	SUFFIX	SUFFIX
		Spice	y	
		silent	ly	
	bi	cycle		
		tight	en	
		fright	en	
		sly	lx	
		try	ing	
		cry	ing	
		my•self		
		high	ly	
		slide	s	
		pilot	s	
	tri	cycle	s	
		type	s	
		tieclip	s	
	un	hice		
		light	s	

Homework List Based on Study Theme

Spelling list for the week of _____ Student: _____

Geology words

You are responsible for learning #_____ words this week and the dictation sentence. If you want to learn the words on the other lists, you will earn extra credit.

Initial closed syllable	Silent -e syllable	r-controlled syllable	Consonant -le syllable	Multisyllable
1. crust	6. slate	11. hard	16. mantle	21. mineral
2. magma	7. shale	12. sharp	17. marble	22. metamorphic
3. fossil	8. limestone	13. force	18. candle	23. sedimentary
4. lava	9. ignite	14. current	19. table	24. obsidian
5. crystal	10. site	15. quarry*	20. sample	25. geology

*The *arr* in *quarry* sounds like the *ar* in *war*.

| q | u | arr | y | | w | ar |

/ ô r /   / ô r /

Dictation sentence: The geologist was looking for metamorphic, igneous, or sedimentary rock samples at the geology site.

_____ *Monday:* Use the attached syllable paper to write your words in syllables. Study 10 minutes.

_____ *Tuesday:* Write each word three times in cursive. Study 10 minutes.

_____ *Wednesday:* Put your spelling words in ABC order. Use the cut-and-paste grids if you need to. Study 10 minutes.

_____ *Thursday:* Take a pretest. Have a parent give and correct the test. Write any misspelled words five times.

_____ *Friday:* Test.

Note: This homework list supports a geology theme in the classroom. The words are arranged by syllable type, and were chosen because of the likelihood that they will appear in thematic readings.

Syllable Boxes

(Tuesday's Homework)

Crust						
mag	ma					
fos	sil					
la	va					
Crys	tal					
Pum	ice					
bas	alt					
gran	ite					
Slate						
Shale						
lime	stone					
ig	nite					
Cal	cite					
man	tle					
mar	ble					
can	dle					
ta	ble					
Sam	ple					

Note: As part of their weekly spelling assignment, students are asked to write their words in syllables. On another day, they use this paper to sort their syllables by syllable type on the Syllable Sorting Grid (Appendix B). On Friday, they can take their spelling test on syllable paper and are given credit for the number of syllables spelled correctly. This is often a great motivator for students who cringe at reading and writing multisyllabic words.

Making Alphabetical Order Easy

Provide students with the following directions for putting words in alphabetical order.

1. Write one spelling word in each box on the abc sort paper. (see Appendix B) (You may have some extra boxes depending on the number of words you have this week.)

2. Cut the boxes apart.

3. Arrange them in ABC order on your desk by following these steps:

   a. Put all "A" words in a pile, "B" words in a pile, etc. You may not have a word or words for every letter of the alphabet.

   b. Arrange your piles of words in ABC order on top of your desk.

   c. Put the words within each pile into ABC order according to the order of the letters in each word.

   d. Check the order of the words on your desk to be sure they are alphabetized correctly. (Number each word in case you drop them.)

   e. Glue your words in ABC order on another sheet of paper.

References

Adams, M. (1980). *Beginning to read*. Cambridge, MA: MIT Press.

Anderson, C. W., Cross, T. E., & Stoner, J. (1992). Lincoln, NE: Spelling Poster Set. Educational Tutorial Consortium, Inc.

Blachman, B., Schatschneider, C., Fletcher, J., & Clonan, S. (2003). Early reading intervention: A classroom prevention study and a remediation study. In B. Foorman (Ed.), *Preventing and remediating reading difficulties*. Baltimore: York Press.

Bradley, L., & Bryant, P. (1985). *Rhyme and reason in reading and spelling*. Ann Arbor: University of Michigan Press.

Ehri, L. (1996). Development of the ability to read words. In R. Barr, M. Kamil, P. B. Mosenthal, and P. D. Pearson (Eds.), *Handbook of Reading Research: Volume 2* (pp. 383–418). Mahwah, NJ: Lawrence Erlbaum.

Hanna, P. R., Hanna, J. S., Hodges, R. E., & Rudorf, E. H. (1966). *Phoneme-grapheme correspondences as cues to spelling improvement*. Washington, DC: Department of Health Education and Welfare.

Henry, Marcia. (2003). *Unlocking Literacy-Effective Decoding & Spelling Instruction*. Paul H. Brookes Publishing Company.

Meyerson, R.F. (1978). Children's knowledge of selected aspects of sound pattern of English. In R. Campbell and P. Smith (Eds.), *Recent Advances in Psychology of Language: Formal and Experimental Approaches*. New York: Plenum.

Moats, L. C. (2005). *Language Essentials for Teachers of Reading and Spelling (LETRS)*. Longmont, Sopris West.

Moats, L. C. (2000). *Speech to print: Language essentials for teachers*. Baltimore: York Press.

Moats, L. C. (1995). *Spelling Development, Disability, and Instruction*. Baltimore: York Press.

Perfetti, C. A., Beck, I., Bell, L., & Hughes, C. (1987). Phonemic knowledge and learning to read are reciprocal: A longitudinal study of first grade children. *Merrill-Palmer Quarterly, 33*, 283–319.

Tangel, D. & Blachman, B. (1995). Effect of phoneme awareness instruction on the invented spellings of first grade children: A one year follow-up. *Journal of Reading Behavior, 27*, 153–185.

Torgesen, J., Rashotte, C., Alexander, A., & MacPhee, K. (2003). Progress toward understanding the instructional conditions necessary for remediating reading difficulties in older children. In B. Foorman (Ed.), *Preventing and remediating reading difficulties*. Baltimore: York Press.

Tyler, A., & Nagy, W. (1987.) The acquisition of English derivational morphology. (Technical Report No. 407) Urbana, IL: Center for the Study of Reading

White, T. G., Sowell, J., & Yahagihara, A. (1989). Morphological analysis: implications for Teaching and Understanding Vocabulary Growth. *Reading Research Quarterly*, 24, 283–304.

Wyosocki, K., & Jenkins, J.R. (1987.) Deriving word meanings through morphological generalization. *Reading Research Quarterly* 22:66081.

Appendix A
Phoneme-Grapheme Mapping:
Step-by-Step Process

Phoneme-Grapheme Mapping: Step-by-Step Process

Day One: Teach Concept and Segment Sounds	
PREPARE: Compile lesson word list. Students need sound tiles.	
TEACH: Teach the new sound, spelling concept, and pattern.	
SEGMENT: Instruct students to use colored tiles to segment dictated words. Tell students the tiles represent sounds, *not* letters.	
CHECK: Check each word immediately by having students touch and say each sound. Remember, one tile represents one sound, *not* one letter.	Circulate among the group to ensure students are segmenting correctly.
Day Two: Read Words, Find, Circle, and Say Target Sound	
PREPARE: Compile Day One word lists for students.	
READ: Instruct students to independently read the list silently. Then lead the group to read the words chorally.	
FIND AND CIRCLE THE SOUND FOR EACH WORD: a. Instruct students to find, point to, and say the target sound. "Say the sound." b. Instruct students to circle and say the letter(s) for the target grapheme. "Say the letter(s).*"	*Instruct younger students to say the sounds when circling the letters.
Day Three: Phoneme-Grapheme Mapping	
PREPARE: Supply students with phoneme-grapheme mapping paper and sound tiles. Prepare word list.	Demonstrate specific mapping procedures.
SEGMENT: Dictate word. Student says each sound and positions one tile in each grid square for each *sound*.	Advanced students may dot each square.
SAY SOUND AND GRAPHEME: a. Point to the first tile. Say, "What do you hear?" Students say sound. b. Ask, "What do you write?" Students say grapheme, move the tile up, and write the grapheme in the square. c. Repeat a and b for each sound/spelling until the whole word is written. When the word is completely written, the student should have the exact spelling of the word on the paper with the letters distributed across the boxes based on their phoneme-grapheme correspondences—one sound, one grapheme per square.	Some lessons instruct students to apply specific color coding for vowels and to note syllable divisions with colors and/or dotted lines.
REVIEW: Instruct students to restate in their own words the sound/spelling relationship.	Can students think of any other words that share the same relationship?

Appendix B
Blackline Masters

Phoneme-Grapheme Mapping
(A Method for Bridging Sound to Print)

Name: _____ Date: _____

Appendix B Blackline Masters

Sound/Spelling Boxes—Primary Paper

Name: _____ Date: _____

Short Vowel Cue Cards

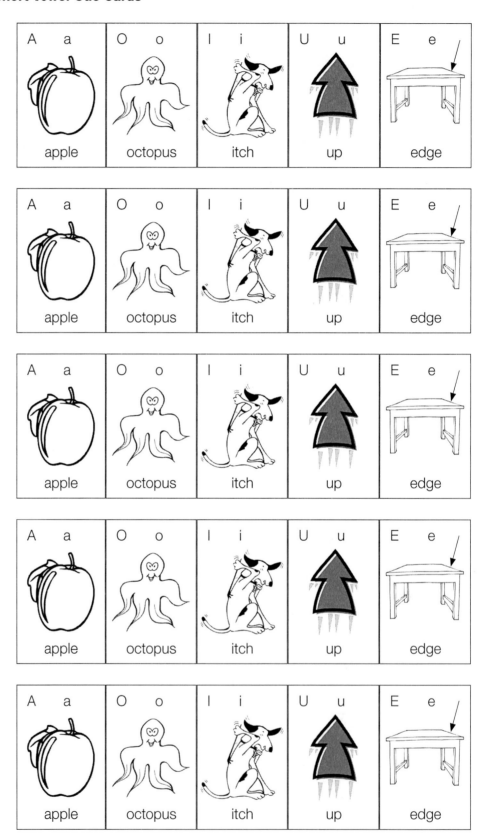

Short *a* Vowel Picture Match

Key words (left to right): hat, bat, basket, mask, cat, tag, apple, backpack, rabbit.

Appendix B Blackline Masters 293

Short *o* Vowel Picture Match

Key words (left to right): otter, octopus, frog, dolphin, golf, dog, clock, box, stocking, soccer, top, blocks.

Short *i* Vowel Picture Match

Key words (left to right): hippo, lips, fish, gifts, swim, disk or diskette, pig, lizard, gymnast or gymnastics.

Short *u* Vowel Picture Match

Key words (left to right): skunk, drum, pumpkin, butterfly, sun, duck, up, cupcake, puppets.

Short *e* Vowel Picture Match

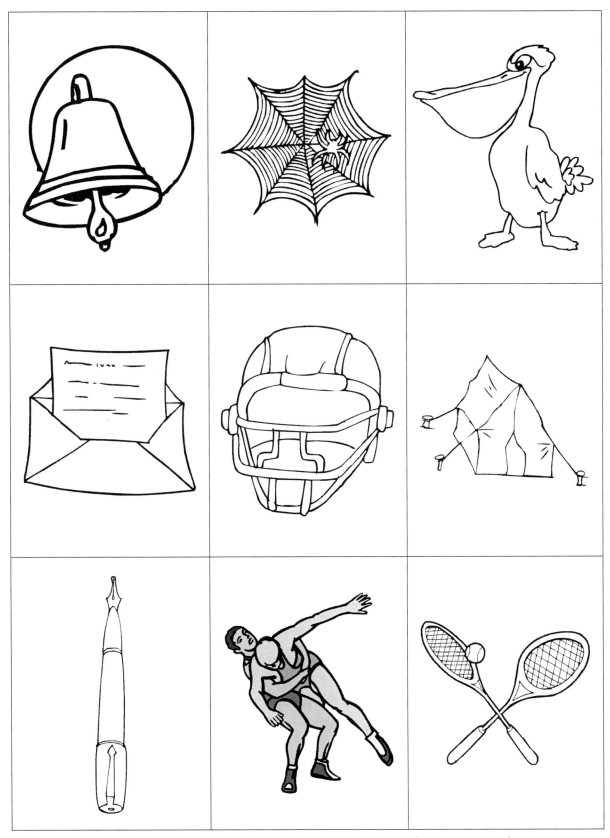

Key words (left to right): bell, web, pelican, letter, helmet, tent, pen, wrestlers or men, tennis.

ABC Order Activity Sheet

1. Write one of your spelling words in each of the boxes below.
2. When you have filled in all the boxes, cut them apart on the solid lines.
3. Using your desktop, sort the words into piles according to their initial consonant.
4. Begin to arrange the words in abc order on your desktop by starting with your Letter A words and then proceeding through the other letters of the alphabet. If you have more than one word that begins with the same letter, use the second letter in the word to help you, and so on.
5. Once you think you have arranged your words correctly in abc order on your desktop, recheck your work.
6. Glue the words you have arranged on your desktop on to a blank piece of paper in abc order. Be sure to write your name on the paper.

Affixo Chart

Name: _____   Date: _____

Prefix	Prefix	Prefix	Base Word or Root	Suffix	Suffix	Suffix

Syllable Writing Grid

Name: _____ Date: _____

Write your words in syllables in the boxes below. Then use this grid to help you sort your syllables onto the Syllable Sorting Grid.

Write the first syllable here.	Write the second syllable here.	Write the third syllable here.	Write the fourth syllable here.	Write the fifth syllable here.	Write the sixth syllable here.	Write the seventh syllable here.

Syllable Sorting Grid

Closed syllables

These syllables have a vowel followed by one or more consonants. The vowel sound is short and spelled with one letter.

| Schwa Closed Syllables: |

Open syllables

These syllables end in a single vowel. The vowel sound is long, or sounds like the vowel's name.

| Schwa Open Syllables: |

Silent -e syllables

These syllables have one vowel, followed by one consonant and a final e. The first vowel is long. The e is silent.

| Schwa Silent -e Syllables: |

Vowel team syllables

These syllables contain teams of letters that come together to make a distinct vowel sound (*ou* as in *out*, *oi* as in *oil*, *eigh* as in *eight*.) Sometimes they can be a vowel team pair, as in *team* and *boat*.

| Schwa Vowel Team Syllables: |

r-controlled syllables

These syllables contain a vowel followed by an *r*. The *r* controls the sound of the vowel.

    ar   or   er   ir   ur

| Schwa r-Controlled Syllables: |

Consonant -le syllables

These syllables end in a consonant followed by -*le*, as in the -*ble* in *table*. The *le* sounds like /ul/.

All consonants -*le* syllables have a schwa vowel, so they are placed in the main syllable box above.

Long Vowel Spelling Choices

Name: _____ Date: _____

	Frequently Used Spellings				Less Frequently Used Spellings			
Spellings of . . . at . . .	**At the END of a syllable (open syllable)**	**In the MIDDLE of a base word or syllable**		**At the END of a base word**	**These spellings are not used as often**			
Long _a_	a ta ble	a-e* name	ai (n, l) rain, rail	ay day	eigh eight	ei vein	ey they	ea break
Long _e_	e be gin	ee feet	ea seat	y funny	e-e* eve	ie chief	[c] ei ceiling	ey key
Long _i_	i si lent	i-e time	igh night	y my	ie pie	y-e type	—	—
Long _o_	o o pen	o-e* robe	oa boat	ow snow	ou shoulder	oe toe	—	—
Long _u_ /y/ /o͞o/ (two phonemes)	u [yu] mu sic	u-e* cute	—	ew pew	ue cue	eu feud	—	—
Long _u_ /o͞o/ (one phoneme)	u ru by	u-e rule	ou/oo soup food	ew grew	ue clue	—	—	—

*These patterns are silent _e_ syllables. The dash means a consonant sound needs to come between the vowel and the final, silent _e_.

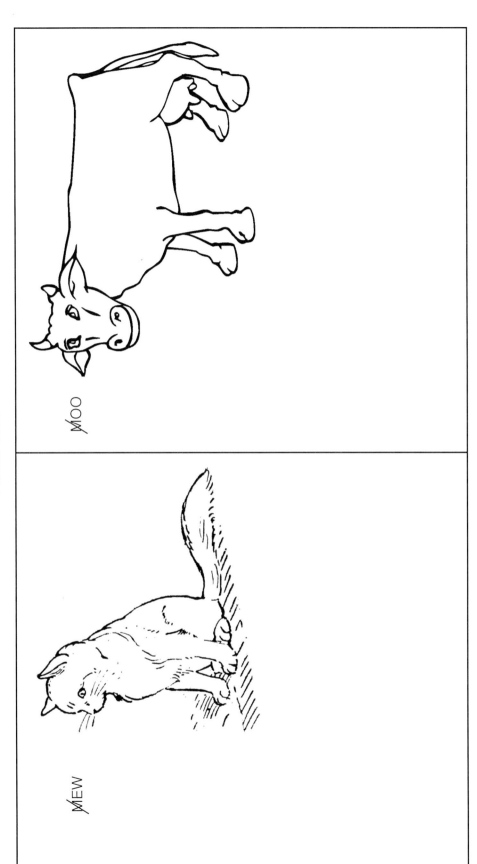

MOO

MEW

Name: _____ Date: _____

Doubling Rule Chart for Single Syllable Base Words

Base word	Suffix or ending	Does the base word have one syllable?	Does the base word end in a short vowel sound?	Does the base word end in one consonant sound?	Does the suffix begin with a vowel?	Double the final consonant if answer to all questions is yes.	Do not double the final consonant if answer to any question is no.
Example: stop	-ing	yes	yes	yes	yes	stopping	
Example: play	-ed	yes	no	no	yes		played

Name: _____   Date: _____

Doubling Rule Practice Chart for Multisyllabic Base Words

Base word	Suffix or ending	Does the base word have more than one syllable?	Does the base word end in a consonant with just one vowel before it?	Is the accent or stress on the last syllable in the base word?	Does the suffix begin with a vowel?	Double the final consonant if answer to all questions is yes.	Do not double the final consonant if answer to any question is no.
Example: propel	-er	yes	yes	yes	yes	propeller	—
Example: profit	-able	yes	yes	no	yes	—	profitable
1. equip	-ed						
2. equip	-ment						
3. control	-ing						
4. gallop	-ed						
5. inhabit	-less						
6. national	-ism						
7. excel	-ent						

Doubling Rule Chart for Multisyllabic Base Words

Name: _____   Date: _____

Base word	Suffix or ending	Does the base word have more than one syllable?	Does the base word end in a consonant with just one vowel before it?	Is the accent or stress on the last syllable in the base word?	Does the suffix begin with a vowel?	Double the final consonant if answer to all questions is yes.	Do not double the final consonant if answer to any question is no.
Example: propel	-er	yes	yes	yes	yes	propeller	—
Example: profit	-able	yes	yes	no	yes	—	profitable
1.							
2.							
3.							
4.							
5.							
6.							
7.							

Phoneme-Grapheme Mapping Rule Paper

(For use with the silent *e* rule)

Name: _____ Date: _____

b	ā	k	i	ng					
□	□	□ ⟋e	□	□	□	□	□	□	□
□	□	□	□	□	□	□	□	□	□
□	□	□	□	□	□	□	□	□	□
□	□	□	□	□	□	□	□	□	□
□	□	□	□	□	□	□	□	□	□
□	□	□	□	□	□	□	□	□	□
□	□	□	□	□	□	□	□	□	□

Phoneme-Grapheme Mapping Rule Paper

(For use with Change the *y* to *i* Rule)

Name: _____ Date: _____

h	a	p	p	i	e	s	t		
☐	☐	☐	☐	☐	☐	☐	☐	☐	☐
☐	☐	☐	☐	☐	☐	☐	☐	☐	☐
☐	☐	☐	☐	☐	☐	☐	☐	☐	☐
☐	☐	☐	☐	☐	☐	☐	☐	☐	☐
☐	☐	☐	☐	☐	☐	☐	☐	☐	☐
☐	☐	☐	☐	☐	☐	☐	☐	☐	☐

Appendix C
Spelling Program Evaluation

Spelling Program Evaluation

Name of program: _____ Grade(s): _____ Date: _____

Does the spelling program I use in my classroom meet the principles of effective instruction?

Questions about your spelling program	Yes	No	No, but I add it. How? What resource?
1. Does the program include instruction in phonological awareness skills?			
2. Does the program teach how letters link to sounds? (phoneme-grapheme relationships and phonics)			
3. Does the program include instruction in orthographic word study skills? a. Orthographic placements (e.g., Long Vowel Spelling Choices chart) b. Visual memory of high-frequency words			
4. Does the program include instruction in syllable types? a. Syllabication division rules b. Spelling multisyllabic words			
5. Does the program teach basic morphology skills? a. Base words b. Endings c. Suffixes			
6. Does the program teach basic spelling rules?			
Questions about effective teaching practices	**Yes**	**No**	**No, but I add it. How? What resource?**
1. Does the program provide for teacher-directed, systematic practice?			
2. Does the program utilize the modeling of strategies?			
3. Does the program provide immediate feedback?			
4. Does the program utilize multisensory instruction?			
5. Does the program utilize organized and sequential instruction?			